# RECOVERING HISTORIES

## STUDIES OF THE WEATHERHEAD EAST ASIAN INSTITUTE, COLUMBIA UNIVERSITY

The Studies of the Weatherhead East Asian Institute of Columbia University were inaugurated in 1962 to bring to a wider public the results of significant new research on modern and contemporary East Asia.

# RECOVERING HISTORIES

LIFE AND LABOR AFTER HEROIN IN
REFORM-ERA CHINA

Nicholas Bartlett

 UNIVERSITY OF CALIFORNIA PRESS

University of California Press
Oakland, California

© 2020 by Nicholas Bartlett

Library of Congress Cataloging-in-Publication Data

Names: Bartlett, Nicholas, 1978- author.
Title: Recovering histories : life and labor after heroin in
    reform-era China / Nicholas Bartlett.
Description: Oakland, California : University of California
    Press, [2020] | Includes bibliographical references and
    index.
Identifiers: LCCN 2020014434 (print) | LCCN 2020014435
    (ebook) | ISBN 9780520344112 (cloth) | ISBN 9780520344136
    (paperback) | ISBN 9780520975378 (epub)
Subjects: LCSH: Heroin abuse—Social aspects—China—
    Gejiu. | Drug abuse—China—Gejiu—History. |
    Recovering addicts—Employment—China—Gejiu.
Classification: LCC HV5840.C62 G453 2020 (print) |
    LCC HV5840.C62 (ebook) | DDC 362.29/34095135—dc23
LC record available at https://lccn.loc.gov/2020014434
LC ebook record available at https://lccn.loc.gov/2020014435

Manufactured in the United States of America

29  28  27  26  25  24  23  22  21  20
10  9  8  7  6  5  4  3  2  1

*To my parents, with love and gratitude*

# CONTENTS

# ILLUSTRATIONS

# ACKNOWLEDGMENTS

This book has emerged slowly, drawing on nearly two decades of study and research. I have incurred many debts of gratitude along the way.

From my undergraduate years, I would like to recognize the lasting influence of Gary Wilder, Sam Yamashita, and Kevin Platt, all fantastic and dedicated educators. From my first years in New York, I would like to thank John Chin, Richard Elovich, Kate Hunt, Dorinda Welle, and Carol Vance. Kasia Malinowska-Sempruch and Daniel Wolfe at Open Society Foundations were wise, kind, and supportive bosses and mentors.

In the Bay Area, Vincanne Adams and Liu Xin shaped this project in crucial ways. In her capacity as chair of my dissertation committee, Vincanne Adams was a kind and responsive mentor, a talented teacher, and an insightful reader. Liu Xin had his office door open at crucial moments and saw early on that this project might focus on temporality. Matthew Kohrman and Deborah Gordon have been cherished mentors. Alex Beliaev, Anthony Stavrianakis, and Eric Plemons were key readers of my dissertation. My fellow UCSF cohort mates Jeff Schonberg, Kelly Knight, and Liza Buchbinder provided support and friendship. Other people I would like to thank include Saleem Al-Baholy, Philippe Bourgois, Lawrence Cohen, Katie Hendy, Judith Justice, Eugene Raikhel, Laura Schmidt, Ian Whitmarsh, and Emily Wilcox. Emily Chua requires special mention for well over a decade of friendship and impactful conversations.

My deep appreciation to wonderful colleagues and friends who made working and living in China over the years a pleasure: Bao Xiuhong, Vincent Chin,

Ge Rongling, Feng Yu, Ted Hammett, Sandra Hyde, Tom Kellogg, Li Dongliang, Li Jianhua, Ralph Litzinger, Liu Yu, Jen Liu-Lin and Craig Simons, Carrie Luo, Tim Manchester, Morgan Philbin, Michelle Rodolph, Kumi Smith, Victor Shih and Maria Goff, Wang Zhenxiu, Stephanie Weber, Xia Ying, Zhang Wei, Zhao Chengzheng, and Zhang Konglai. A note of gratitude as well to my Chinese teachers. I want to thank IHRD grantees in China and Indonesia whom I had the privilege of working with and learning from.

In Los Angeles, thank you to Jason Throop, Cheryl Mattingly, Josh Goldstein, Doug Hollan, the MMAC community, and the anthropology departments at UCLA and USC. A preliminary thank you as well to Esther Dreifuss-Kattan, Peter Loewenberg, Jeff Prager, and Bettina Soestwohner, my cohort mates and teachers at the New Center for Psychoanalysis, the Valley Community Counselling Clinic, and the international group relations community for your kindness in allowing me to explore an endlessly fascinating and enriching field.

At Barnard College and Columbia University, Rachel McDermott and Max Moerman in AMEC have been extraordinary senior colleagues and mentors. Lesley Sharp has gone above and beyond. Thanks as well to Ron Briggs, Michael Como, Nadia Abu El-Haj, Kathy Ewing, Sev Fowles, Guo Jue, Eugenia Lean, Lan Li, Lydia Liu, Elliot Paul, Haruo Shirane, Emily Sun, Christina Vizcarra, Carl Wennerlind, Ying Qian, and other colleagues in EALAC, AMEC, and anthropology. I also express gratitude to my excellent students, who have provoked my thinking and scholarship in important ways. A big thank you to the wonderful caregivers who have watched Naomi and Lucian.

I am particularly appreciative of the manuscript readers whose comments dramatically improved this book. Jennifer Hirsch, Kim Hopper, and Lesley Sharp generously organized a workshop through the Columbia Population Research Center that gave me valuable feedback on a nearly completed draft. The Weatherhead East Asian Institute at Columbia sponsored a book workshop later that year. Myron Cohen, Dorothy Ko, Rachel McDermott, and Max Moerman provided enormously constructive and insightful comments. Special thanks to my outside readers: Ann Anagnost's detailed feedback inspired additional attention to the legacies of the 1980s and unexpectedly enhanced my teaching; Bob Desjarlais's perceptive comments and ongoing discussions in lunch meetups have enriched my understanding of the possibilities of fieldwork and sharpened the phenomenological focus of this book; and Angela Garcia's suggestions and encouragement, alongside her inspiring work on addiction, have influenced this project for many years.

Sara Appel, Chris Bartlett, Lyle Fearnley, Emily Ng, Yang Jie, and Bharat Venkat made constructive suggestions on sections of the manuscript at various points. Discussions with Yukiko Koga, Jeremy Soh, and Allen Tran in recent years have been helpful. Two reviewers from UC Press, subsequently revealed to be Josh Burraway and Zhang Li, provided generous, careful, and perceptive comments that significantly improved this text. The book also benefited from comments at talks given over the years at UCSF, the Mind Medicine and Culture seminar at UCLA, Bucknell University, the Boas seminar and Modern China Seminar at Columbia, and numerous AAA, AES, and SPA panels.

Naor Ben-Yehoyada and Mara Green deserve special thanks. In our regular meetings, Mara and Naor have been the kindest and most provocative of interlocutors, energetic readers, and generous friends who on many occasions helped me to remember the joys of collaboration.

At the University of California Press, I owe thanks to Reed Malcolm, who patiently guided this project over several years, and to Archna Patel, who served as an expert and careful guide in ushering it into its final form. Thanks as well to Sharon Langworthy for superb, eagle-eyed copy edits, and to Heather Altfield for creating the index and additional attention to the text. Many thanks as well to Ariana King and Ross Yelsey at Weatherhead Books, Josh Jacobs for photograph-related coaching, Jennifer Schontz for help with the appendix table, former WEAI visiting fellow Zhang Fuyu and Wang Chengzhi for help in securing permissions, Jenny Zhan for interview transcriptions, and Mary Missari and Jessica Xu for departmental assistance.

I feel a special debt of gratitude to the residents of Gejiu. My initial intention was only to stay for a few months. However, I quickly found this was a special place, with many people whom I felt deeply connected to. Thank you for your generosity, hospitality, patience, and friendship. And a special thanks to the individuals whose experiences make up this text. To you I owe the greatest debt of gratitude. I wish you health, happiness, and a respite from the past to pursue futures of hope and possibility.

I have been able to conduct this research thanks to generous support from the Fulbright-Hays Doctoral Dissertation Research (DDRA) Abroad Fellowship, a National Science Foundation (NSF) Dissertation Improvement Fellowship, Foreign Language and Area Studies (FLAS) Fellowships, a UCSF Graduate Dean's Health Science Fellowship and Presidents' Research Fellowship in the Humanities, and the UC Humanities Graduate Dissertation

Fellowship Society of Fellows in the Humanities. Early research in China and recent costs related to publication were supported by the Columbia Weatherhead East Asian Institute. The Freeman Foundation deserves special thanks for funding a post-college table tennis project that provided me with my first opportunity to live in China.

Earlier versions of chapters 2 and 4 have been published elsewhere as "The Ones Who Struck Out: Entrepreneurialism, Heroin Addiction, and Historical Obsolescence in Reform Era China" (*positions: asia critique* 26, no. 3 [2018]: 423–49) and "Idling in Mao's Shadow: Heroin Addiction and the Contested Therapeutic Value of Socialist Traditions of Laboring" (*Culture, Medicine, and Psychiatry* 42, no. 1 [2018]: 49–68).

I would like to finish by expressing my profound gratitude to family and friends who have sustained me over these many years. Adam deserves special recognition, not just for a lifelong friendship, but also for his role in helping to instigate my first trips to China and, later, pursuing a career in anthropology. Dave, Joe, and Mike deliver annual doses of sanity, twenty years and counting. Long live Team Oak! Thanks to Greg and Lee, Julie, Jeff, Zane and Sebastian, Cynthia, Josh, Abram and Dalya, Valerie, Anjali, Jon, Kate, and Phil, Kiran, Erica, Josh, Nazia, Najam, Seth, and Rachel for being there.

Thank you to my caring and wonderful mother-in-law Liz, as well as new family members Kristin and Omid. Liz, thanks for being your ebullient, hilarious, fun-loving self since before you became Cool Aunt Liz. Andrew, thank you for being such a caring, sensitive, and generous presence in my life from our first games of catch. Mom and Dad, your unconditional love and encouragement, and the inspirational example you show in how you live, have made everything else possible.

The arrival of Naomi and Lucian has been a source of joy and a welcome escape during the writing of this book. Naomi, your kindness, curiosity, and ability to connect to others astounds me. And Lucian, your sense of fun, restless spirit, and love of cooking bring me great joy. It is an honor to be your dad. I look forward to many future adventures with you both, including enjoying rice noodles followed by a climb to the top of Old Yin Mountain.

And finally, a last and most crucial thank you to Diana. You have been there for me through all the frustrations and small victories that have accompanied turning this project into a book. Your literary sensibility and intuitive understanding of this project dramatically improved my attempts to tell these stories. Much more important, your companionship over the last years has brought joy, security, and contentment to my life in ways I could never have imagined. Watching you flourish in your new profession and laughing while making sense of the world together have given me great pleasure. You are the most supportive and thoughtful partner a person could wish for.

# Introduction

*Toward a Phenomenology of Recovery*

## BACK ON THE MOUNTAIN

On a crisp spring morning in 2004, just before dawn, Xun Wei left his apartment. Most of his neighbors in Gejiu, a city of 310,000 residents crowded into a narrow valley floor in a mountainous area in southern Yunnan, had not yet awakened.[1] Xun entered Huawei Park, a wooded area to the east of the city center. Old Yin Mountain loomed above him. Its peak was accessible by mounting a winding staircase of more than twenty-five hundred carved steps.

He set forth for the mountain that morning, like many other times in his life, in pursuit of a work opportunity. Xun had once been a wealthy tin mining boss, enjoying a lavish lifestyle while overseeing more than two dozen employees at a nearby mountainside site. That was many years earlier, before his heroin habit contributed to his losing his mining tunnel to competitors. In recent months he had enrolled in a newly opened government clinic that provided him with daily doses of methadone to stave off his heroin cravings. Determined to heal his body and stay busy, Xun filled his days with walks around the lake and badminton games with his fiancée. When he saw signs posted by local government officials offering cash rewards for harvesting rodents in the nearby hills, Xun eagerly pursued the opportunity to reenter the legal workforce.

As he trudged up the steep slope, Xun passed a group of residents hiking to the top of the mountain. Approximately four hundred people, many of them unemployed or furloughed state workers, made the trip every day, with

FIGURE I. Abandoned tracks on Old Yin Mountain. Photo by author.

a thousand or more regularly summiting on the weekends. Veering off this busier paved path, Xun passed over a defunct railway line that had once transported tin from tunnels on Old Yin to the city center (see figure 1). The minerals in these mountains had attracted human settlers for more than three thousand years. Remnants of infrastructure from various eras of mineral extraction were still visible on the mountainside and throughout the city center. In the new millennium, mining outfits drilled ever more deeply into the earth—now as far as two kilometers underground—to find unclaimed, high-grade ore.

Nearing a cluster of trees, Xun heard the rattling of a mountain rat inside a metal cage. He carefully picked up the device by the handle, then walked to another spot nearby, then another. Within a few minutes he had retrieved all six of his traps, five of which held large, squirming rodents. He walked back down into the city center. The rats struggled furiously, and the cages occasionally bumped against his legs. Once back at his apartment, Xun carefully released this group into a holding pen in his living room, where they joined others he had captured in previous days.

"You should have seen all those rats!" Xun Wei paused in his retelling for dramatic effect. His narrow, angular face was framed by closely shaven hair, chunky black eyeglasses, and a pronounced Adam's apple. A T-shirt tucked into acid-washed jeans accentuated his skinny frame. His voice was raspy, some might say grating. Like many residents in a prefecture famous for its tobacco, he constantly smoked cheap Red River cigarettes. As we sat in his apartment in early 2010, he took a puff, cleared his throat, and continued his story.

Twice a week Xun delivered his cargo to the disease prevention station (*fangyizhan*), where he collected a prearranged payment of 10 yuan per live rodent. He never learned the rats' fate. Xun excelled at this job; in total, he secured close to 2,000 yuan in that first month, a sum equivalent to the salary of a midlevel government cadre or manager of a respectable local business. But the venture did not last for long. Overexploitation of the mountain's rodents— several dozen other rat catchers competed with him for the government payouts—resulted in a decreased supply and smarter rats. His fiancée, unhappy sharing their apartment with such houseguests and worried about the gashes on his legs left by their teeth and the metal bumping against his skin, eventually convinced Xun that this business was best abandoned.

When talking about the role of the mountains in Gejiu life, local residents during my time in the region taught me an old Chinese slogan: "Mountain dwellers *kao* the mountains, shore dwellers *kao* the sea," with *kao* translatable as "rely on," "make use of," or "exploit." I initially imagined that this phrase referred to the stable rhythms that had emerged between this mountainside community and the natural resources that surrounded it. What became clear to me from my time in Gejiu was that in recent decades the possible futures nurtured by the extraction of natural resources in this region had been rapidly shifting. The mountains, of course, were always there, but the careers and rhythms of living they supported were in a state of flux.

People with a history of heroin use faced particular challenges adapting to the changes that had swept the region. Xun's career is exemplary in this sense.

A child during the last years of the Cultural Revolution in the mid-1970s, he scavenged steep nearby slopes for wild vegetables when state-rationed food did not provide enough calories for his large family. In his teenage years, during Deng Xiaoping's tenure, Xun submitted to the rigid schedule of state-affiliated mining enterprises before striking out on his own to become a wealthy private-sector mining boss. Following a stint in a compulsory labor center, he returned to the nearby mountains in the mid-1990s to start a trucking venture that helped connect sellers in regional open-air markets.[2] In the early 2000s, after he gave up rat catching, Xun opted to stay in the city, taking on a series of temporary, low-paying jobs that included helping his in-laws sell lottery tickets. But the mountains—and dreams of other futures—were never far from his thoughts. For Xun, like others I met in Gejiu, recovery from heroin use merged with striving to find a way to *kao* the mountains and achieve a "normal person's life" (*zhengchangren de shenghuo*) in changing times.

At the time of our conversation in 2010, Xun was serving as director of a grassroots nongovernmental organization (NGO), managing three part-time outreach workers and a financial accountant. Living in an apartment he and his wife had bought at a reduced rate from his father's state employer, Xun was one of a relatively small group of people I knew with heroin use history in the region who had found desirable, full-time work. The mountains provided him with a venue for periodic team-building and outreach activities. Peer educators from competing nonprofit organizations prowled mountain mining outposts searching for heroin-using miners, to whom they could provide HIV testing and referral services.

Xun finished his cigarette in silence. Despite his recent successes, he was unsure about how long he could successfully find donors to support his organization. We could hear the clanging of construction outside; another high rise was being built next to the lake, part of a seemingly endless expansion upward from the narrow valley floor. Partially visible through the window, Old Yin Mountain silently loomed above us.

## OUT OF TIME? AN EPIDEMIC OF THE RECENT PAST

Drug users—and in particular those consuming heroin—have often been depicted as lacking an awareness of history. William Burroughs describes the heroin user as living in "junk time," in which his "body is his clock, and junk runs through him like an hour-glass. Time has meaning for him only with reference to his need" ([1953] 1977, 180).[3] Caught up in the self-contained thoughts and actions born of physiological craving, drug seeking, and withdrawal, addicts, in this Beat writer's account, are radically disconnected from a broader social world and, by extension, shared historical time. Focusing on experiences of those attempting to rebuild lives after extended periods of heroin use, *Recovering Histories* argues that the men and women I encountered in Gejiu were especially attuned to what we might call the fraught historical times of the nation. Achieving recovery for this group was inextricably linked to responding to the challenges of the historical moment, a struggle not only to find a position within society but also to become oriented to shifting experiences of social time.

A brief history of my own relationship to this topic and place may help introduce the reader to what follows. I first heard about Gejiu city in 2002 while working as an assistant programs officer in the Beijing office of a social marketing organization operating under the umbrella of the China-UK HIV/AIDS Prevention and Care project. Public health experts at the time warned of a looming "titanic peril" and potential "fault line" that could threaten national development (UNAIDS 2002; Wolf et al. 2003). Located fewer than two hundred kilometers from the Vietnamese border, Gejiu was identified in early epidemiological surveys as a priority area for HIV programming because of a concentration of heroin use and sex work in the region.[4] Buoyed by a post-SARS commitment to effective public health and supported by deep-pocketed international donors (cf. Mason 2016; on surveillance see Fearnley 2020), Gejiu officials in the mid-2000s spearheaded dozens of projects targeting "high-risk" populations. International news media soon lauded the city as a "model" for China's HIV prevention efforts (Yardley 2005). Service providers offered local drug users access to methadone maintenance therapy, needle exchange, targeted medical care, and expanded social support. Peter Piot, at that time the director of UNAIDS, and a handful of international public health luminaries made brief visits to Gejiu to inspect what was billed as an innovative and progressive local response to the country's HIV/AIDS epidemic.

In 2008, when I was working part time for the International Harm Reduction Development Program (IHRD) at Open Society Institute (now Foundations), I visited the city for the first time to meet with a number of recovering drug users who had formed a regional network dedicated to improving the lives of their community. IHRD provided the group with a start-up grant to fund work in five cities across the prefecture. As a result of my initial connections with members of this network and my growing interest in the dynamics of drug use in the region, I moved to Gejiu in August 2009 to begin my dissertation research, a project that I believed would focus on a widespread and visible heroin epidemic.[5]

Hyper-alert for drug references and struggling with the local dialect, my ears during my first weeks living in the city would prick up every time I heard the city's nickname; "tin capital" shares the same phonetic pronunciation as "using drugs" (*xidu*). I quickly found that my initial assumptions formed through reading reports about the local crisis were mistaken. Following a pattern of "drug generations" identified in many parts of the world (Golub, Johnson, and Dunlap 2005), consumption of heroin in Gejiu had in fact been confined primarily to a single historical cohort. Born during the second half of the 1960s or in the 1970s, most local users first encountered the drug in the late 1980s or early 1990s. At the start of the new millenium, as many as 15,000 of the city's 310,000 residents experimented with the opioid (Li and Zhang 2003). By the early 2010s, its use was limited to approximately twenty-five hundred predominantly middle-aged local residents.[6] A heavy toll of overdoses and infectious diseases, as well as intense stigmatization of the drug by nonusers, had contributed to the rapid reduction of what was once a sizable heroin-using community.

I was also mistaken in thinking that most heroin users I encountered would be heavy users. Though "sneaking a puff" (*touxi*, the intermittent heroin use sometimes referred to in English as "chipping") was not uncommon, few of the individuals I came to know well were engaging in the "ripping and running" often associated with acute physiological addiction (cf. Agar 1973). By the time I arrived in Gejiu, the availability of methadone substitution therapy and intense police crackdowns on organized crime and drug dealing had noticeably constricted supply and demand in the local heroin market. In addition, supporting heavy habits had become more difficult for aging users, who were increasingly excluded from licit and illicit forms of economic activity. Cumulatively, this shifting scene led drug users and non–drug users alike to remark that I was "late" to arrive; if I was interested in experiences of an epidemic, I should have been in Gejiu to witness the widespread use that started in the 1980s and peaked in the 1990s.

Unlike many studies that have focused on encounters taking place in a clinic, service agency, or residential center (Carr 2010; Waldram 2012; Hansen 2018), my fieldwork in Gejiu was conducted largely outside of spaces dedicated to drug treatment. As I lacked an official hosting institution, Green Orchards, an internationally funded, government-affiliated drop-in center for heroin users, became an important fieldwork site. During frequent visits to the patio where "members" (huiyuan) congregated, I met a rotating group of people with heroin use history—some actively using and others abstaining—who stopped by to while away the afternoon hours. In addition, former IHRD grantees from the regional network introduced me to their friends. Meals and tea in private homes and at outdoor restaurants, wedding celebrations, family and job-related events, and weekend hot springs retreats provided occasions for me to form longer-term, more intimate relationships with a smaller group of recovering users. Through these interactions, my initial interest in the intersection of drug use practices and state policing came to be replaced by a desire to better understand lived experiences of recovery.

The people with heroin use history I came to know in Gejiu fundamentally challenged my own preconceptions about addiction and recovery. Rather than seeing themselves as individual patients suffering from a relapsing brain disease, this group often spoke about their struggles as a generation of workers who had become lost while attempting to "get ahead" of other local residents as teenagers and young adults. Forging a life after heroin required searching for opportunities to live and labor in a world that bore little resemblance to either the Maoist work units of their childhood or the disorienting but opportunity-filled chaos associated with the mining boom of their early careers. Personal experiences of recovery were thus intimately shaped by their understanding of the collective horizons of their heroin-using cohort, the city, and the nation.

*Recovering Histories* describes distinct ways that individual members of this generational cohort conceptualized and moved toward life after addiction. In contrast to the government's attempts to define distinct *phases* of recovery defined by bodily recovery, long-time heroin users in Gejiu frequently disagreed about what bodily habits, friendships, and career ambitions they should preserve from their pasts and what vision of a future life they should pursue. If the addicts in Burroughs's fictional accounts existed outside of historical time, the recovering drug users who appear in these pages were intensely concerned with both the lived temporality of their own lives and the shifting collective time associated with China's reform and opening. Close attention to their experiences reveal a complex temporal politics of healing and conveys powerful, rarely considered perspectives on China's historical trajectory.

## APPROACHING HISTORICITY

Conversations about historicity in anthropology, philosophy, and related disciplines provide conceptual scaffolding and methodological inspiration for this investigation. Phenomenologist David Carr argues that scholars interested in historicity "want to know how history is encountered, how it enters our lives, and in what forms of consciousness and experience it does so" (2014, 47). Carr's formulation immediately raises important questions: What is the relationship between lived individual and collective experiences of time? To what degree are ways of encountering, living, and becoming conscious of history distinct processes? How might centering these philosophical questions inform a study of recovery from heroin addiction?

This account starts with a phenomenological interest in the lived time of individuals. While early phenomenological work aimed at developing a technical vocabulary to describe the unifying structure of temporal experience (Husserl [1928] 1964), more recent phenomenological attention to temporality by anthropologists has shown how individuals' lived relationships to past and future horizons are shaped by concrete experiences in the world (Desjarlais and Throop 2011).[7] Historicity grapples with the overlapping lived relationship between an individual's immediate past and future (the flux or flow of qualitative time); more habituated ways of engaging the world (temporal orientations or shifting horizons of approaching the past or future); and the reflexive, shared narratives, discourses, and events that connect individuals to broader groups (Stewart 2016, 86). Historical time understood as the connection between the lived time of individuals and groups has been approached as social experience; a type of narrative; a form of consciousness; and shared knowledge, intuitions, and feelings. I briefly introduce three distinct approaches to historicity.

Certain cultural Marxist scholars emphasize the importance of historical consciousness as a critical means of gaining a perspective on the present. One author defines historicity as "a perception of the present as history; that is, a relationship to the present which somehow de-familiarizes it and allows us that distance from immediacy which is at length characterized as a historical perspective" (Jameson 1990, 284). Whether struggling in a "thick present" of the post-9/11 global order (Harootunian 2007) or living "pure and unrelated presents in time" in late capitalism (Jameson 1990, 27), historical actors often struggle to understand how the collective past shapes the present. Particular individuals—often academics and cultural producers, but also workers (cf. Comaroff and Comaroff 1992)—through attention to historical process come to effectively diagnose, grasp, and critique events in an otherwise opaque historical present.[8]

If the writers in this first group see historicity as enabling a critical perspective on the complex reality of the present, postcolonial scholars and some anthropologists have emphasized the potential dangers of drawing on European ways of accounting for social time. This historicity scholarship discusses the cultural assumptions and political implications associated with historicism, the tradition undergirding modern understandings of history. Originating in the writings of eighteenth-century scholars in Europe and disseminated through commerce and conquest, the principles associated with historicism—including assumptions about chronology, historical linearity, and ideals of progress—spread around the world, partially displacing other modes of understanding the past and the present and shaping commonsense ways that individuals and groups experienced the movement of time (Anderson 1983; Koselleck 2004; Iggers 1995; Bambach 1995; Hodges 2019).

Assumptions associated with historicism inflect academic writing, national media campaigns, and individual narratives in potentially destructive ways (Fabian 1983; Young 1990; Chakrabarty 2000). In exposing the relationship of "Westernization," modernization, and development, anthropologists have shown how tenets of historicism justified the spatialization of global hierarchies and advanced European and American colonial and imperial ambitions (Ferguson 2006; Pursley 2019). For example, at the height of the Cold War, Zambian urban residents were encouraged to embrace "expectations of modernity" and focus on the "not-yet" of a future horizon of imminent economic and social prosperity (Ferguson 1999). Dreams associated with narratives of Zambia's future position in a global order worked to silence workers' dissatisfactions in the present. In the new millennium, historicism continues to exert powerful effects on how people in many parts of the world experience and narrate their own positions within a shifting global order.

A final cluster of historicity scholarship has focused on "forms of human awareness of being and becoming in time" that emerge from "nonhomogeneous social field(s)" (Palmié and Stewart 2016, 210, 223).[9] Rather than rely on experience-distant attention to discourses and social ideology, this work has been attentive to intuition, fantasy, and imagination in exploring historical sense (cf. Berlant 2011). Complicating culturalist formulations that emphasize sharp divisions between European and other conceptions of history, recent anthropologists' attention to historicity has shown how concrete dramatic performances, shared rhythms of laboring, dreams, and perceptions of landscapes contribute to intimations of historical time (Lambek 2002; Hirsch and Stewart 2005; Stewart 2017; Stewart and Strathern 2003).[10]

I approach *historicity* broadly through attention to individual and social experiences of time. Following Paul Ricoeur's (1990) creative engagement with aporias in human time and Victoria Browne's (2014) multilayered approach to lived historical time in feminist conversations, the chapters in this book adopt diverging approaches and temporal scales. I attend to verbal and nonverbal experience, cognitive thought and embodied feeling, rhythms produced through everyday embodied routines, and the politics of negotiating personal and collective pasts in the present. Some chapters, for example, foreground the existential challenges of reckoning with difficult pasts, while others look at how recovering heroin users participated in public conversations about Gejiu's future. I also explore how contemporaneity—the intimate relationships that develop between long-term heroin users—functions as "a mediating structure between the private time of individual fate and the public time of history" (Ricoeur 1990, 113). The next three sections show how the three approaches outlined here—historicity as critique of the historical present, historicity as exploration of the legacies of historicism, and historicity as ethnographic attention to experience in concrete encounters—help to elucidate the dynamics of the recovering histories featured in this book.

## ADDICTION AS A HISTORICAL PROBLEM: LABORING, IDLING, AND SOCIAL CRITIQUE

The complicated temporal politics of recovery became clear to me in the tension that emerged between two common Chinese phrases: "quitting drugs" (*jiedu*) and "returning to society" (*huigui shehui*).[11] Though each could be translated under the English umbrella term "recovery," these two phrases register important divergences in how efforts to build a life after heroin in China came to be conceptualized and lived. The most widely used term, *jiedu* or "quitting drugs," referred to breaking physiological addiction to the substance—a potential synonym for "detoxification" (*tuodu*), though it also encompassed longer-term efforts to live an abstinent life. Focused on preventing relapse, private hospital doctors, "folk" minority practitioners, employees at the national methadone maintenance clinics, and other service providers tended to speak about recovery as *jiedu*. They did not, as a rule, address broader questions their patients faced in building a life and finding work after drugs.[12]

The phrase "return to society" appeared frequently in government documents, on posters, on banners, and in everyday conversations during my time in China. Government propaganda campaigns encouraged a variety of "marginalized groups" (*bianyuan renqun*), including orphans, street children, government officials convicted of corruption, and former Falungong members to "return to society." The Chinese characters for "return" (*huigui*) are the same ones used to describe the process by which Hong Kong "came back to" Chinese rule in 1997 after more than 130 years under British control, an event commonly known in English as "the Handover." To return thus connotes a reintegration into a previously existing set of relationships, the taking back of a position that one has left in the past. If "quitting drugs" tended to emphasize the accumulation of quantitative, linear "drug-free time," the temporality of this state-sponsored call to "return to society" drew attention to heroin users' relative position in relation to the contested historical time of the nation.

The importance of distinguishing between "return to society" and "quitting drugs" became clear to me through a blunder I made during one of my early visits to the Green Orchards drop-in center. I had learned that Old Kaiyuan, a frequent attendee at the center identifiable by his bald head and slight limp, had abstained from opioids for more than three years. Curious how others viewed this figure, I asked a small group of regular attendees if Old Kaiyuan might be a candidate for having successfully "returned to society." Li, his frequent companion at the center, responded to my question with incredulity. Barking at me in a frustrated tone, he protested, "Someone like Old Kaiyuan? How could you think that he has 'returned to society?'" Li noted that this aging, penniless idler was estranged from his family and came to the center in part because slightly better-off friends would buy him snacks and alcohol. That I would attempt to nominate this socially marginalized and unemployed—albeit opioid-free—middle-aged man as someone who had "returned" struck Li as a cruel joke.

The encounter underscored the centrality of laboring to ideas of recovery in China. With close to 80 percent of registered drug users across the country reporting that they were jobless (National Narcotics Control Commission

2009), many people with heroin use history whom I met spoke of persisting unemployment—referred to by my interlocutors as "idling" (*xianzhe*)—as the primary barrier they faced in their attempts to "return."[13]

While having a job was a crucial part of any return, my interlocutors held diverging understandings about which forms of labor were healing, what living conditions and career ambitions they might aspire to, and perhaps most important, who was responsible for ensuring that they worked.

A closer exploration of how the "society" was conceptualized by heroin users helps to explain these diverging attitudes toward labor. *Shehui* is a relatively recent addition to the Chinese language, appearing as a translation of the European term by way of a Japanese loanword at the end of the nineteenth century (Vogelsang 2012). Two coexisting meanings in the English etymology of the word are relevant to how *shehui* came to be used by my interlocutors in Gejiu: society conceptualized in a Durkheimian sense as a national modern collective, and society understood as an exclusive group or club. Future chapters explore the attitude that my interlocutors held toward shifting national regimes of labor in China during and after Mao's reign.[14] People with heroin use history in Gejiu also spoke about their past involvement in "society" best understood as a club or special group. The great majority had grown up "inside the state system" (*tizhili de ren*) as members of the exclusive "small society" (*xiao shehui*) that Yunnan Tin and its partners created for their workers under Mao. In addition, chapter 1 documents the importance of "mixing in Society" (*hun shehui*) early in their careers, a usage I distinguish through capitalization to refer to a group of pioneering private sector workers who had great influence in the city in the 1980s and early 1990s.

The multivalence of this group's understanding of *shehui* combined with the ambiguous temporal politics of *huigui* converged in their frequent discussions about how recovering addicts might be expected to labor. Maoist, Deng, and post-Deng state regimes espoused different ideas about collective life, state employment, and the therapeutic value of laboring for individual addicts (see the appendix). Echoing the rhetoric of laid-off state employees in Beijing and the Bolivian and Tswana miners who traced their own struggles to broader market forces (Yang 2015; Nash 1979; Comaroff and Comaroff 1987), my interlocutors offered critical analysis of the harms of market-oriented policies guiding the state's contemporary approach to governing. In debating how they might reenter the workforce, Old Kaiyuan, Li, and other idlers with heroin use history sometimes drew on Maoist imaginaries, or what Michael Dutton refers to as "the ever-present specter of another type of politics" (2008, 110) to imagine alternate ways of participating in collective laboring.

## BEHIND THE TIMES? THE FRAUGHT TEMPORAL POLITICS OF CATCHING UP

Historicist assumptions, numerous observers have argued, thrived in recent decades in China (e.g., Sahlins 1990; Ferguson 2006). Interactions over the years in China exposed me to the concrete ways that assumptions about development and historical movement appeared in everyday conversations. Acquaintances, including people with heroin use history, on occasion asked me to quantify in years how far the Middle Kingdom was behind the United States. References by Gejiu residents to how Laos or North Korea existed "decades behind" the People's Republic underscored the commonsense perspective that China was moving in homogenous, linear, and global time. Historical modes of reckoning supplemented by embodied sensations of movement and its absence also appeared in my interlocutors' descriptions of addiction and recovery.

Meng's views on his own recovery introduce these themes. I first met Meng just after he had been released from a two-year stint in a compulsory labor center at the office of a grassroots NGO that was part of the Honghe Prefecture drug-user network in a nearby city. His parents had recently passed away, and unusually for someone born before 1980, he had no siblings. With nowhere else to go, the thirty-six-year-old temporarily slept on a couch in the NGO office while working as a volunteer.

In our early encounters, Meng had intense anxiety about his own position in contemporary society, which came to be expressed in frequent comments about how he lagged behind his contemporaries. For example, he told me one day that he liked to watch tennis and named a few of his favorite players. I teased him that he must not have been a very committed fan, as those he mentioned had all retired in previous years. He looked at me seriously. "It's not that I don't like tennis. It's that I've been using drugs and in labor camps for much of the past twenty years!" Shuttling between periods of heroin use and stints in state detention, Meng argued, had removed him from historical time and led to deficits in his ability to navigate city life.

In another of our early meetings, Meng complained to me that until very recently he had not known how to operate a smartphone, use the internet, or withdraw money using a bank card. He asked me rhetorically how this could be possible in 2009. When I pointed out that I had been in a bank the previous week when a worker from a nearby farming community—likely in the city for seasonal employment—had struggled to operate an automated teller, Meng sighed and noted with frustration that *he* had been born and raised in one of Honghe's biggest cities; his own expectations about the trajectory of his life should not be compared to that of a peasant (for an exploration of the category of peasant in China, see Cohen 1993). Meng felt that the combination of periods of heroin use and bouts in state detention had kept members of this cohort from responding to the needs of the national trajectory: "While others are moving with the development of society (*genzhe shehui de fazhan*), we [long-term heroin users] are still stuck in (*tingliu*) the '80s or '90s!"

Other middle-aged, long-term heroin users I came to know in Gejiu also saw addiction as an affliction that impeded workers from keeping up with the historical present. For some, recent feelings of obsolescence tied to their own repetition of behaviors associated with the past contrasted sharply with their early careers, when they "moved with the waves of society" (*genzhe shehui de langchao zou*) and "caught the latest fashion" (*ganshimao*) by taking advantage of entrepreneurial opportunities in their youth.[15] Bodily symptoms including complaints of remaining stationary or being stuck in a previous era functioned as socially recognized symbols communicating shared pressures of responding to a rapidly changing local economy (cf. Geertz 1968).

Attention to state discourses on development help to explain how experiences of addiction came to be linked to a presumed historical movement of the country. China scholars have shown that assumptions of historicism have undergirded nationalist rhetoric in China for over a century and across differing political projects.[16] In recent years, government directives in a range of fields, including real estate regulations, mental health guidelines, statistics bureau operations, and national and regional labor policies, evoked the necessity of national development to frame their programs (Greenhalgh 2003; Zhang 2006; Liu 2009; Hoffman 2010). Workers negatively impacted by shifting policies and emerging regimes of labor in the post-Deng economy complained of feeling "pushed backward, toward the socialist past . . . and obsolescence" (Solinger 2013, 60).

Building observations of the prevalence of this language into an expanded criticism of contemporary Chinese society, Yan Hairong argues that keywords promoted by the Chinese government "coded the social landscapes" beginning in post-1980s China. Migrant workers were taught that they "lack a consciousness of development that the post-Mao Chinese state has been striving to foster through reform and opening" (Yan 2008, 114). They came to understand their own movement to the city to work as a pursuit of "self-development" that mirrored the country's purported work of "catching up to," "advancing," and "getting on track with" wealthier nations in the global market economy (2, 115, 189; see also Yan 2003; Pun 2005). In moving from observing the prevalence of this developmentalist discourse to critiquing its effects, Yan argues that state messages about the inevitability of following particular historical trajectories served to distort and mask a new "subterranean" reality (2008, 24, 249): the exploitation of a massive rural workforce for the benefit of "new masters" in China's reform and opening.

While recognizing the power of Yan's account, this book eschews embracing overarching arguments to focus on the situated ways that individuals and groups debated and internalized their positioning within a broadly shared "cultural anxiety about temporality" (Zhang 2000, 94).[17] For long-term heroin users, questions of who was exploiting whom under what conditions were contested. Moreover, these conversations were always linked to immediate existential and practical challenges of attempting to forge new lives in changing, uncertain times.

Meng adopted a pragmatic attitude toward an understanding of recovery that he conceived of as "catching up" to the demands of the contemporary economy. He saw the need of immediately addressing the "huge" gap that he sensed existed between his own "psychological development" and an imagined urban dweller who was "a similar age and background to my own." In the first months after his release from the compulsory laboring center, he prioritized learning how to operate computers, type, Microsoft Office programs, and participate in various online communities. He also argued that people with drug use history needed to learn to be content with and embrace an "ordinary" (*pingpingdandan*), frugal lifestyle—typical urban residents in the new millennium could enjoy basic comforts, but not the pursuit of gratuitous pleasures that he had embraced as a teenager in an earlier moment of market opening. A few months after we first met, Meng obtained an entry-level job at a private security firm and was quickly promoted to a management position. The quiet, stable life he enjoyed in the later stages of my fieldwork for Meng validated his self-diagnosis and response.

## DISORIENTATION: MOVING IN THE HISTORICAL PRESENT

Interactions I had with Pan, a long-term heroin user who appears in chapter 5, provide an opportunity to explore how historicity impacted recovery from addiction on a more intimate scale. Sitting on his living room couch one afternoon, Pan complained that he felt his heroin use history continued to cast a shadow over his future plans. At the time of our conversation, he noted that he had managed to "keep his integrity" (*baochi caoshou*—i.e., abstain from heroin use) for more than two years. He said he believed he had "walked half the road" (*zoulebanlu*) out of addiction. When I asked him what remained for him to do to "return to society," he grew apprehensive and again brought up the question of time. "One, two, three, four years. Who's to say I won't be good by then? That's my thought, but I'm not able to make sense of this question. In the end, where is the place that [a return] exists?" (*wo gaobudong zhege wenti, [huigui] daodi cunzai zai shenme difang?*).

Pan's interest in locating a "place where return exists" drew attention to his anxiety about the type of future he should strive for, a crucial question confronting every figure appearing in this book. Pan's musing also drew attention to how recovering drug users might assess if they were moving closer to a "return" in a given moment, and what facilitated a shift in these feelings shift over time.

In *Queer Phenomenology*, Sara Ahmed speaks of the concept of orientation as crucial to how we both "find our way" and come to "feel at home" as we extend our bodies into space (2006, 7). Ahmed's critical acumen foregrounds queer, critical race, and feminist mediations; she rereads foundational texts in the phenomenological tradition, challenging their white European male creators' heteronormative presumptions and expanding on possibilities for queer life. Her focus on the power of disorientation in embodied everyday experience deeply resonates with how the recovering addicts at the center of this book perceived their failure to fully inhabit the current historical moment. "Collective direction," as Ahmed puts it, comes to be imposed on individuals by outside groups—we are asked to turn in particular ways, and our bodies take shape as a result of the accumulation of how we are directed through time (2006, 16–17, 20). Disorientation occurs when we lose the taken-for-granted sense of following established ways of moving—that is, when we stray off of the paths or lines that others have made before us (11).

Ahmed's phenomenological attention to orientation offers inspiration for approaching long-term heroin users' recovery on a more intimate scale in attending to how bodies acquire shapes in relation to particular gatherings and objects. In thinking about how this perspective applies to my encounters with Pan, one day in particular comes to mind. In 2011 I accompanied a group of recovering drug users on a trip to a hot springs. Though three of my companions were experienced drivers, I ended up behind the wheel as the only person with a valid license. Never having mastered manual transmission, I was slightly apprehensive operating the "bread van" we had rented for the occasion. Pan volunteered to sit next to me. He deeply identified as a driver, which had been his professional vocation for a number of years when he was in his twenties and thirties. I learned on this trip that he was intimately familiar with the particular model we rented, as he had repaired and driven these vehicles during a stint when he worked as a mechanic. From helping secure the rental to coaching me on when to switch gears to sharing trivia about driving in the area, Pan seemed happy and at ease throughout the day, particularly when we were in the car.

After dropping off the other passengers, I drove with Pan and his wife, Su, to the outskirts of the city to return the vehicle. He asked me if he could take over driving. We pulled over, and he slipped into the driver's seat. With Su growling from the back seat that he needed to be careful, he pulled onto the road. Though it had been close to a decade since he had been at the wheel, Pan effortlessly returned to the road, moving through the various gears. After a couple of minutes, Su began to chide him, saying that he shouldn't be driving in the city center without a license. When we returned the car, Pan eagerly told the proprietor of the rental business that he expected to be back in the future. In subsequent weeks he energetically renewed his search for delivery positions that might help him reenter the workforce and spoke more frequently about hoping to take the test to have his license reinstated so he could work again as a driver.

One way of thinking about "return to society" is an attempt to find a new equilibrium after becoming "disoriented" (*mimang*), a term that my interlocutors used to describe both the effects of past heroin use and their early efforts to rejoin society. While some in this book questioned their acquired orientations and saw the need to deviate from previous lives, others hoped for a "return" to familiar lines. This book at times focuses on these attempts at reorienting—unearthing old skills such as playing table tennis or mahjong—or finding pleasure in gaining new competencies, ways of connecting, or bodily habits that made moving in unfamiliar spaces easier. Our day of driving was not a significant moment in Pan's life. And yet, small actions like orchestrating a ride in a familiar car might become more substantial parts of recovering histories, opening individual future horizons and deepening visions of lives that were worth living. "Hope," Sara Ahmed writes, "is an investment that the 'lines' that we follow will get us somewhere" (2006, 18).

## CHAPTER BY CHAPTER

Attention to historicity in this account unsettles persistent assumptions that undergird popular understandings of recovery. Derek Summerfield, for example, writes that recovery is what "happens in people's lives rather than in their psychologies. It is practical and unspectacular, and it is grounded in the resumption of the ordinary rhythms of everyday life—the familial, sociocultural, religious, and economic activities that make the world intelligible" (2002, 1105). While informed by a sensitivity to lived experience, Summerfield here fails to address a crucial recurring concern of my Gejiu-based interlocutors: What if the "activities" and "ordinary rhythms" that *once* "made the world intelligible" fail to correspond to opportunities available in contemporary social and economic life?[18] This book describes diverging understandings of recovery that are inextricably imbricated with sensing and responding to a dynamically shifting historical present.

In chapter 1, I show how heroin use for Gejiu residents took on meaning within shared horizons of a young generational cohort's early laboring experiences. Recounting events occurring more than two decades before my arrival in the region, the chapter documents how early encounters with the opioid were shaped by a tin mining boom that occurred in the late 1980s and 1990s, a time I call the Rush years. Three coming-of-age stories focus attention on the shared existential challenges of young people who came to believe that the ways of laboring and navigating the world associated with their parents were increasingly inadequate to the changing times. In attending to how these young workers shared ideas about the possibilities and challenges of rejecting local Maoist traditions, this chapter foregrounds the lasting impact of risk-taking on the experiences and outlook of a group I call the Heroin Generation.

Each of the remaining five chapters focuses on how individuals during my fieldwork defined and moved toward life after heroin. Chapter 2 begins by describing how Sam, a onetime mining boss, and his friends struggled to navigate a private sector economy that had changed dramatically since the 1980s. An account of my trip to the nearby mountains documents the radical reorganization of labor that had taken place since this group first came into contact with heroin. I then show how Sam came to understand his heroin habit as intimately connected to a broader crisis in his self-conception as a worker. Recovering from heroin for Sam required "adapting" to social realities of the new millennium by breaking habits accumulated in the Rush years and emulating later-arriving entrepreneurs who had replaced him.

Chapter 3 explores the struggles of a small group of long-term heroin users who, in contrast to others in this book, argued that the window when they might have returned to society had closed. Focusing on particular encounters when my interlocutors communicated severely diminished expectations concerning their own futures, I show how a particular mode of narrating and experiencing their lives as "sacrificial offerings of the Reform era" facilitated connection with their peers even as it contributed to individual suffering and shared, overwhelming feelings of obsolescence.

Drawing on conversations with regulars at Green Orchards, a drop-in center and harm reduction NGO, chapter 4 shows how idling long-term heroin users turned to the therapeutic potential of two distinct legacies of socialist laboring. Members of this group spoke about the care provided to employees by state-owned enterprises in the 1980s as well as the radical revolutionary power of collective "remolding through labor," imagined to have existed in the first years of the People's Republic, as potent examples of how the state could encourage—and even force—drug users to "merge into" society as productive workers. In questioning what constituted appropriate interventions into citizens' lives, Green Orchards members drew on the country's past to criticize contemporary state policies that they argued contributed to a condition of addiction that they saw as inseparable from their involuntary idling.

Chapter 5 starts with a detailed description of a wedding ceremony. The rituals associated with this event helped make visible a more general set of opportunities and risks that Su, the bride, faced in her attempts to return to society. Drawing on the concept of caring labor to foreground the importance of maintaining and renewing relationships with others, I show how Su's efforts to improve her own life came to be entangled with attending to aging family members, restarting her career as a saleswoman in a multilevel marketing organization, expanding her family, and forging new connections with "normal people." In these activities, Su confronted gendered expectations of where and how she should labor and negotiated relationships complicated by the specter of her history of heroin use.

Chapter 6 documents the career of Yan Jun, a controversial NGO leader and onetime colleague of Xun Wei. I explore two distinct ways that Yan came to narrate his civil society work: first as building a grassroots network and later as embodying the position of brave protector of the rights of people with drug use history, including his own. Observers who knew him questioned not only his motivations but also the very principles of civil society that he claimed to embody. My struggles in making sense of Yan Jun's experiences prompt me to revisit the book's phenomenological approach to recovering histories and briefly consider how a psychoanalytically informed attention to the dynamics of the encounters described in this book might open up other perspectives.

Drawing on observations from a trip to Gejiu made a decade after my first visit to the city, the epilogue offers a brief meditation on how recent changes in this community impacted collective ways of experiencing the future. The book finishes with Xun Wei and me taking a trip to the nearby mountains to visit his former mining site a decade after my first visit to the city.

The structure of the book aims to pluralize understandings of addiction as each chapter explores how historicity—the complex interweaving of personal and collective experiences of time—impacts recovery. Some focus on narratives of life events and diagnosis of contemporary society, while others work to examine how nonverbal ways of relating to the past and future, impact individual and collective outlooks. All draw attention to the importance of labor in thinking about possibilities for living in the fourth decade of the country's reform and opening.

Most of the figures appearing in this book are men. This is in part due to my own difficulties in forging close relationships with women recovering heroin users in Gejiu. But it is also a reflection of the fact that men made up the great majority of heroin users throughout the country: 85 percent according to national public security registers (National Narcotics Control Commission 2009). In this particular corner of the country, heroin had initially spread most quickly among entrepreneurs connected to the male-dominated mining industry at a time when such ventures were a "sign of risk, glory, and masculine strength" (Rofel 1999, 54). Chapters 1 and 4 in particular explore how historically particular gendered division of labor impacted the lives of my interlocutors.

## LOCATING ADDICTION

This book joins a body of scholarship that has pushed against waves of medicalization that depicted addiction as a pathological personality disorder or, more recently, a relapsing disease of the brain (Lindesmith 1938; Acker 2002).[19] Anthropologists have contributed to broader conversations about addiction by showing how patterns of structural violence perpetuated through race, gender, and class differences shape the distribution of illicit drugs as well as harms associated with use (Bergmann 2008; Bourgois 2003; Bourgois and Schonberg 2009; Knight 2016). Occasionally in some of this important scholarship, ethnographers have argued substance abuse is an "epiphenomenal expression" (Bourgois 2003, 319) of underlying societal inequalities, as marginalized subjects "self-medicate the hidden injuries of oppression" (Baer, Singer, and Susser 2004, 169). In a similar vein, Pierre Bourdieu depicts drug addicts as individuals who, due to "the smooth functioning of habitus," remain largely unaware of their "hidden" suffering and the broader social conditions that fuel their misery (Eagleton and Bourdieu 1992, 121). The sage social scientist in these accounts helps users to "make their situation explicit" through rigorous socioanalysis—including historicizing the roots of drug-related suffering (Eagleton and Bourdieu 1992, 121). My discomfort with the move to understand problem drug use as primarily an unconscious or "hidden" expression of suffering is that it risks homogenizing how people with drug use history come to inhabit the historical present and potentially overlooks the critical role that analyzing, reflecting up, intuiting, and feeling shared historical time has for long-term heroin users in how they understand and respond to their condition.[20]

Angela Garcia's attention to temporality and history in *The Pastoral Clinic* (2010) has influenced my approach. She describes the Hispano heroin users in her account as "melancholic subjects," figures for whom the use of opioids is connected to intergenerational experiences of dispossession and "endless" suffering. Garcia argues that experiences of loss come to be inflected by a Hispano tradition of mourning that "commemorates the singularity of death while insisting on the inevitable repetition of it" (2010, 73).[21] Throughout her account, she shows how the pain and relief of heroin use mingles with the psychic legacies of events occurring months, years, or even centuries in the past. If, as a local saying puts it, "history is a wound," Garcia's phenomenologically oriented study of the heroin epidemic in Espanola Valley documents the deep, collective scars created through familiar cycles of painful loss and attention to collective ways of reckoning with this past (97).

My exploration of historicity in Gejiu draws attention to a markedly different temporal dynamic. Though residents in this tin mining community, too, reckoned with individual and collective pasts as part of the recovery process, my interlocutors often understood themselves as grappling with a pernicious form of obsolescence. Many members of this generational cohort of predominantly Han urban residents saw themselves as having once played a central role in implementing the early marketization policies touted by Deng Xiaoping at a time when engaging private sector activity was deeply stigmatized; they thus were haunted by missed possibilities associated with unpredictable ruptures, openings, and fault lines in the country's ongoing development rather than living through a perceived "endlessness" of exclusions and loss.

I also want to underscore that this is an ethnographic study of recovery rather than of drug use. During my fieldwork, I was rarely in the presence of the drug. Some might argue that a phenomenologically oriented account of people whose lives had been deeply affected by their consumption of this potent drug needs to give extended attention to direct experiences of heroin use.[22] My response is that my relationships with many of the people in the book emerged in part because I became deeply invested in their attempts to start new lives. In following their struggles to break from painful parts of their pasts, aspects of my interlocutors' lives became central to this research, while others were either inaccessible to me or failed to find their way into this account. I came to believe that this group's efforts to "return to society"—and by extension to diagnose, explore, and move through a rapidly shifting social world—offer important perspectives on broader experiences of labor and life in contemporary China and beyond.

## BACK ON THE MOUNTAIN?

On a spring day in 2015, Xun took me to visit his office. Funding that had been available in previous years had become difficult to come by, and the spacious two-bedroom apartment that had formerly served as the organization's headquarters had been replaced by two tiny, separate rooms on the ground floor of an apartment building. As director, Xun sat at a single desk in a closet-sized space at the front of the building, while peer educators and the group's financial officer crammed into a room across the hall. After closing the door to leave for dinner, he cursed softly when he realized he had left his keys inside his office.

Now in his late forties, Xun appeared both thinner and frailer than when I had first met him. After a nasty motor scooter accident, a metal bar had been inserted along the right side of his collarbone. This bar had subsequently broken, and the pieces visibly protruded from underneath his skin. For years after the accident, he struggled to carry even light packages with his injured hand. Xun was acutely aware of his own appearance. Once, while telling me a story about his youth, he actually apologized for his diminished physique, as if the discrepancy between his earlier actions on the mountain and his present appearance strained his credibility.

Looking in through a window protected by an iron grating, we could see his keys were on the far side of his desk, several feet away from us. I suggested that we call the locksmith to open the door. Xun replied that he had another idea. He plucked a bamboo rod from a nearby flowerpot and unwound a metal wire that was holding up a nearby window plant. Fashioning this metal into a hook that he attached to the rod, Xun began slipping this quickly constructed fishing device through a slit in the open window.

A young man in his early twenties, wandering to his parked car across the street, stopped to watch. "You really think you can get it?" he asked incredulously. Xun ignored him.

Although his initial attempts fell far short of his target, Xun adjusted his grip and extended the makeshift pole. By flexing his arm to allow the rod to move a few more inches inside the office, he bumped the hook up against the keys. "It won't take long now," he noted. Sure enough, with a few more flicks of his wrist, he managed to catch his keyring on the metal hook and carefully retracted the pole until his keys had reached the windowsill. He then pulled them through the metal bars, placed them in his pocket, smiled briefly, and turned to walk home.

Though it lasted less than twenty minutes, this scene holds an enduring significance for me. It reminded me of Xun's vulnerability; leaving his keys was part of a growing forgetfulness that he frequently commented upon, and the strangely configured office was a sign of the tenuous status of his NGO— and civil society actors more generally—under the Xi government. I saw, in his quiet indifference to the incredulous comment of the younger passerby, his strength in enduring frequent slights that included discrimination at hotels and an encounter with a shop operator who (knowing his history) refused to touch money that Xun placed on the counter to make a purchase. But this was also an instance of Xun's self-reliance and stubborn ability to forge his own way. His patient resourcefulness also helped him to produce a budget, write grant applications, and become a steady leader of his NGO. These were qualities he attributed to his entrepreneurial past on the mountain. More than anything, Xun's successful recovery of his keys, to me, represented his tenacity in keeping his future open at a time when many with his background faced difficult prospects.

Xun and I never discussed the key-fishing episode. Indeed, perhaps the meaning I have bestowed on this event is more a product of my own projections and associations than a reflection of the significance it held for him. In making these connections, however, I draw on conversations that occurred over a number of years as well as my sense of his patterns of moving in and making sense of the world. I thought I could feel Xun finding the pleasures of rediscovering his own inventiveness as he opened doors that appeared to have closed on him. Subtle, situated acts like this one were part of how the past came to be negotiated and a "return to society" enacted.

# CHAPTER I

# Mayhem on the Mountains

*The Rush of Heroin's Arrival*

First-time visitors to Gejiu cannot help but notice the presence of the mountains. While Old Yang Mountain's modest profile hugs the western side of the city, Old Yin Mountain towers far more dramatically to the east, a geographical characteristic that, according to local legend, provided women in the region with greater strength than their male counterparts. In the early 2010s lights illuminated the eight floors of a pagoda that had been built on the peak by the local Buddhist monastery. From the valley floor at night, this tower appeared to float in the sky above the city (see figure 2).

Despite the mountains' intimate proximity, I rarely heard residents discuss their allure. Occasionally members of the city's growing middle class of car owners might drive into the nearby hills for a weekend meal; the "one hundred year continuous broth chicken restaurant," for example, was a (very) minor attraction located near mining tunnels in the mountains behind Old Yang. For the most part, those whose careers had involved extracting minerals referred to their interest in the mountains in the past tense. The dreams and energy of urban residents were focused elsewhere. Young people with ambition tended to talk about potential futures in the new prefecture seat Mengzi, the provincial capital Kunming, or if they were especially adventurous, a major city on the east coast.

This neglect of the surrounding topography was not a permanent feature of this community. In the late 1980s and early 1990s, more than ten thousand workers, many of them young local residents, sought opportunities in privately run mining enterprises. The mountains briefly became places of possibility

FIGURE 2. Old Yin Mountain, visible from the valley floor. Photo by author.

that beckoned to a group of young men and women who broke from established ways of moving to seek out their own fortunes.

Residents in Gejiu had a saying—"Open the Big Door, but forget to draw the curtains" (*damen dakai, chuanlian wangle lashang*)—to characterize the destructive aspects of the local implementation of Deng Xiaoping's reform and opening policies in the 1980s. The arrival of heroin, alongside the re-emergence of sex work and gambling, were often referenced as unintended consequences of the opening. Heroin had traveled to Yunnan alongside—and sometimes within—shipments of fruit, clothes, electronics, and other consumer goods that increasingly flowed into the country from Vietnam, Laos, and Myanmar as part of the country's efforts to promote trade and growth (see map 1).

Yet such characterizations tend to elide the question of who the people were who came to use the opioid that circulated in this early period of experimental market reforms. A Kunming-based addiction expert involved in drug treatment since the 1980s told me that users of heroin during Deng's tenure tended to come from the lowest rungs of society (*diceng*) and had "little to

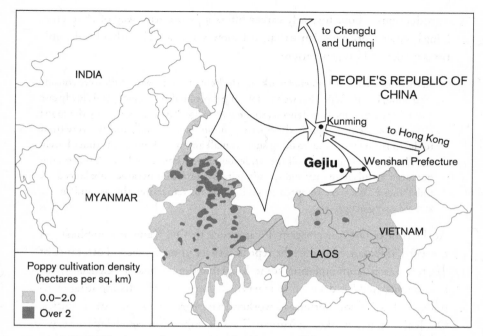

MAP I. Regional opium production and overland heroin trafficking routes, 1999. Adapted from Beyrer et al. (2000, 78).

lose" by turning to illicit drugs (Li 2009).[1] This type of characterization fails to grapple with the fact that inherited Maoist class and social status labels were themselves radically questioned in these years. An anthropologist conducting research among the Yi minority in nearby Sichuan province concludes that "desire to take part in the development going on all around them, in China's modernity" (Liu 2011, 17) led young male workers to participate in circuits of migrant labor and engage in illicit drug use. Early users of this drug in Yunnan have been described as "fun seekers" with entrepreneurial backgrounds who deployed their newly available disposable incomes to pursue emerging consumptive opportunities (Zoccatelli 2014).

My interest in this chapter is to examine how events associated with the "opening of the big door"—and in particular the possibility of laboring opportunities outside the purview of the state on the mountains in and around Gejiu—came to shape young people in common ways. A comment made by Old Kaiyuan—the unemployed Green Orchards regular appearing in the introduction—about his early career offers a provocative way of characterizing his own work experience that, as I show, was shared by other local ambitious workers of his generation:

> In the '80s when I first started working, the benefits at my work unit were considered good, but in Gejiu city, we saw lots of people [making money] and slowly our mental state became unbalanced (*xinli bupingheng*). The local scene, by the 1990s it wasn't ok, seeing people in the Society (*shehuishang de ren*), while we were tired to death from work, only making such a small amount of money, at times barely even having enough to eat, all the while looking at those people, each one taking out large fistfuls of money and spending it. So our minds became unbalanced . . . unbalanced. We were tempted to go looking for dangerous things, and slowly started using drugs.

At the time of our conversation, I was struck by Old Kaiyuan's emphasis on the word "unbalanced," which he repeated twice upon his second utterance of the term as if contemplating some long-abandoned puzzle. Crucially, his account situated his decision to start using heroin *after* a disorienting reappraisal of his self-conception as a worker. In his early teens and early twenties, Old Kaiyuan had worked at Yunnan Tin's Number One Smelting Factory, a highly desirable lifetime position at a respected state employer.[2] The taken-for-granted, established ways of living that had kept him laboring at this state job—including the "good" benefits he, like his parents before him, had enjoyed—suddenly came to be reevaluated in the light of his exposure to a different *type* of worker, one who consumed in new and conspicuous ways. Old Kaiyuan understood his lack of balance as precipitated by a historically particular and, as I show, broadly experienced crisis of laboring.

This brief reflection also draws attention to the shifting way that young people came to relate to each other during these years. In his first evocation of a "we," Old Kaiyuan refers to a group of childhood friends who had grown up in households of state-owned enterprise (SOE) employees and were working in state-provided jobs. The "we" at end of the paragraph, however, references a collective who, after being exposed to changes in the "local scene" and wealthy "people in the Society," were seeking a world beyond the state factory and housing compounds. Importantly, this latter group in his telling was unified by the shared trait of being "tempted to go looking for dangerous things" rather than drug-seeking behavior.

In the following pages, three coming-of-age stories elucidate the shared existential challenges associated with a period in the late 1980s and early 1990s that I call the Rush years, a name meant to evoke both the opportunities associated with the beginnings of a short-lived mining boom and the shared sensations experienced by workers who pursued these newly possible careers. The first account describes a young miner's process of entering into the Society—a loose collective of workers at once widely stigmatized and envied—that grew rapidly in size and influence starting in the mid-1980s. The second section focuses on a bitter argument between a father and son about the latter's career that highlights the profound generational divide in historical and temporal orientations associated with different laboring regimes. The final narrative, of the disillusionment of an unhappy "iron rice bowl" worker, documents the emotional toll of radically questioning inherited ways of living.[3] Across these stories, I explore how Gejiu youth made the decision to break from the socialist iron rice bowl ways of laboring and living to pursue emerging opportunities in a nascent private sector.[4]

This chapter offers a revisionist account of what others have identified as a "turbulent moment" in China's recent history when "it wasn't clear which type of person would represent the nation, which group of people the state should favor in its post-Mao vision of modernity" (Rofel 1999, 103). Rather than understanding the young workers appearing in this book through inherited class positions or fixed occupational categories, this chapter draws on the work of Karl Mannheim and others interested in historical experience of generations to argue that a young cohort of intrepid workers shared new ways of intuiting the movements of collective history and facing uncertain futures. Attending the common challenges faced by this generational cohort allows a better understanding of the conditions under which heroin circulated broadly in the city. Examining the opportunities and challenges of entering adulthood under these conditions also provides a shared background for diverging attempts to realize a "return to society" more than two decades later.

## A BUSINESS OF HIS OWN: XUN WEI BECOMES A SOCIETY MINING BOSS

Xun Wei, the rat catcher and NGO worker introduced at the start of this book, moved from plans of becoming a "traditional" worker to becoming a notable "person of Society" (*shehuishang de ren*) in the span of less than three years. Attention to this period of his life introduces us to the historically specific allure of the mountains, as well as the charged economic and social activity associated with private sector actors in the Rush years.

The youngest of four brothers, Xun had grown up as part of Team 308 (*sanlingba dui*). This highly respected SOE was responsible for conducting exploratory geological work that guided Yunnan Tin's mining operations.[5] Xun's father served as a Team 308 office worker while his mother was a well-liked head of a neighborhood canteen, a "collective enterprise" (*jiti*) operating under the auspices of this SOE. Due to the needs of the work unit, the family had moved to a nearby mining town when Xun was a young child, returning to the city center for his junior middle school years. Though their income rarely allowed splurging beyond life's basic necessities, family members enjoyed generous iron rice bowl benefits, including living in 308 employer-provided housing, accessing medical care provided by the work unit, and attending SOE-run schools.

Xun initially assumed that his laboring life would unfold within Team 308's sprawling network of enterprises.[6] However, while his oldest brother was able to land a stable SOE job through family connections, and his second oldest brother "held up" their father's job when the latter retired, there were no iron rice bowl positions available for Xun Wei after his vocational senior middle school graduation.[7] Instead, Xun initially took a less secure position as a roaming book salesman in a newly formed collective enterprise bankrolled by 308. In this new role, he traveled around Honghe prefecture peddling books, including a massive hardcover tome with color photos that sold for several times his monthly salary. When the business disbanded after failing to turn a profit, Xun Wei, still only eighteen years old, joined dozens of other young men from his neighborhood to work for yet another 308 collective, based in the nearby Hongqi and Huangmao Mountains. This was Xun's first foray into tin mining.

His arrival at the 308 campsite in 1986 corresponded with the promulgation of new national mining policies and rapid expansion of private sector actors on the mountainside (State Council of the People's Republic 1986). Liberalization policy directives from Beijing urged local governments that oversaw mining operations to "open large mines up, unleash small mines, intensify extraction, and let the water flow."[8] Following this national trend, in the second half of the 1980s Yunnan Tin turned its focus to lucrative, mechanized deep mining (the "large mines"), leaving tin deposits close to the mountain's surface for excavation by private outfits. At the same time, extracting, washing, refining, and selling tin—activities long overseen by Yunnan Tin and its SOE partners—were also opened to private businesses for the first time since the last years of the Republican period in the 1940s.

Xun arrived on the mountainside as an early wave of workers representing hundreds of new businesses had appeared to take advantage of these new opportunities. He thus found himself in a dynamic context where state and private sector actors were mining side by side and frequently interacting. His own collective employed a total of about three hundred workers. Nearby, other mines were staffed by the employees of cash-hungry state organs, including the military. Meanwhile, separate from these government-affiliated collectives, local "mining bosses" (*kuang laoban*) opened their own operations. Although national laws still on the books at the start of the Rush years specified that businesses be limited to eight or fewer non-kin employees—a number that the Communist Party had adopted following Karl Marx's warnings about the inflection point for the creation of a rentier class (*Economist* 2011)—private mining bosses often employed dozens of day laborers to work in their mines. The daily wages these laborers received were more than ten times what Xun made in the 308 collective.[9]

Xun's ambition of becoming a Society mining boss emerged through the relationships that he cultivated in the mountains. His first mentor was a retired former colleague of his father who had recently entered the labor force to earn extra money in the 308 collective. When the two men were assigned to watch over a remote Yunnan Tin tunnel, this longtime miner taught Xun Wei crucial aspects of the mining trade, including how to assess the quality of tin by using a prospecting bowl. The older man told Xun stories about life on these same mountains in the 1940s, when "Old Society" (*jiu shehui*, i.e., pre-1949) bosses had grown wealthy from mining. Vilified as exploitative during "speaking bitterness" sessions and decades of Maoist propaganda campaigns, stories about pre-Liberation mining bosses now fueled Xun Wei's aspirational hopes of earning personal fortunes and growing the local economy. He began to wonder if he might create his own "enterprise" (*shiye*), a business that, he began to imagine, "would belong to me."

A few months later, Xun Wei struck up a close relationship with a Hui mining boss whose private outfit was located a few hundred meters away from the 308 collective's base. The Hui, a Muslim minority community who lived in farming settlements on the valley floor a few kilometers away from Gejiu, pioneered the production and regional distribution of a range of products, including chili peppers, grains, chemical fertilizer, guns, opium, heroin, and various minerals. A Chinese academic expressed a sentiment shared by many of my Han interlocutors when he wrote that the Hui tended to "swar(m) like bees" to any profitable enterprise.[10] This group had had a contentious history with the Han Chinese, who in addition to making up 92 percent of China's total population, constituted the great majority of Yunnan Tin's employees.[11] Due to the Hui's reputation as fierce fighters and local policies that offered them preferential policies to alleviate tensions over past conflicts, city and SOE security forces initially avoided interfering with their mountainside businesses. As a result, the Hui were highly represented among the earliest bosses in the mountains around Gejiu. In return for materials Xun pilfered from the 308 collective, this seasoned mining boss taught the younger worker about the intricacies of running a private mining business, including how to find and employ short-term laborers—groups of migrant Hani workers from the nearby mountains were beginning to show up around the train station in Gejiu looking for employment as day laborers—and manage local government relationships.

Equipped with a basic understanding of the economics and techniques associated with private sector mining, less than a year after arriving on the mountain Xun decided to go out on his own. In contrast to his father's dismissive attitude to this new career direction, his mother, a woman he idealized for her free spirit and spark, actively supported his decision to start his own business.[12] With several hundred yuan (approximately $100) put together from his own and other family members' savings, Xun Wei bought basic cooking supplies, picks, drills and other tools he would need; hired a small group of Hani and Guizhou day laborers; and began to dig.[13] After achieving moderate success in his first mountainside dig, Xun's second effort struck an abandoned 308 exploratory tunnel that offered access to ore with high tin content.[14] Benefiting from the untapped bounty of the mountain and abandoned infrastructure from local SOEs, Xun Wei began to make hundreds of dollars a day from his mine. As his profits grew, he hired more laborers, eventually overseeing a team of more than twenty workers, most of whom slept in tents near the mining entrance. Before his twenty-second birthday he had become a "hundred-thousand-aire" (shiwanyuanhu), with more money stored under his bed than his parents could make in several lifetimes of working at their SOE jobs.[15] In the process, he had become a living example of what moving onto the mountains—and into the nascent private sector—might bring to workers who dared to break free of established routines.

Xun Wei's success in running his own mining operation was relatively rare among my interlocutors. However, his account of becoming a "person of the Society" (*shehuishangderen*) helps to introduce a broader reconfiguration of Gejiu city—and China more broadly. In the twenty-first century, as well as in its pre-Maoist usage, the Society, an abbreviation for "black society" (*heishehui*) or organized crime, was often opposed to *legal* private sector activity. This distinction did not hold in Gejiu during the Rush years. In addition to those engaging in explicitly criminal activities, including extortion, drug trafficking, operating casinos, pilfering tine from state mines, pickpocketing, and robbery, workers in what would today be designated "legal" private sector professions, including restaurant proprietors, "little brother" assistants to bosses, hair-dressers, cab drivers, clothing sellers, nightclub staff, trucker drivers, and mechanics, also described themselves as members of the Society. Even certain state employees referred to themselves as "mixing" as they began to spend time with Society figures in consumptive evening entertainment or moonlighted in money-making ventures while holding onto their traditional employment.

Similar understandings of the Society as a transgressive community were deployed in other contexts in Deng Xiaoping's China, where the boundary between private sector and world of crime were blurry. For example, Fujianese businessmen who joined sworn brotherhood associations, participated in unregistered businesses, and carried firearms were referred to as "people of (S)ociety" (*shehuishangderen*) (Chen 1999, 287). Commercial discotheques in the "chaotic marketplace" in Shanghai in the 1980s were also referred to as "(S)ociety" spaces. At once cosmopolitan, expensive, rough, and associated with foreign influence, these venues in the early post-Mao years were con-trasted with "noncommercial" dancehalls run by the state, which had con-trolled admissions, promoted decorous behavior, and were often located in neighborhood settings (Farrer 1999, 153). While overlapping with "descending into the sea" (*xiahai*), a phrase broadly used in Reform-era China to designate the pursuit of a private sector career, "mixing in Society" during the Rush years references a set of charged practices and attitudes that must be attended to in their historical particularity.

Xun Wei's gradual adoption of new rhythms of laboring and consuming during the mining boom helps to elucidate the charged forms of social connection that proliferated in the Society during the Rush years. Work on the mountains was far more dangerous for Society workers than for state employees. With private mining sites potentially worth hundreds of thousands of dollars, mining bosses and their crews in the Rush years were frequently attacked by competitors; hand grenades and unregistered cheap "double-barreled" guns from nearby Pingyuan county flooded the campsites. Members of Xun's team slept with swords and other weapons nearby, while Xun obtained a permit that allowed him to keep a gun in his tent. He also brought a dog to stay at his site to help detect intruders.

Labor was at once more sporadic and intense than the slow, repetitive grind that had defined Xun's earlier state positions. Xun noted that at times, especially when the team seemed on the verge of unearthing high-grade tin, he threw himself into the manual labor with an intense energy, knowing that he would be the primary beneficiary of whatever the group unearthed. And yet returning to his mine day after day required discipline and bravery. Unlike the well-lit, spacious tunnels that the Communist Party had promoted as part of its worker-friendly approach to mining, Xun and his colleagues worked in hastily constructed, narrow tunnels that collapsed and nearly killed workers on more than one occasion (Kusnetzky 2011).

New activities on the mountains profoundly shaped social life in downtown Gejiu for early Society participants. Whereas in his previous job he had worked six or more days straight on the mountainside before going back to the city, Xun, who bought a motorcycle with early profits from his mine, began to spend most evenings in Gejiu. Though at one time it had offered little after-dark entertainment beyond a walk around Golden Lake, the tin capital was in the process of transforming into a thriving regional nightlife hub, with restaurants (early 1980s), mahjong parlors (1984), dance halls (1985), an indoor ice skating rink (1987), bars (1990), and clubs hosting traveling professional entertainment troupes (1990s) opening in rapid succession.[16] Xun was in a position to enjoy new consumptive opportunities as they arrived. For example, while his father had waited for years to take a trip to the nearby Workers Springs, a facility that had been built to reward both exceptional and ailing state employees with an all-expenses-paid opportunity to soak in healing mineral waters, after becoming a private miner Xun could go to the same facility whenever he wanted, staying in a new section opened to those who had the disposable income to pay.

At a time when corruption within local SOEs was limited and public salaries low, mining bosses and their associates were key consumers in a city where spending money on public leisure activities was still viewed as a potentially morally transgressive act. Part of Xun's motivation to spend additional informal time in Society spaces was a strategic interest in building relationships with people willing to help him protect his mining site. He frequently took out a group that included his siblings, work associates, childhood friends of 308 employees, and other potential allies to eat, drink, and sing in the city's nightspots. Confrontations between groups celebrating in newly opened night venues were common, as spending money at times reproduced the all-or-nothing, violent behavior with which it was earned.

Xun Wei's evening activities helped to show others the possibilities associated with Society careers in the Rush years. In visible, unapologetic economic activity, he was what Old Kaiyuan identified as "those people": a different *type* of worker embodying the possibilities of a new way of moving onto the mountains and through this urban community. The remaining two narratives explore complex lived experiences of young workers attempting to navigate shifting possible futures.

## GAMBLING WITH HISTORY: LI ZHIJUN'S REFUSAL OF HIS FATHER'S *DANWEI* VISION

Li Zhijun and his father over the years had had their share of disagreements, but their quarrel in 1985 was an especially unpleasant and consequential one. The family patriarch expected his son, a recent high school graduate, to take over his iron rice bowl position at Yunnan Tin. Zhijun refused, declaring that he would instead start a motorcycle repair business with a couple of his friends. His father forbade him to pursue this private sector career. Neither relented, and the confrontation resulted in an extended period of estrangement between them.

The Li drama focuses our attention on the particular way in which rapid changes to the local economy and society came to be understood by members of two distinct generational cohorts. In times when challenges to established ways of living are minimal, the "cultural product" of "the world of everyday life" becomes, as Clifford Geertz once posited, "the established scene and given object of our actions. Like Mt. Everest, it is just there, and the thing to do with it, if one feels the need to do anything at all, is to climb it" (1973, 111). In the 1980s in Gejiu, new workers challenged the reproduction of socialist ways of living. The disagreement between the Lis can be understood as an example of the failure of the cultural transmission of a Maoist way of life, realized not just in different ideas about decisions in the present, but also in the way that these two men conceptualized the collective future of the city.

In his 1927 essay "The Problem of Generations," sociologist Karl Mannheim directs our attention to how shared knowledge and lived experiences come to be shaped by the "location" of particular generational cohorts. Mannheim is particularly interested in understanding social dynamics in periods of rapid change where, as he puts it, "the latent, continuous adaptation and modification of traditional patterns of experience, thought, and expression is no longer possible" (Mannheim [1927] 1952, 309). In these moments, "youth"—a category he defines as between seventeen and thirty years of age—leave the "appropri-ated memories" of their elders and educators and feel the "real binding power" of "personally acquired memories" ([1927] 1952, 300).[17] Young people in this phase of life have the potential to become "dramatically aware of a process of de-stabilization" and "take sides," while older workers tend to "cling to the re-orientation that had been the drama of their youth" ([1927] 1952, 301). The clash between the Lis can be productively interpreted as confrontation of two ways of conceiving historical time, forged from their respective experiences as youths.

The senior Li had been deeply shaped by national and local events influenc-ing his own early career. He had moved to Gejiu in the late 1950s from a nearby city to take a position as a mechanic with Yunnan Tin at a time when the Chinese state was undertaking a national project of converting decadent and exploitative "consumptive cities" (*xiaofei chengshi*) into "productive cities" (*shengchan chengshi*) (cf. Brown 2012). His lifetime position at Yunnan Tin had provided him and his family with what was in Maoist times a highly desirable quality of life. During the senior Li's years at Yunnan Tin, the SOE had built schools, hospitals, and parks; expanded sorting and smelting plants; improved roads; and created newer, wider mining tunnels. The Yunnan Tin standard-issue fur work hat and wool clothes he and other employees had received were considered a key symbol of a desired potential spouse.[18] Drawing on his own direct early career experiences, Li was convinced that taking a job at Yunnan Tin was the single best way that Zhijun could attain a stable job and beneficial environment for raising his own family.

Li's strong feelings about passing on his job to his son were also bolstered by his intuitions about the historical movement of the country. Only two years before their argument, the local implementation of a national crackdown on "bourgeois" behaviors had resulted in the arrest and public humiliation of local "speculators" and other "hooligans." Engaging in small-time unregistered business activities or committing petty crime such as the pilfering of Chairman Mao–style hats resulted in detainment for up to three years in reeducation through labor centers. During mass arrests associated with this crackdown, police resorted to using thick string rather than handcuffs to tie together detainees—many self-identified "Society" members—in the local drained swimming pool. Young men dressed in the bell-bottom or tight-ankled pants associated at the time with Hong Kong crime movies were subject to special scrutiny during this sweep. Given that the government at any moment might launch a new "political movement" (*xingdong*) signaling a return to a past era's intolerance of private sector activity, the senior Li believed that the pursuit of "Society" activities was not just morally questionable but also constituted an unwise gamble with history. The People's Republic as he had come to know it would ultimately reward cautious and loyal state workers.

Born in 1966, Li Zhijun experienced the growth of the city—and by extension the trajectory of the country—in different ways from his other family members. For nearly a decade during the Cultural Revolution, many local youth, including his older sister, had spent years working in nearby rural poor minority communities as part of the national Maoist "up to the mountains and down to the countryside" campaign. Zhijun speculated that this experience helped to instill in his sister a seriousness, capacity to labor, and political commitment that bound her to the worldview of their parents; she heeded their advice and focused on her studies before becoming a local government official.[19] Zhijun, the baby of the family, by contrast was among the first group of teenagers in the post-Mao years who were not asked to do manual labor outside the city.

Instead, Zhijun in his adolescence began to "mix" in the Society, working sporadic hours as a street salesman. At first he made extra income by selling brand-name cigarettes outside the school gates to older men who wanted an alternative to the rationed "public cigarettes" (*gongyan*) that his father preferred. Cultivating contacts with "illegal smugglers" (*zousifan*), he was soon also peddling electric lighters, calculators, and fake Casio digital watches, which could be sold for as much as 50 yuan ($25), ten times their purchase price. Many of these products came into the country from Vietnam, passing through Pingyuan county before reaching Gejiu—the same trade route that would supply the younger Li with heroin several years later. Meanwhile, he displayed a penchant for getting into trouble in class, changing schools multiple times and repeating grades in two different academic years.[20]

As a teenager, Zhijun found that the activities that satisfied members of his father's generation, such as fishing in Golden Lake, riding bikes to the city outskirts, and walking in Baohua Park, no longer held his interest. Instead, he frequented Society nightspots accompanied by girlfriends or ventured out in larger groups of business associates and friends. Zhijun enjoyed gambling, dancing, eating at restaurants, and trying out the latest fashions, including the "refugee" (nanmin) garments from Japan that had just begun to arrive in the city. His "mind for business" (jingji tounao), antiauthoritarian tendencies, skill at fighting, and appetite for risk made him a valuable worker in Society circles. The idea of curtailing his own business aspirations to work long hours at his father's work unit for a salary of 35 yuan ($12) a month, an amount that could barely cover his basic living expenses let alone his evening pursuits, was unacceptable.

Zhijun's convictions derived in part from an explicit rejection of his father's mode of historical reckoning. He saw Gejiu residents of this older generation either as "traditional" (chuantong) fools stuck in increasingly irrelevant "orthodox" (zhengchuan) thinking associated with the country's recent past or jealous, "red-eyed" (hongyan) figures who lacked the courage to pursue the wealth that they secretly desired. By contrast, he was convinced that his fate was tied to a private sector that he believed would continue to grow. Indeed, Zhijun and his friends at times explicitly spoke about themselves as part of a "vanguard" (qianfang) group who were realizing the goals of China's marketization. As one former Society member recalled, "People mixing in Society wanted whatever had just entered the country; we wanted to be the one to try it (changshi) first!" Some felt the continual expansion of the private sector throughout the second half of the 1980s and beyond vindicated their life choices and helped to "prove some things" (zhengming yixie shiqing), as "this way of doing things maybe is acceptable after all" (zheyangzuoyebushibukeyi). It was precisely Zhijun's openness toward and ability to exploit the "formation of new trends" (qushi xingcheng) that convinced him that the only acceptable future was one in the nascent private sector economy.

The battle of wills between father and son in 1985 thus cannot be reduced to the younger Li's self-described "coarse and wild" (kuangye) personality or the enactment of universal family conflicts, Instead, following Mannheim, their disagreement can be interpreted as a collision of generational modes of understanding the historical trajectory of the country. We might say that the two Lis were co-temporal but not contemporaneous; they lived in the same moment but had divergent understandings of how individuals should be oriented in relation to the historical time of the nation.[21] While the younger Li retained confidence in his ability to anticipate changes in the local economy, others sharing his generational outlook were less successful in definitively breaking from the Maoist iron rice bowl world they had inherited.

## AN UNACCEPTABLE FUTURE: YAN JUN'S DISILLUSIONMENT WITH AN IRON RICE BOWL EXISTENCE

This chapter's third and final coming-of-age story draws attention to the ways in which shifting regimes of laboring contributed to the intensity of the "unbalanced" feelings alluded to in Old Kaiyuan's reflections at the outset of this chapter. In contrast to the enthusiasm that Zhijun and Xun Wei found in their early careers, Yan experienced his own entry into the labor force as a series of failures characterized by feelings of anxiety, frustration, and confusion stemming from his dissatisfaction with established ways of living.

Born in 1967, a year after the start of the Cultural Revolution, Yan Jun described himself as a patriotic, idealistic child. When his father, an iron rice bowl worker at Yunnan Tin, received an assignment in the mountains, Yan, his mother, and his two older sisters moved there with him. After returning to Gejiu a few years later, Yan Jun became the top student in his class at Yunnan Tin technical high school, where he received a scholarship of eight yuan ($2.60) per month as he prepared himself for life as an SOE miner.

As a teenager, Yan began to question whether he would follow in his parents' footsteps. Lively conversations with college students who returned to Gejiu for the holidays inspired Yan Jun to read newly available books that were trickling into the country. After years in which he had been encouraged to read the Four Great Classics, Yan devoured translations of Nietzsche and Schopenhauer, John F. Kennedy's autobiography, and the critical essays and novels of Bo Yang, an activist and founding president of Amnesty International's Taiwan chapter. Like Old Kaiyuan, Xun felt profoundly unsettled by the idea that life elsewhere was better than the socialist routines that structured his own days. He described feeling increasingly "cheated" and "duped" by his education, which he came to believe had fostered his own "cultural ignorance" (wenhua mengmei).[22]

Upon graduating from high school, Yan Jun received a respectable iron rice bowl job at Yunnan Tin. After relocating to Laochang, a mining town eighteen kilometers from downtown Gejiu, he was only able to return to the city center once a week. The unease initially created by his intellectual discoveries in school was exacerbated by the realities of the harsh conditions and long hours of the laboring life on the mountain.

Yan Jun quickly came to the realization that he had material and spiritual needs that Yunnan Tin's low monthly salary and grueling work schedule could not fulfill. He conceived of the problem as one of generational differences. While his parents cherished the stability of a lifelong position, the assumed security of his iron rice bowl benefits felt to him like a suffocating life sentence. In contrast to his older relatives' attempts to put away any money that they could, forgoing basic comforts to ensure longer term financial security, Yan Jun felt a compulsive need to spend his salary immediately on fashionable clothes, food, or a night out. For example, while meat had been considered a rare luxury in his early childhood, Yan Jun would skip meals in his work unit canteen if it wasn't available on a particular day.

Vowing not to grow old as a "simple-minded worker" (han gongren) but not daring to disobey his parents' shibboleth that he remain at Yunnan Tin, Yan Jun engaged in a series of escalating rebellious acts against the traditions instilled by his parents and employer. Whereas only a few years earlier he had proudly worn the ribbon awarded to him by the Young Pioneers mass youth organization, Yan Jun allowed his Communist Youth League membership to lapse in a symbolic expression of his crumbling faith in the political system that he had been raised in. When a boss at his new work unit assigned him to work deep in the mines, Yan protested that he was unfit to labor in tunnels due to his poor eyesight. After his request for a transfer was rejected, he stormed off the mountain in protest. His parents eventually intervened, and Yan was reinstated in the same work unit as a chef in the canteen. Unable to fully sever his link with Yunnan Tin but convinced that his future required he follow other opportunities, Yan's disillusionment deepened into an existential crisis.

During this time of deep resentment, Yan began supplementing his income by participating in other opportunities that were proliferating on the mountainside at that time.[23] His first foray into Society activities occurred at gambling tables. Strictly forbidden in the Cultural Revolution, when families did not risk keeping mahjong tiles or playing cards in their homes, gambling began to flourish in the region beginning in the 1980s. Yan discovered he had a talent for mahjong. After first playing with friends in his work unit dorm, he soon began to seek out games with local mining bosses, who frequented the parlors that had begun popping up in the mountain community around the time of his arrival.

In 1988 Yan took a leave from work to travel with a friend to Guangxi, a neighboring province, with money from a strong winning streak at the table. While traveling, he became consumed by the idea of opening a fast-food restaurant like the ones he had seen in larger cities. Upon his return he began reading cookbooks in the hope of learning skills that could help him launch a new career as a restaurant owner. However, he was unable to raise start-up funds to start the business, and the idea languished. Xun's unhappiness on the mountain deepened.

While still based in Laochang, Yan accompanied tin thieves—a group that included "brave" young disaffected SOE employees and poor migrant workers from nearby Yuanyang, Xuanwei, and Guizhou—on trips into his employer's tunnels. The sudden marketization of the mineral had created new opportunities for enterprising scavengers, who would haul away up to fifty-five pounds of high-grade tin ore on their backs each night.[24] Working under the protection and guidance of local "Big Brothers" (dage), who as former Yunnan Tin employees often possessed intimate knowledge of the mines that they pilfered, scavengers could make 50 or 100 yuan ($10–$20) for two or three hours' work. Yan Jun was caught by Yunnan Tin police on one of his first trips and had to ask his parents for help to pay a fine of over 1,000 yuan ($200). While maintaining his residence on the mountain, Yan frequently failed to show up for his job as he embraced his "daring" traits.[25]

The tumultuous feelings and increasingly reckless actions that marked Yan Jun's early career can be interpreted as part of the desperate search for meaning that often accompanied entry into adulthood in the 1980s. Poet Gu Gong's "The Two Generations" offers reflections on the divide that the author felt between himself and his son, also a poet. Whereas the elder Gu wanted him to "sing the battle songs that we had sung in the days of our youth," his son responded to this revolutionary tradition with anger. The young Gu's alienated reflections on his experiences in early Reform-era China included a poem declaring that the "sun is gone"—a reference to the collapse of the orienting authority of the Communist Party that had guided his father's life (Gu 1985, 9–16).

Yan Jun described his early adult experiences as "disorienting" (*mimang*)—which, as we saw in the introduction, can be understood as referencing the sensation of leaving the established paths of elders in periods of tumultuous change. In reflecting on the challenges he and his contemporaries faced, Yan explained, "Suddenly, the beliefs we had held were gone. [Our assumptions from our youth] had been overthrown, and we were looking for something new to believe in, but couldn't find it." His contemporaries made similar observations about the particular challenges surrounding their generation's entry into adulthood. As a colleague of Yan Jun once put it, "What had been inculcated (*guanshu*) in us [as children] and the trends in society we encountered [as we entered the workforce] were two very different things."[26] For Yan, the new horizons for personal and collective life opened up by Deng-era policies fueled his own feeling of frustration with the realities of his day-to-day existence as a worker. His own growing "unbalance," produced by the new possible horizons associated with the Rush years, pushed him into the burgeoning Society world.

## THE RUSH OF HEROIN'S ARRIVAL: AN OPIOID FOR SOCIETY WORKERS

The timing of heroin's arrival in Gejiu played a crucial role in how the drug came to circulate and the meaning it initially took on for its overwhelmingly young and Society-affiliated users. In the early 1980s, illicit drug use in the region had been largely confined to opium, smoked by an aging population with chronic ailments.[27] Army enlistees who had been stationed on the border with Myanmar in Dehong Prefecture brought small quantities of heroin to Gejiu around 1983. Police set up the city's first compulsory detoxification center for local heroin users in the mid-1980s.[28] By the late 1980s, many Society workers had come into contact with the drug. However, even then supply was inconsistent, with regular users often taking bus rides to nearby Kaiyuan to purchase the drug. Use of heroin peaked in the early 1990s, when the drug had become "as easy to buy as vegetables."

Heroin in its early years in the city quickly became a symbol of wealth, bravery, and belonging for a group actively questioning inherited economic and social traditions. Even though the drug is derived from opium and both drugs flowed along the same trade routes, my interlocutors consistently told me that when heroin first appeared in the region, early users understood it as a different *type* of narcotic from anything that had come before it.[29] Circulating alongside food, alcohol, and sexual services, heroin in Gejiu initially played a key role in the Society's gift economy, helping to strengthen the "strong interpersonal ties" (*nong renqing*) that characterized long-standing relationships among Society members. The drug also moved through childhood networks forged in parents' SOE work unit housing blocks that had preceded the mining boom.[30] As heroin came to be smoked in mountainside camps, at meetings, and in newly created consumer spaces such as clubs and barber shops, even entrepreneurs who did not use the substance found they were often exposed to the drug in business and social venues.

Heroin in the 1980s had a reputation for soothing injuries sustained in tin wars and easing the nerves of "tyrants" (*ba*) fighting and gambling their way to unknown futures. Even after realizing that their practice of smoking created physiological and psychological dependency, newly rich users played down the drug's addictive properties by boasting that they could "afford to smoke" (*chideqi*) for life. In the Rush years, this group could spend more each day on brand-name imported cigarettes—priced at more than 15 yuan ($3) a pack—than on maintaining their heroin habits. For Society bosses, distribution of the drug could bolster loyalty among associates, who initially were unlikely to demand regular wages. The fact that many young workers were first offered the drug by more successful business associates added to its initial aura of exclusivity.

While the young men in this chapter encountered heroin under different circumstances, they had each first pursued "dangerous things" associated with new opportunities to labor and consume in Society. Xun began smoking heroin soon after finding success as a private mining boss. In addition to preparing meals, the cook employed at his mountainside mining camp was responsible for having a water pipe ready for Xun and his workers when they emerged from their tunnel for a break. For many months the drug did not affect his ability to work; the thought of making more money by reaching unearthed tin was enough to draw him back to his mine. It was not until 1993 that Xun, still overseeing a lucrative mining operation on the mountainside, was arrested and sent to a compulsory labor center.

A lover of alcohol since his teenage years, Li Zhijun declined countless offers to smoke the drug in his first several years in the Society. His eventual decision to use was connected to a shift in his business fortunes. The motorcycle repair shop that he started with his friends was moderately profitable but left Li wanting more. Upon receiving money from his maternal grandmother, he bought a truck and traveled around the country as a long-haul driver, carting bananas and live pigs. In 1989, after the engine of his overloaded truck gave out, he decided to try his luck mining in the nearby mountains. He lost his savings when a collaboration he funded failed to find tin deposits. Out of money, he began to work for friends, managing hired laborers, "protecting" the mines of associates, and working in tunnels. Eventually he sought out work as a "life seller" (*maiming*), joining raiding teams funded and led by ambitious bosses who offered cash payouts to those willing to help them seize competitors' mines. He married and divorced within less than a year. Disheartened by the gap between the fortunes he knew were achievable and his own increasing economic desperation, Li first tried "Number Four," as heroin was initially known in Gejiu, with a friend in 1992.[31] He was soon smoking regularly.

Yan Jun began smoking heroin in the Yunnan Tin dorm rooms on the mountainside when he was offered the drug by a coworker and fellow gambler in the late 1980s. Heroin had become a popular distraction for disillusioned, aimless iron rice bowl workers. Like most early users, Yan initially "chased" the drug from aluminum foil or smoked it with a water pipe rather than injecting it. He found the opioid helped to dampen the angst and hopelessness he felt as a Yunnan Tin worker. Despite his increasingly erratic work habits and deepening Society ties, Yan held his job at the canteen until 1992, when, exhibiting the signs of full-blown physiological addiction, he moved back to Gejiu's city center to gamble, steal from stores, and swindle out-of-town visitors.

Instead of viewing heroin consumption as the primary inflection point in my interlocutors' narratives (e.g., Song 2000; Wang 2004), this chapter has argued that the drug circulated among workers who were already grappling with the consequences of breaking from the iron rice bowl world associated with their parents to pursue Society careers. Whether initially providing distraction from boredom and disillusionment, relief from the pain of injuries to and stresses of career disappointments, or a means of celebrating in the city's bourgeoning nightlife, the pharmacological effects of heroin responded to and amplified the opportunities and dangers associated with this cohort's understandings of the historical moment.[32]

## INTRODUCING THE HEROIN GENERATION

This conclusion considers the implications of calling the men and women in Gejiu who appear in this book members of the Heroin Generation, a term that I use in future chapters.[33] My use of "generation" here is not to be confused with demographers' and epidemiologists' narrowly defined "drug cohorts." Instead, the term implies a shared set of early adulthood experiences, a common discursive landscape of historical problems, and the potential for forging connections based on shared projects and experiences of social time. Membership in this group provides a common background that shapes the recovering histories that I describe in future chapters.

Numerous studies in recent decades have shown how expectations of the future, ideas about collective life, health-seeking behaviors and experiences of illness in China tend to be shaped by birth cohorts (Ng 2009; Kleinman 1982; Yan 2003; Pun and Lu 2010). Set on the floor of a state-owned silk factory, Lisa Rofel's *Other Modernities* (1999) shows how three distinct generational cohorts of Chinese women workers articulate strikingly different desires for their laboring lives and expectations of the Chinese state.

Following Rofel and others who document how common early life experiences produce enduring assumptions about the world, I argue that the young people in Honghe who ventured into the Society in the Rush years were shaped in lasting ways by the specific opportunities of the liberalizing economy. In contrast to their parents, who were likely to stay within their work units, young workers saw the potency of a new idealized worker, based on the figure of the mining boss, who was a "brave" individual who "grabbed what he could" and "made a mess trying to live."[34] They encountered moral condemnation and envy, bodily risk, and uncertainty about the future in pursuing murky opportunities at a time when Society and private sector activities converged. Xun Wei's convictions about making the mountain his own, the younger Li's ferocious tenacity to push against the wishes of his father, and Yan Jun's increasingly reckless attempts to avoid growing old as a "simple-minded worker" were all responses to the shared challenges of embracing new ways of living and laboring.

David Scott's (2014) reflections on generation as a social institution of time offers a way of thinking about the relationship between early adulthood experiences and later shared orientations of historical actors. In his interpretation of a series of dialogues with older Caribbean intellectuals who came of age during decolonization, Scott argues that generation cohorts share an internal discursive landscape of historical problems and a social imaginary of a horizon of future possibility. As part of a long-standing interest in theoretical practice that might enable a refashioning of futures, Scott is focused specifically on "which pasts (and which *notion* of pasts) [his interviewees, all from an older generation] mobilized to inform their sense of what their present demanded and how the present could be made into the futures they hoped for" (1999, 2014, 159).

Like the Caribbean activists and leaders in Scott's account, my interlocutors did not agree on the significance of their shared past or on visions for their own post-addiction life, still less the future of the country. However, their feelings about and reflections on the future in the 2010s were shaped by a shared internal discursive landscape particular to their generation—the *only* cohort in recent memory whose entry into the labor force had occurred at a time when the mountains appeared radically open for the taking. Two decades later, my interlocutors still reckoned with the consequences of their earlier participation in the Rush years: Was their turn away from socialist traditions prescient, tragic, or something else? At what moments and in what ways had their laboring lives deviated from a promising trajectory? How should their early career identifications and skills influence their later-life professional ambitions? The project of recovery required returning to and making sense of the charged emotions and events described in this chapter.

Approaching this group as a generational cohort also draws attention to the ways in which individuals in this book came to define and experience community. This chapter tracked the different ways in which "we" came to be evoked by young local residents. Old Kaiyuan and Yan spoke of a "we" encompassing disillusioned iron rice bowl workers pursuing trouble; Li referred to a "we" that included Society collaborators who shared his values and skills; and the collective that Xun Wei invoked when describing his mining operation included childhood friends, hired laborers, and more recently encountered business partners. These unstable and shifting understandings show that heroin users cannot be assumed to constitute a distinct and stable subculture. Feelings of belonging, moreover, often grew from shared commitments to embrace new forms of laboring and intuitions of social time.

Yan Jun once argued that he and his contemporaries in the Rush years were connected by their need to embrace the unknown: "Regarding our future, all we knew is that the present situation [of staying in state positions] is unacceptable (*buganyuxianzhuang*)." Future chapters show how later connections and evocations of community returned to and extended these themes as one-time Society workers faced challenges of living and laboring after the closing of the mountains.

# CHAPTER 2

# Recovery as Adaptation

*Catching Up to the Private Sector*

After nearly two hours of sitting silently in a far corner of the karaoke room, Sam stood up, microphone in hand. The forty-three-year old offered a well-practiced, pitch-perfect rendition of a Cantopop song from his youth. The forlorn, heartfelt song was accompanied by grainy concert footage from a 1980s performance by a Hong Kong pop idol.

When Sam finished singing, the group of twenty-somethings who surrounded us in the room clapped politely and quickly replaced him at the microphone. The energy and style of performance changed as they belted out song after song of the rap-influenced, chart-topping tunes of the moment. Our host, a fast-talking twenty-seven-year-old policewoman whom we had met earlier in the evening at a nearby bar, ordered two additional cases of beer and multiple rounds of her favorite food, chocolate Cornetto ice cream cones.

Sam was once a successful Society figure who had capably pursued opportunities in the mountains and city center associated with the private sector mining boom described in chapter 1. In 2011 he still maintained an imposing physical presence, standing nearly six feet tall, with a stout build, ruddy cheeks, military crew cut, and a deep, calm voice. His physically imposing looks and violent past were accompanied by careful manners, seriousness, and a sensitivity to others. On this evening he wore jeans and an athletic Adidas T-shirt.

Over the years Sam had been out hundreds of nights in Gejiu's evening nightspots. His status as someone who was once well-known in the city's evening life had been brought to my attention a few hours earlier when the forty-something leader of the house band at the bar where we had first met recognized Sam from the stage and quickly dedicated a song to him. The subtle swagger of Sam's movements conveyed the presence of someone who was used to being seen and respected. But from the moment we joined this younger group, Sam seemed out of place, unsure of himself.

Our talkative host attempted to elicit our collective advice about a problem unique to her position as a privileged "wealthy second generation" (*fuerdai*) member of the "post-1980" (*balinghou*) cohort: Should she continue her career as a government official or quit to take over her mother's highly profitable cosmetic distribution company? Sam did not appear to have much to say in response to her concerns. He sat at the end of a sofa, generally ignored, as the festivities continued. Empty beer bottles multiplied on the floor, and the group of twenty-somethings became louder and more raucous.

Later, as the two of us wandered out into the warm June air well after midnight, Sam confided to me that he had felt out of his element for most of the evening. His feelings of marginalization in the karaoke room—visible in his lack of knowledge of recent music and difficulty engaging in the banter of workers nearly two decades his junior—were reminders of his broader ejection from a social world that he had once moved through with impunity. For years, local workers who "had guts" and cultivated an "evil name" had excelled on the violent, unpredictable mountainside and in nascent private sector businesses that flourished around the lake. Like Gao, the computer enthusiast whom I quoted in the introduction, Sam felt he was stuck in the recent past. Gejiu had changed, but he continued to repeat habits he had acquired in the Rush years.

In their landmark essay "How Bodies Remember," Arthur Kleinman and Joan Kleinman explore how the tumult associated with the Cultural Revolution (1966–1976) lived on in the embodied worlds of its survivors. In pushing for greater specificity regarding the "largely unanalyzed" ways in which bodies come to incorporate societal processes, they ask, "How does the societal disorientation caused by a crisis of cultural delegitimation become a bodily experience? How are disoriented bodies socially experienced?" (1994, 711). This chapter explores these questions in relation to legacies of the Rush years rather than the Cultural Revolution. Sam's reflections on his struggles to find a place in contemporary Gejiu offer a vivid depiction of a societal disorientation that came to be experienced in a particularly acute form by certain members of the Society, including those who used heroin.

This chapter is divided into two sections. The opening offers an account of how Sam and a group of his friends understood their economic marginalization in Gejiu during my fieldwork. As the initial "release" of the mountains in the Rush years gave way to new state policies, early-arriving entrepreneurs frequently found they were crowded out of the private sector by different *types* of actors who had arrived in the late 1990s and 2000s. I then describe a mountainside satellite community in which this post-Rush division of labor was readily visible. The second part of the chapter explores how Sam's heroin habit related to other bodily dispositions he acquired in his early career. This one-time boss speaks about his recent struggles in terms that echo what Pierre Bourdieu describes as the "hysteresis effect," a condition in which historical actors find that previously efficacious strategies and bodily dispositions are ill-adapted to a rapidly shifting social environment (Bourdieu 1990, 59, 62). For Sam, recovering from heroin required "adapting" to social realities of the millennium by breaking habits accumulated in the Rush years and emulating later-arriving, successful entrepreneurs.

## REPLACED: DRUG USERS AS ENTREPRENEURS OF THE COUNTRY'S RECENT PAST

Public memorials to workers were difficult to miss in Gejiu. Life-sized statues erected a few years before my arrival captured the physicality of mining techniques endured by laborers working in capitalist- and colonialist-owned mines in the nineteenth and early twentieth centuries (see figure 3). Appearing around the city in central public spaces, these figures were part act of commemoration, part local government scheme to lure domestic "tin culture" tourist dollars.

Another effort to commemorate the sacrifices of early twentieth-century Chinese workers was visible in the back rooms of "the French Building" (*faguolou*), a onetime office for foreign railroad administrators that had been converted into a fashionable restaurant that served Western and Chinese food to well-off urban residents. A small museum behind the restaurant displayed photos of brutal labor conditions and statistics about the loss of Chinese workers' lives in the construction of a railroad that stretched from Kunming into the French Indochinese empire. Employing 100,000 Chinese laborers and thousands of foreign engineers and contractors, the 466-kilometer-long railway line had enabled tin unearthed from the nearby mountains to flow south to feed French colonial ambitions (Xinlan Lishi 2015).

FIGURE 3. Monument to nineteenth-century tin workers. Photo by author.

Next to Golden Lake, a train car from the competing Gebishi railway offered visitors coffee drinks and cocktails in refurbished, if still cramped, train cars. This attraction was a reminder of the ingenuity and resilience of Chinese business leaders and the workers they employed. Through a mix of patriotism and self-interest, local entrepreneurs, with the implicit backing of the Chinese state, worked to diminished foreign influence in the region by building a narrow "meter track" (cungui) railway that bought coal to Gejiu and enabled moving tin unearthed in the region east and then north to Chinese distributors (Zoubian Zhongguo 2017).[1]

Testaments to Maoist work units and iron rice bowl workers were visible throughout the downtown area. Much of the city's still-visible mining infrastructure, including Yunnan Tin's regal headquarters and the Number One Ore Dressing Factory, had been put up by local SOEs. Soon after Mao's forces defeated the Guomingdang and formally established the People's Republic in 1949, the newly seated government merged privately held companies that had profited under the Nationalists into state-run Yunnan Tin. In the 1950s this SOE generated more foreign currency for the Party than any other business in the country (Kusnetzky 2011, 11). Partnering with the city government and other SOEs, Yunnan Tin constructed newer, more comfortable mining tunnels for its miners; expanded sorting and smelting plants; improved roads;

FIGURE 4. Upscale mall and luxury apartment buildings in the city center. Photo by author.

and built schools, hospitals, and parks. Though its influence in the new millennium had been greatly reduced, Yunnan Tin still operated a host of businesses, including a large hotel and a network of factories and real estate holdings.

Visitors to Gejiu had to look a bit harder to find traces of the entrepreneurial activity that Sam and his contemporaries had undertaken in the Rush years. Private sector businesses, of course, were everywhere. Recently arrived, high-end luxury retailers such as Lacoste, which during my stay in Gejiu launched an aggressive billboard campaign urging local residents to indulge in "unconventional chic," had proliferated alongside a host of national chains and small businesses (see figure 4). Walmart and KFC opened franchises in Gejiu while I was living in the city, while a myriad of small shops sold clothing, consumer goods, and food.

Some Society workers continued to thrive in this business-friendly environment. Many of the ventures operating in the Rush years, however, had disappeared without a trace.

One night Sam and four of his friends met at a local outdoor market near the old train station. Each was attempting to reestablish his or her career after many years of intermittent heroin use. Earlier in their working lives, the attendees had participated in a range of licit and illicit Society activities, including working in clothing and other retail stores; operating private loan businesses; managing casinos; helping to mine, sell, trade, and steal tin; extracting money from local businesses; participating in traveling dance troupes; and running bars and other nighttime venues. Their frank discussion of their displacement from Society jobs and difficulties navigating the contemporary economy offers a succinct introduction into how marginalized Society workers experienced the shifting economy in the millennium.

On the surface, criticisms of Gejiu's contemporary private sector seemed out of place: per capita spending in the city had increased sevenfold and consumer spending elevenfold since 1990 (Honghezhou Weixuanchuan 2009). With the growth of a large middle class and the emergence of a smaller group of ultra-wealthy families, how could there not be opportunity in the contemporary moment?

My dinner companions argued that the particular developmental trajectory of the local economy had eroded their own initial advantages in the private sector. Starting a business had been relatively simple in their youth. A clothing seller in the mid-1980s, for example, had to make the trip to Kunming to purchase goods from a wholesaler, then transport clothes back to Gejiu. For early vendors, selling these consumer items once they had arrived in Gejiu had been easy. Mountainside trading or mining, bars, restaurants, pop-up clothing stores, food stalls, and other ventures had low start-up costs and often offered substantial profits that could support an extravagant lifestyle by the standards of the time for the select few who took the risk.

The situation in Gejiu in the 2010s was very different. Competition in every corner of the private sector was intense. Lucrative high-end retail, real estate, and construction sectors had come to be run by a select group of "self-made rich" (baofahu) or their children, who over the past decade or few years had forged deep connections with key government workers or emerged from their ranks. Young college graduates returning from the provincial capital, laid off and retired local state workers, and tradespeople from other parts of the country had all subsequently rushed into private sector opportunities. "Captains of industry" (qiyejia), "heads" (zong), or "businesspeople" (shangren) had replaced self-made tin mining bosses (kuang laoban) as the wealthiest, most influential private sector actors in the city.

While we were waiting for our ordered food to arrive, I asked Ling, a woman in her late thirties who supplemented her welfare payments by reselling jewelry she bought online, how her street-based jewelry business was doing. She noted that her margins were small and the competition was intense. Customers these days could always turn to internet websites like Taobao, which had superior selection and cheaper prices. Sam, too, spoke about his own job with dissatisfaction. He had recently taken a job as an errand runner and laborer at a company owned by a friend's relative and was working twenty-nine days a month renovating the new villas that were sprouting up in nearby expanding suburbs. Though he had been happy when a connection helped him land this entry-level construction job, he complained that his pay was so low that he could not afford to move out of his parents' home. He noted that Gejiu remained a comfortable place to grow old if one could afford it. However, it was no longer a good place to make money. The others at our table nodded in agreement.

These observations of life in Gejiu are supported by studies of labor market shifts in the Reform era. While there were only 150,000 recognized *getihu* in the whole country in 1978, the number of private sector workers had swelled to 8 million in 1992 and 24 million by 1999. In the early 2010s, one study estimated that the private sector had expanded to 253 million people, about two-thirds of the urban workforce (Bray 2005, 167; Lardy 2016, 39). As the government formulated increasingly probusiness policies and laws, the meaning and skills associated with laboring outside the state sector underwent dramatic change.[2] In making the distinctions between "speculators," "workers," and "former functionaries," Wank (1999) argues that there was a gradual shift from the first group, generally less educated and willing to take on bodily risks; to the second, better connected SOE workers; to the final group, white collar and well-educated, who entered in greater numbers starting in the 1990s.[3] Early-moving entrepreneurs who found success in the 1980s often "quickly went under" (Wang 2003, 529) as other types of workers arrived in the private sector.[4]

My dinner companions noted that regional labor flows also contributed to the remaking of the local private sector. The city had long been a destination for workers from around the country.[5] However, when my interlocutors were growing up, most out-of-town workers arriving in the city were accepting jobs assigned by the state. As a result of decollectivization of rural areas, the easing of travel restrictions, and enforcement of the national resident permit (*hukou*) system since the 1980s, more than 100,000 workers—close to one-third of the city's population—were members of the "floating population" (*Gejiushi Shimin*

*Duben* 2011). Wealthier out-of-towners often arrived with the resources to start businesses, including regional restaurants, locksmith shops, and hair salons. "Workers" from poor parts of the country who could "eat bitterness" (*chiku*) decided to come to vie for a range of lower-paying jobs, including physical labor in the mines themselves. Sam and his friends saw these more recently arriving migrants as unwelcome competition.[6]

The influence of the Society—once predominantly composed of "sons and daughters" of SOE workers—had radically diminished since the Rush years. Government crackdowns on illegal mining and racketeering thinned out the ranks of people supported by bribes, stealing, and mountainside fighting. As private sector careers were no longer stigmatized, ambitious private sector actors did not need to "mix in Society" to make business connections. Local residents who continued to pursue illicit activities found they were being displaced here as well. During my fieldwork, holdups, home break-ins, and street- and bus-based scams were increasingly performed by "fearless" young migrant laborers.[7] Would-be lawbreakers in their late thirties and forties grumbled that they could not keep up with the skills or physical vigor of younger, later-arriving criminals. A sense of failing to meet the challenge of increased competition contributed to my companions' anxiety. Bo, one of the men at the table, reported that his middle school education, never a barrier to employment in previous years, came to feel like a serious limitation in the new economy. He noted that even twenty-somethings with undergraduate degrees increasingly struggled to find decent private sector jobs. Middle-aged workers like themselves had truly fallen behind the times.

Toward the end of our dinner, an aging itinerant performer carrying a violin approached our table. Zuo, a former dancer, remembered from a previous conversation that I had once played the violin. She handed the man a few yuan and asked him to perform for us. After he had finished his song and wandered off to another table, she told me she wished he had brought his *erhu* instead. She explained she had once worked alongside this man at a local nightclub (*yezonghui*). Packed with bosses and other Society workers, local clubs in the 1990s had tried to outdo each other by putting on lavish nightly performances employing dozens of performers and staging elaborate shows. As consumer tastes had shifted and the influence of mining bosses waned, large-scale performance-oriented spaces like the one that had employed them both had all but disappeared. While not a heroin user, this musician had also been displaced in the "transition" that had called forth new types of workers.

## INTERLUDE: "PICKED DRY": A NEW DIVISION OF LABOR ON THE MOUNTAINSIDE

The longer I stayed in Gejiu, the more curious I became about the nearby mountains. While often described as "giant casinos" attracting aspiring workers from around the country in the Rush years, the mining industry was often characterized by Sam and his friends as "no good to do" (*buhaogan*). Hoping to better understand the tin industry in the aftermath of the Rush years, I began to make trips up to nearby mining outposts to visit members of the Heroin Generation who had remained on the mountainside.

To reach the half dozen mountain towns located within twenty kilometers of Gejiu, passengers had to make their way to a dilapidated local depot rather than the large, privately owned bus station that serviced other destinations. Soon after boarding an old fifteen-seat bus with a side door that did not fully close, I was immediately struck by the fact that most of the passengers were speaking unfamiliar dialects rather than local Gejiuhua. These "outsiders" (*waidiren*) included Hani and Yi minority workers who came from other parts of the prefecture, as well as workers from Xuanwu prefecture and Guizhou province, areas that were among the poorest in the country.

After traveling nearly an hour on a winding, bumpy road, we arrived in Laochang, a tin mining outpost made up of several winding streets where a number of my interlocutors had spent time during their working careers. Old Passout (Laodiao), a longtime heroin user whose nickname referred to his tendency to overdose, had come to meet me at the station. At age fifty, Old Passout was one of the oldest drug users I met during my initial fieldwork. Suggesting that we go to his mother's apartment to chat, he led me down a dusty street while telling me about the town's history.

Before Liberation, this area had been settled predominantly by male miners, who had often squatted in semipermanent camping sites on the mountainside. By the 1970s the population had swelled to more than thirty thousand residents, including doctors, engineers, machinists, miners, and their families, who had accepted government work assignments. A regal, elevated theater in a central park once showed Maoist propaganda films and hosted traveling performances. Though SOE iron rice bowl employees often cycled through Laochang for relatively short periods of time, Old Passout had spent his whole childhood in this community, receiving his education in mountainside Yunnan Tin–run schools before joining Yunnan Tin as a worker.[8]

Unlike in Gejiu, where the great majority of the housing stock had been built in the past three decades, most residential buildings in Laochang during my fieldwork had survived from the Maoist era, though a new block of housing had been built in the 1990s to accommodate what turned out to be a short-lived influx of fortune-seekers. During my visit, sheets hung behind broken windows and sheds originally used for storing coal in the winter were strewn with trash. Old Passout turned into one of the five-story apartment complexes and led me up three flights of stairs to a simple one-bedroom apartment with concrete floors and no bathroom. He noted that his mother, still benefiting from subsidies first created under Mao, paid less than $10 a month from her state pension for rent and utilities.

Over tea in his living room, Old Passout recounted the dramatic changes that had resulted from the sudden marketization of tin in the mid-1980s. Thousands of workers—initially Hui and then Han residents living nearby—arrived to supply labor to hundreds of private mining operations on what had been exclusively state-controlled land. Tents—canvas structures and then more permanent concrete barracks—popped up in increasingly dense concentrations on the nearby mountains. Dozens of karaoke bars, mahjong parlors, and sex work establishments quickly opened their doors. Clashes between Han and Hui workers, police raids and counter-raids, and assassinations of well-known entrepreneurs were common occurrences in those years.

Old Passout had been working at Yunnan Tin in the mid-1980s when, against his parents' wishes and despite his employer's threat that it would suspend his benefits, he quit his iron rice bowl job.[9] He began organizing groups of thieves to carry out tin raids in his former employer's tunnels. Over time he gained a reputation as a local "tyrant" (*ba*) and collected fees in exchange for helping to facilitate access to state tin mines. However, his heroin habit increasingly interfered with his Society activities.

By the end of the 1990s, the combination of early exhaustion of resources and the regularization of public-private cooperation helped to quell the violence and reduce the revenue streams that had nourished many local "tyrants" and their associates.[10] Part of the shift was due to the rapid exhaustion of shallow "edge mining" (*bianyan caikuang*) as "high-grade" (*gao pingwei*) tin accessible through low-cost methods came to be "picked dry" (*taokong*), a fact that was recognized nationally in 2008, when Gejiu was named one of the country's first eight "resource-depleted" cities.

New government regulations and controls also played an important role in the shift. After several years of tolerating lawlessness and violence on the mountainside, officials in the region concluded that the rapid expansion of private sector entrepreneurial activity during the late Deng period had been "excessive," "disorderly," and "scattered" (Li and Xu 2009). In a campaign starting at the end of the 1990s, a coalition of government forces set to work to "tidy up the mountainside" by curbing "wild" and "wasteful" activity in favor of a "sustainable" approach. As part of these efforts, city police and Yunnan Tin security forces confiscated seven hundred tents, made more than two hundred arrests, and destroyed dozens of "illegal" tunnels ("Gejiu Moshi" 2008; Li and Xu 2009). Close to one hundred mining outfits—more than one-third of all private bosses on the mountain—were forced to leave when they could not produce documents proving legal rights to their claims ("Gejiu Moshi" 2008). The local government and Yunnan Tin successfully reasserted control over much of the mountain range and implemented standardized subcontracting (*chengbao*) to vetted, "legal" private sector partners, in what become known as the "Gejiu model" of mountain management.

After we finished our tea, Old Passout offered to take me around the Laochang downtown area to show me how the mining labor population had changed in the post-Rush years. On the street we encountered weary miners trudging back to their homes who wore hardhats and headlamps and wielded pickaxes that seemed to be similar to the tools used in Republican China. At a glance, Old Passout could tell from a worker's outfit whether he was employed at one of the SOEs or by a smaller, private subcontractor. The majority of residents in Laochang were migrants officially designated as "contracted laborers" (*hetonggong*). Unlike the predominantly Han workers who had once been assigned to the city, this group was generally not provided job security or local residence permits. This turn to short-term contracts over the last two decades allowed state producers increased flexibility to adjust production to fluctuations in international tin prices. Subcontracting also allowed larger companies to reduce spending on benefits, as well as the payouts for injuries and death resulting from mining accidents.

As we arrived on the main street, a fancy air-conditioned bus decorated with Yunnan Tin's insignia passed us on the road. Old Passout explained that SOE managers and technical professionals now commuted to mining sites from apartments in the city center to oversee work in the mines. The SOE's radically egalitarian ethos had been replaced by a rigid hierarchy that separated investors and well-compensated upper management from workers.[11] Most of the onetime iron rice bowl miners had retired or been reassigned furloughed status (*daigong*). In a sign of the times, the Laochang elementary school that Old Passout once attended had been closed and replaced by school that provided education for the children of migrant workers. Old Passout's mother, who was playing mahjong with her friends down the street during my visit, was one of a dwindling number of onetime SOE iron rice bowl employees who had chosen to remain stationed in this mountain town rather than make the move to Gejiu's city center.

Old Passout led me into an unmarked, single-story building on a side street. Three men and a woman, all in their thirties or forties, sat in the corner around a mahjong table. They nodded to Old Passout as we entered but did not take their attention away from their game. We watched as the players pulled individual bills from thick stacks of 100 yuan bills to bet on each hand. Once outside, Old Passout explained that this was a group of Guizhou bosses, some of the most powerful figures in Laochang. One of the men sitting at the table had worked for him more than twenty years earlier. This former migrant laborer had successfully avoided the dangers of heroin, violence, government crackdowns, and shifting alliances to achieve success as a legal Yunnan Tin subcontractor in the new order on the mountains.

As we approached the bus that would take me back to Gejiu, Old Passout began to speak about his own feelings of having been left behind. He noted that two decades earlier, migrants arriving from poorer parts of the country had been "simple" (*chunpu*) workers who tended to act "like mice afraid of an elephant" when in the presence of local Big Brothers like him. "They didn't dare to disobey us!" he said with a laugh. But the collective "us" in this sentence—Han Society bosses—had lost their clout. Some had been "eliminated" (*taotai*) by violence and the heroin consumption that had reached its apex two decades earlier. Others, including his friends whom I met on other trips and who now lived in tents on the outskirts of the town and in a cramped, hollowed space underneath the staircase in a Yunnan Tin housing block, survived on the edges of the mountain community. A lucky few had managed to turn their businesses into legal companies or started new ventures. Old Passout wondered out loud what his life would have looked like if he had put away some of his money and left this mountain outpost years before.[12] Displaced like Sam, Old Passout struggled to find a new position in a post-Rush regime of laboring.

## LAGGING BEHIND: SOCIETY HABITUS AS LIABILITY

In this section I explore Sam's diagnosis of his own embodied struggles in the post-Rush years. In our frequent conversations, Sam foregrounded the importance of his body—what Marcel Mauss refers to as our first "natural technical object" ([1934] 1973, 75). His descriptions of his formation as a laborer emphasize his own cultivation of "habits of living" (*shenghuo xiguan*)—the perspectives, strategies, and outlook that he adopted in his youth—a notion that strongly resonated with the habitus of Pierre Bourdieu's practice theory.[13]

Sam prided himself on his abilities as an athlete; he had been a basketball player in his youth and later became a weightlifting enthusiast. On one of our first meetings, he took me on a tour of a local barebones gym that he belonged to. His size and strength had played an important part in the process of finding his vocation.[14] Though he initially attended a local technical school and worked at Yunnan Tin as craftsman of fine tin products for two years in the mid-1980s, he made the decision to break from his Yunnan Tin iron rice bowl job to start a business with an older brother buying and reselling tin ore. His early career trajectory represented a gradual intensification of the rhythms and behaviors associated with economic activity in the Society. When a more powerful boss put a stop to his family tin reselling business, Sam continued to make a healthy living by making periodic trips to the nearby mountains as a miner, protector, and freelance fighter or "life seller" (*maiming*). The work he did as a freelancer offered the most extreme version of the Society disposition: Sam engaged in frenzied, increasingly dangerous efforts to protect and seize territory on nearby mountainsides, supplemented by extended periods when he spent freely on evening entertainment in Gejiu's newly opened discos, bars, and karaoke parlors.[15]

Sam drew attention to his years in the Society as a form of bodily training. At a time when "protecting" (*hukuang*) had increasingly become an inseparable part of "prospecting" (*tankuang*) (cf. Yunnan Net 2011), workers who displayed "guts" (*danzida*), built "evil names" (*eming*), and "wanted money, not life" (*yaoqianbuyaoming*) were most likely to rise to prominence on the mountainside and in the city center. Sam became adept at coming up with strategies for "collecting money" (*kuqian*) or "grabbing at money" (*gandaoqian*) through "fighting and troublemaking" (*dadanaonao*). As a daring Society worker, Sam cultivated an ability to "attract a crowd" (*haozhaoli*) of companions through socializing, networking, and accumulating debts that would oblige others to respond to his call. The goal of those years, he noted, was "being a bit happier, having a few more friends, and being able to try something new every day."[16]

In the early 1990s, after a few years of doing Society work, Sam hit a rough patch in his entrepreneurial career and temporarily attempted to reprise the SOE tin craftsman job that he had held as a teenager.[17] Upon his return, he watched iron rice bowl workers toil on the clock and observed the urgency with which they scurried to pick up their paltry monthly salaries. He confessed that he felt he had "no words to speak" to these government employees whom he had once considered his colleagues. Their outlook and skills seemed pathetic when compared to what he had experienced—and obtained—in the Society. Sam left this iron rice bowl job for good after only a few weeks. The encounters on the old shop floor made him realize that he had become a different type of worker.

In reflecting on the arc of his Society career, Sam noted that for a significant period of his adult life his cultivated ways of moving through the world had been rewarded. Despite absences from the private sector labor force, Sam had been able to bounce back after setbacks and find new opportunity through his Society contacts.[18] As late as 2000, his reputation and skills helped him find high-paying work as the manager of a popular underground casino. In the new millennium, however, Sam lamented that the characteristics that had helped distinguish him as a valuable asset in Society businesses increasingly sabotaged his own goals.[19] His involuntary repetition of actions from the past had become increasingly costly with the passing of time.

Sam's analysis of the source of his own difficulties resonated with Pierre Bourdieu's ([1962] 2008) early ethnographic work documenting the discomfort experienced by middle-aged French male farmers who found themselves unprepared to dance to fashionable music at the local Bachelor's Ball. In this ethnographic work, the French sociologist documents how the crisis of the collapse of the bucolic world into which these rural workers were born, punctuated by their growing anxiety over looming failure to produce offspring, became palpable and present in their newfound struggles to move their bodies in an unfamiliar social space. Bourdieu called this condition the hysteresis effect, a Greek term meaning lagging behind. This description appeared to perfectly capture Sam's growing anxiety that his embodied status as a worker—the habitus that he had cultivated through years of mixing in the Society—made him ill-suited to occupy the well-paying jobs he most desired.

Sam depicted his relationship with heroin as a habit linking him to the recent past. Once smoked with impunity among groups in public spaces, heroin in the early 2010s in Gejiu was often used by individuals or pairs in squalid conditions. Although heroin had previously enabled a high characterized as blissful, potent, experimental, and powerful, Sam noted that the drug circulating in Gejiu during my fieldwork was laced with impurities and could often have dulling and even unpleasant effects.[20] Once associated with dangers attributable to "playing with one's life" that could lead to economic gain and social prestige, heroin had become linked to mundane lingering injuries; chronic medical conditions; and the weak hearts, lungs, and brains of "scary and pathetic" aging, unemployed idlers.[21] Sam's opioid use, like other bodily habits, was associated with his "daring" past career, a career that no longer fit with the times.

Absorbing the way this former Society boss viewed his own condition, I became more attuned to Sam's bodily capabilities in different contexts. When operating within familiar implicit rules and expectations associated with the Society spaces of his youth, Sam continued to thrive, moving in ways that were highly efficacious. He was a valued guest at reunions, wedding celebrations, and other gatherings. For a World AIDS Day event organized by local harm reduction NGOs, for example, organizers sought out Sam to serve as emcee. Dressed in a handsome suit, he oversaw the event with confidence and skill. The gap between bodily habitus and field was minimal. Mahjong tables in the city were another venue where Sam appeared to feel at home.[22] I also learned that he found success in navigating Chinese prison and compulsory labor centers. When in an environment in which physical prowess and daring attitude still held sway, Sam's fearlessness, his ability to make connections and willingness to display physical toughness through "threatening displays of force" (*weishe*), allowed him to take on "management" (*guanliceng*) positions that afforded him special privileges and exempted him from heavy labor.

However, when Sam was in environments in which Society norms were less accepted, his confidence and charm left him. As the karaoke scene with younger entrepreneurs at the beginning of the chapter demonstrates, in these moments he became unsure of himself, quiet, and even awkward in the presence of actors whom he viewed as having a feel for moving in contemporary Gejiu that he lacked.

Others from his generational cohort also demonstrated self-defeating behaviors that Sam might have interpreted as unhealthy connections to the past, maladaptive dispositions, or "historical bodily stutters" (Farquhar 2002, 17). For example, a number of my interlocutors were impulsive, less than savvy consumers. The combination of eagerly searching for impossibly good deals and a lack of familiarity with payment and delivery of online goods made them easy targets. One recovering heroin user I knew received multiple calls a week from scam artists, the result of her having responded to several previous cons. Another made a down payment on an impossibly inexpensive motorcycle he found online that never arrived. My interlocutors also at times engaged in the aggressive behaviors once associated with Society bosses. A stab wound a friend received after starting an argument in a low-stakes mahjong game, an impromptu fight on a crowded bus, and an episode in which Sam lost his temper and attempted to break down his colleague's door could all be interpreted as part of a socially learned destructive impulsivity. In each of these instances, the person later claimed to know better and yet in the moment had followed deeply engrained patterns of behavior. It was the increasing failure of Sam's intuitive ways of moving—the misfiring of his Society bodily habitus—that marked him as "stuck in" the recent past.

## RECOVERY FROM HEROIN AS "ADAPTING" TO A NEW HISTORICAL MOMENT

One evening while we were chatting in my living room, I asked Sam what he thought he needed to do to achieve a "return to society," deliberately choosing a phrase that I knew had a complicated meaning for people with heroin use history. In responding to my question, Sam took issue with my use of "return" (*huigui*).

In a frustrated tone, Sam responded, "[I must] now find a new way of living or a new perspective on life, to go live and work. . . . If you were to say, 'What about going back to how things were before?', that would be empty talk! How could that be possible?" Sam had first encountered heroin in the late 1980s and had been sent to compulsory labor centers twice for positive urine tests. Since arranging a home-based detoxification with the help of friends a year before my arrival, he had abstained from all opioids, including methadone. The question of recovery from addiction for Sam appeared embedded within his broader ambition of overcoming a pernicious form of obsolescence. Sam explained that rather than "return" to the iron rice bowl work he associated with his parents' generation or the Rush-era opportunities that had opened and then disappeared, he needed to break his connections to the city's past and "adapt" (*shiying*) to the historical changes that unfolded around him. With this response, he blurred the boundary between overcoming his patterns of problem drug use and reinventing himself as a private sector actor in the mold of those who had replaced him in the local economy (cf. Wu 2007).

In the summer of 2011, Sam became reacquainted with a former mining boss and onetime colleague who had become a wealthy entrepreneur engaged in mining, tea, and real estate investments. This businessman had recently taken Sam and other guests to an underground garage to show them his three most prized possessions: a Ferrari, a Lamborghini, and a Maserati, one of each of Italy's most coveted sports cars. Sam commented that this acquaintance had had the good fortune and savvy to turn himself from a violent, law-breaking mining boss into an owner of a legitimate, tax-paying company. He had become a "forward-facing" (*chaotian*) citizen, a "legal businessperson" (*hefa de shangren*) who oversaw a complex business empire instead of "grabbing at money" and engaging in "briefcase" (*pibao*) behavior—a term locals used to describe businesspeople from the Rush era who borrowed money with no intention of repaying it.[23] Sam envied not only this onetime colleague's success in business but also the habits he had cultivated to make this success possible.

Sam also spoke with grudging respect about successful younger business-people from the "post-1980" (*balinghou*) generation. Supported by their parents, teachers, and others, this group, Sam noted, had often been encouraged to study business, management, and other skills designed to fuel the pursuit of well-paying private sector careers.[24] These younger workers were often able to formulate "their own life goals" (*ziji renshengmubiao*) while avoiding the various pitfalls that had been common in Society life during the Rush years. In acknowledging their frequent prowess in navigating business opportunities, Sam noted enviously that this younger generation had benefited from having "their parents pave their roads for them" (*luzi shi fumu bang tamen pudinghaole*). They, too, were worthy of study and emulation.

When comparing Rush-era workers like himself to those who found success in the new millennium, Sam differentiated between the attitudes these types of private sector actors held toward their futures—what Pierre Bourdieu in his work on Algeria refers to as distinct "temporal dispositions" ([1960] 1979, 6).[25] This idea that different historical moments have required diverging dispositions was the topic of a pun that circulated widely in China in the 1980s, *wangqiankan*. Two different statements emerge depending on whether the *qian* sound is taken to mean "the future" or "money."[26] When applied to the Maoist period, *wangqiankan* described the Chinese people as "looking toward the future," a phrase corresponding to a time when the Communist propaganda machinery insisted that citizens cast their eyes toward a collective horizon unfolding under the guiding hand of the Leninist-Maoist state. In the early years of the country's reform and opening the phrase became "looking toward money."[27] This second meaning referenced the emergence of a new disposition associated with the pursuit of personal wealth.[28] Sam understood himself as one of the many workers who "rushed ahead" of other historical actors in the Rush years by embodying this short-term orientation, a disposition he described as "grabbing money" and "trying something new every day."[29]

During my fieldwork, however, Sam had concluded that "looking at money" was as at odds with the outlook of the entrepreneurs who had replaced him in the private sector. He explained that to find lasting success in the new private sector, he needed to figure out how to "hold on to" (*bawodehao*) the opportunities he encountered and learn to "accumulate" (*jilei*): a job, savings, contacts, and a family. Sam's car-collecting onetime Society colleague, for example, possessed what Sam called a "professional ambition" (*shiyexin*). Though this figure was also chasing money, he was now oriented toward more complex future horizons, with an ability to make long-term plans and steadily accumulate assets. Similarly, younger entrepreneurial figures, like the karaoke heiress in her careful contemplation of her "life goals," were able to plan for "sustainable" careers and a long-term view of prosperity in a way that continued to elude Sam and many of his friends.[30]

Other long-term heroin users offered similar understandings of recovery as bodily reorientation required by the demands of a different historical moment. Also invoking the concept of *shiye*, a term that can be translated as "undertaking," "project," or "business," a friend of Sam's noted that in the twenty-first century "everyone else has a *shiye*, and they give precedence to that profession. But we've been pursuing money and material things. Others are pursuing their *shiye*. Sooner or later, you have to end up doing a *shiye*, right?" This observer contrasted the idea of a decades-long private sector career to the short-term impulses of Society workers. Another long-term heroin user similarly argued that the key to recovery was a process of "washing [himself] white" (*xibai*). This involved "transferring" (*zhuan*) to a new "economic path," breaking long-established habits and cultivating connections that could enable him to engage in new forms of business activity.

Sam argued that "quitting drugs," understood as the narrow pursuit of keeping his body free from opioids, was not enough to provide him with an adequate life. Fixating on successful twenty-first-century entrepreneurs, Sam hoped to sever his unhealthy repetition of the Rush-era past and cultivate a bodily habitus adequate to thriving in the country's rapidly shifting economy.

## HISTORY, ORIENTATION, RECOVERY

Anxieties relating to feelings of embodied obsolescence that I have described here are not uncommon in times of state-sponsored marketization. Anthropologists of postsocialist societies have shown how planned "transitions" from socialist to market-oriented economies are often complicated by lived everyday realities. Workers forging new lives in unfamiliar local moral worlds often struggle with feelings of alienation and confusion (Verdery 1996; Humphrey 2002; Burawoy and Verdery 1999; Buyandelgeriyn 2008). Elizabeth Dunn observes that while a small group of Polish state workers "acquired the habitus of the Western businessman" and "embodied the idea of the transition from socialism to capitalism," the great majority of *kierownik* (state workers) found that their ways of laboring and living were no longer validated (2004, 73).

The concerns brought up by Sam and other struggling onetime Society entrepreneurs complicate postsocialist anthropological work that focuses on the persisting influences of the socialist past on factory attendants, peasants, and other workers responding to the sudden implementation of market reforms.[31] Sam's feelings of obsolescence and lagging behind, while in part attributable to a more general "politics of lateness" (Zhang 2006, 464) in contemporary China, were inseparable from his complex position as an entrepreneur of the recent past. Contrasting also with accounts of a *transhistorical* Chinese entrepreneurial ethic characterized by a "long-term quest to improve material well-being" rather than short-term gain (Harrell 1985, 216), Sam's efforts at building a Society habitus for a time allowed him to enjoy a life as a potent, powerful, and well-paid worker. In the new millennium, however, he increasingly disavowed his ways of moving as crude, undisciplined, and associated with "low quality," marginalized groups.

In discussing pleasures associated with sex and food in the Middle Kingdom, Judith Farquhar (2002) demonstrates that the formations of particular "appetites" are contingent on their historical moment. Her descriptions of the practices of banquet participants during the Cultural Revolution, the covert pleasures of students sharing newly available fruit in the first years of the country's opening, and insecure aging male government cadres' consumption of select foods to offset their own "red" displacement in the 1990s provide examples of bodily dispositions of historical actors attempting to adjust to shifting political, economic, and social conditions. In contrast to assertions that mindful bodies are inevitably "securely anchored in a particular historical moment" (Scheper Hughes and Lock 1987, 7), these stories, alongside Sam's struggles, show how particular bodily appetites and capabilities leave workers feeling that their bodies remain oriented toward action in the recent past rather than China's present.

Sam's interpretation of his condition as a worker can also be understood as emerging from a particular socialist tradition of thinking about addiction that connected possibilities of recovering to historicist ideas about the demands of the nation. Soviet social campaigns, for example, depicted persistent substance abuse as an inability to respond to deep-seated changes in collective working life. Officials applied the phrase "remnants of the past" to a range of troubled individuals, including severe alcoholics, whose suffering was said to stem from "the socio-economic relations, views, ideas, customs and traditions inherited from the old society" ("Perezhitki proshlogo" 1981).[32] Marginalized Soviet diary writers expressed the hope that if they could learn to "think in step with the marching collective" and become "aligned with history," maladapted bodily habits from the past might give way to new dispositions more appropriate to the demands of the day (Hellbeck 2009, 54–55, 369). The Chinese Communist Party in the mid-twentieth century, as chapter 4 examines in more detail, described opium addiction in similar terms, noting that the drug was a "vile lingering poison of the old society" (*jiushehui de elie yidu*) (Wang 1996; see also Smith 2012). Even as Sam turned to local entrepreneurs rather than state-promoted revolutionary heroes as embodying the healthy "new man" in the twenty-first century (cf. Cheng 2009), his understanding of heroin addiction followed the temporal logic of a socialist tradition that insisted on reframing biomedical accounts of addictive behaviors of individuals as problems of misguided workers rooted in vestiges of the past.

Sam's reflections also offer a testimony to the particular lasting costs associated with entrepreneurial experiences in the early years of reform and opening. Unlike the Lost Generations associated with the First World War or the Cultural Revolution (Kleinman 1982), the frenzied activity in the 1980s and early 1990s is rarely discussed as a time that produced mass disorientation. This chapter suggests that the Rush years in Gejiu and other parts of the country in the 1980s and early 1990s might be conceptualized as one of many historical eddies: a vanishingly brief period of tumultuous experimentation and change that many quickly moved beyond.[33] For Sam, however, the possibilities of obtaining a future he desired required overcoming the stubborn legacies of those turbulent times.

## CODA

As the two of us sipped *pu'er* tea in a café on a hot afternoon in the summer of 2011, Sam brought up the ongoing trial of Ma Zhibao, an infamous Society entrepreneur. Known around Gejiu as perhaps the biggest "evil name" (*eming*) in the region, this forty-something-year-old, self-made mining boss had reigned on the nearby mountains for more than twenty years, successfully eluding crackdowns under the Jiang and Hu governments. After finally being arrested along with forty-two alleged accomplices, including a local judge, Ma was charged with a litany of crimes, including receiving protection fees, breaking and entering, committing murder, and dealing heroin (Wu 2011; Yunnan Wang 2011). Sam had followed Ma's exploits since both men had made their way onto the mountains in the second half of the 1980s. For Sam, the spectacular fall of this local Society legend marked the final act of an era of violent entrepreneurial activity.

While rumors of Ma's impending execution swirled around Gejiu, Sam shared with me his latest tentative plans for the future. One of his older brothers had started a successful hardware store franchise in the provincial capital. It looked like Sam might be offered a position if the business succeeded. A job such as this one, in a growing private company, could lead in new directions, he noted hopefully. Sam told me that he loved this community, but with the mountains closed and Society opportunities gone, he needed to find new ways of navigating a new world.

# CHAPTER 3

# Absence of a Future

*Narrative, Obsolescence, and Community*

### ENCOUNTERING OBSOLESCENCE AND THE LIMITS OF "RETURN"

This book was initially organized around the assumption that my interlocutors were engaged in recovery, broadly defined. Some, however, indicated that they thought the very idea of starting a new life after drugs was impossible, that it was too late for them to overcome their status as obsolescent and damaged workers. This chapter explores my encounters with members of the Heroin Generation who appeared to live with an absence of hope for the future. I argue that these individuals shared a common narrative and structure of experience intimately linked to their broader understandings of historical time.

One way of understanding the shared symptoms of those appearing in this chapter is to consider these individuals as suffering from undiagnosed depression or other mental illness. The ICD-10 lists "bleak and pessimistic views of the future" as a common symptom of a depressive episode (World Health Organization 1993, 119). While I would not deny the possible presence of a somatic component contributing to the bleak outlooks presented here, biomedical understandings of clinical depression common in the United States and larger cities in China were virtually absent from my Gejiu-based interlocutors' accounts of their own struggles. Following Ian Hacking (2006), we could say that living with depression had not become a way of being a person for members of this community. Attention to their way of speaking about their condition leads in other directions.

A short man in his early forties with an oval face, sloping shoulders, and brooding eyes, Bo had a deep interest in China's ongoing transformations and a tendency to ask probing questions. Identifying as a "realistic" (*xianshi*) person, he often served as fact checker for the group of people with heroin use history he associated with. On numerous occasions at Green Orchards, I watched him sit quietly at the edge of a conversation, seemingly not participating, until he suddenly interjected, "That's not possible!" (*na shi bukeneng de shiqing*) to refute a careless or perhaps overly optimistic statement made by another attendee at the center. Though he had numerous criticisms of China—including laments about the rise of selfishness and the corruption of national institutions—he strongly believed that the Middle Kingdom would soon become the wealthiest and most powerful country in the world. Despite widespread anxieties about the region's diminishing natural resources, he also insisted that Gejiu city would find new ways to grow and "be good again" in the future.

When we met, Bo often worked to keep the conversation focused on me. He took a vicarious pleasure in offering commentary on my future plans, particularly enjoying telling me about potential ventures that I might pursue teaching English in the region. The focus he placed on helping me to better understand my horizon of opportunities contrasted starkly with his frequent refusals to speak about his own plans for the future.

One afternoon in the summer of 2011, Bo and I convened in the city center and began walking around Golden Lake. I had recently returned after nearly a year in the United States. He was unemployed at the time. I asked for news of two of our mutual acquaintances. He informed me that one friend had been found dead in his apartment, presumably of an overdose, a few months earlier. The second had been detained after a positive urine test and was in the middle of a two-year spell in a nearby labor camp. Bo shook his head and noted darkly that these types of partings had become "too common" these days.

After a period of silence, he then told me that when he walked with his parents around this lake, whenever his mother saw his father dote on small children they encountered on the path, she could not keep from verbalizing her disappointment with Bo. She would comment that her husband's displays of affection for other people's children came from his knowledge that Bo would never give him grandchildren of his own. In a previous meeting, Bo had told me that Chinese men felt an incredible pressure to produce offspring for their parents, an obligation he argued stemmed from the weight of thousands of years of Chinese civilization. This was a pressure that I, as an American, could never understand.

"That time is over now, for me," Bo said quietly.

Wanting to push back against his bleak assessments about the closing of his future, I actively challenged his characterizations of his life's trajectory. I reminded him of the weddings of mutual friends that the two of us had recently attended and of mutual acquaintances who had started families in their forties. His life, like everyone's, had ebbs and flows. Perhaps his own future might move in positive directions that he could not yet see.

Bo didn't answer my comments directly. Saying nothing about the drug's connection to his own life, he observed, "China has no place in its future for heroin." He paused, then continued quietly, "In five years, maybe ten, you will see. We will be gone."

In this meeting Bo expressed a pernicious form of hopelessness that certain other individuals I encountered in Gejiu appeared to share. Instead of suffering from a medical condition they needed to manage or a set of habits that they needed to try to change, these figures spoke with a grim confidence about the impossibility of their own "return" and echoed Bo's sentiments about the broader fate of their generational cohort, as if their futures had been preordained (cf. Tanya Luhrmann's notion of "social defeat" [2007]). In the moments when these claims were made, I found myself struggling with the uncomfortable thought that my research had inadvertently become a form of "salvage anthropology," a rush to document a group that was "vanishing on the disappearing frontier of an advancing civilization" (Gruber 1970, 1297). This discomfort came to be manifested in a sense of despair—sometimes accompanied by visceral bodily sensations, including an uncomfortable pain in my stomach—that I felt during these encounters, reactions that I thought might be shared by my interlocutors.

David Carr, a philosopher with an interest in the relationship between temporality and historical experience, argues that narrative structure "constitutes the unifying form common to two sets of possible oppositions: it is on the one hand the unity of the *lived* and the *told*, and on the other hand the unity of the *individual* and the *social* or *historical*" (1991, 184; emphasis in original). The relationship between these two sets of oppositions came to be realized in Bo's bleak assertions about his own life—his certainty that he would never have a child, for example—and the broader convictions he held about the historical cohort to which he belonged—a "we" that would be gone in five or ten years.

This chapter explores the dynamics and sources of what I came to see as shared forms of hopelessness. The next section explores the relationship between the lived and the told in individuals. I show how the structure of a particular, pernicious narrative—"sacrificial offerings of the Reform era"— contributed to the bleak way in which the group of interlocutors in this chapter spoke about and experienced their personal futures. A conversation among three childhood friends at a holiday meal provides initial clues to the way in which shared feelings of hopelessness became connected to a feeling of community. I finish by considering how discussions of narrative, hope, and temporality might contribute to understanding when and how particular forms of recovery become possible.

## "SACRIFICE OFFERINGS OF THE REFORM"

Bo referred to himself as a "sacrificial offering of the Reform era" (gaige kaifeng de xishengpin), a phrase that a number of members of the Heroin Generation used to describe themselves during my fieldwork. I came to see this expression as something more than a convenient label. Here, I outline how this phrase referenced a process of shaping lived experience of individuals in relation to their understanding of the movement of the nation.

Though "sacrifice" (xisheng) has appeared in ritual and religious contexts in China for many centuries, the term circulated in China broadly as a "super-sign" suffused with Christian undertones throughout the twentieth century.[1] Media accounts in the early decades of the People's Republic referred to martyrs dying in revolutionary struggle as having given their lives as "sacrificial offerings" for the country. In the 1980s, workers who had fared harshly under Maoist policies, including hundreds of thousands of intellectuals struggling to resume their lives after being "sent down" to rural areas, came to be labeled "sacrificial offerings of the Cultural Revolution." By 2010 there were a number of differently situated marginalized groups who spoke of themselves as "sacrificial offerings of the Reform era."[2]

More than three decades into the Reform, the moniker had come to designate unemployed workers who had lost positions in state work units and failed to find new jobs in the market economy. As one laid-off former state worker in her late thirties in another part of the country remarked, "For China to pro-gress, we have to go through this process, [even if] people like us will be affected by it. . . . We need to sacrifice for the next generation . . . so the country can get stronger. . . . [E]liminating people is a necessary law of social development" (quoted in Solinger 2013, 76).[3] Unemployed workers in other parts of the country described this phenomenon as *xiemo shalu*: "killing the mule immediately after it finishes its work" (Yang 2015, 55). Sacrifice during my fieldwork increasingly appeared to refer to the acceptance of the necessity of obsolescence as part of the country's attempt to integrate into a global market economy.

While drug users were rarely referred to as "sacrificial offerings" in media reports or government campaigns during my time in China, a number of my interlocutors maintained that this label accurately described their cohort.[4] There were reasons for desiring this designation. As opposed to the stigmatizing and individualizing connotations associated with "addict" (*chengyinzhe*), "drug using criminal" (*xidufan*), or even the unspecified "victim" (*shouhaizhe*), "sacrificial offerings of the Reform era" linked the suffering of heroin users to the temporary, dangerous, and "necessary" (*biran*) activities associated with reform and opening in the Deng era that enabled later "societal development" and prosperity for others. An acquaintance of Bo's put it this way: "[W]hen [the country] needs a certain type of person, that type of person comes to do what is needed. Like these cigarettes"—he pointed to a pack of locally produced Honghe brand cigarettes on the table—"if they need a box like this to wrap them, we will make such a box." After performing a needed role at a particular moment in the country's development, members of this group had been abandoned. This retrospective understanding of their early careers helped certain members of the Heroin Generation feel a shared identity by attributing a broader, recognized meaning to their past actions. Disappointments stemming from later life trajectories could be transformed "from something that is private and amorphous into something that is shareable and substantial" (Jackson 2012, 48).

Nevertheless, I came to see that telling and living lives as "sacrificial offerings of the Reform era" had deleterious effects on the outlook of certain members of this group. Medical anthropologists have documented the crucial role that narrative plays in structuring experience of recovery from illness and serious injury (Garro 1994; Hunt 2000; Good and Good 2000). Narrative emplotment, Cheryl Mattingly argues, is the creation of a whole out of a series of events. Ongoing actions come to be formulated into a coherent structure that has a beginning, middle, and end (Mattingly 1998; cf. Ricoeur 1990). Occurring between medical providers, patients, and their families, this process of emplotment can be "acted, embodied, played, even danced" in what Mattingly calls "healing dramas" (1998, 2000, 181). Her work identifies distinct genres—healing as battle, as science detective story, as machine repair, as transformative journey—that help to shape the expectations of sick children, their families, and care providers (Mattingly 2010, 37–76). The often-overlooked, collective work of narrative emplotment helps to move patients from feeling "lost, when there seems to be no 'point' to what they are doing" to a view of the future in which "endings are uncertain," at once "marked by suspense" and hope (Mattingly 1998, 812, 814; 2010).

Bo embraced a "sacrifice" narrative that gave his life a unifying structure. However, in contrast to ordering events in a way that opened up to "the possibility of transformation" (Mattingly 1994, 819), Bo's emplotment contributed to his denial of his own abilities to change his life circumstances: to have children, to marry, to find a job, to leave his home to find work or build a new life after addiction. The barren future that he produced and seemed to experience as inevitable existed as an inversion of the life-giving qualities of a "healing drama."

Broadly shared experiences among people with heroin use history contributed to the potential saliency of this way of understanding their own lives. The Gejiu-based cohort I call the Heroin Generation *was* shrinking over time. While police records from 2005 indicated there were more than five thousand "registered" heroin users in Gejiu (Zhao 2008), estimates by groups I knew claimed that the number had dwindled to approximately twenty-five hundred people with heroin use history. Most heroin users in the early 2010s could rattle off dozens of names of friends and acquaintances who had died—initially primarily from overdoses but in more recent years due to a range of complex medical conditions including liver problems and AIDS-related opportunistic infections. In 2010 the city's younger population gravitated toward an array of "new style" (*xinxing*) drugs, including ketamine and ephedrine, that had become available in karaoke lounges and clubs. Media representations also tended to reinforce the view that heroin use was a disappearing epidemic of the past. Just over two decades after its dramatic appearance in this city, heroin was frequently referred to as a "traditional" (*chuantong*) narcotic. Though the opioid had once been synonymous with illicit drug use in the city, heroin was no longer the focus of national drug campaigns.

Bo and other figures in this chapter linked the steady news of sickness and death among their friends and broader narratives about the users of the drug to feelings of inevitability about their own futures. In one memorable example, after telling me about the "too sudden" death of a friend, Bo remarked to me that health for people with heroin use history is just a "surface thing" (*biaomian de dongxi*). I understood the implications of his statement to have two meanings. First, the disappearance of other members of this community foretold his own early death. Second, he felt he lacked the capacity to create and live a future markedly different from his past. In contrast to facilitating a salutatory shift from temporal confusion, incoherence, and disorder to coherence (Carr 1991, 96; Mattingly 1998), Bo's "genre" of self-sacrificing narrative drew together the lived and the told and the individual and historical in a potent combination that critically impaired his own ability to imagine a life after heroin. Others shared his way of speaking about and orienting toward the future.

## "NO NEED FOR NICE SHOES"

Zhijun greeted me at the door of his parents' home. Sporting a military-style crew cut, he had a slightly crooked nose and moved with the stiff, gingerly gait of a retired boxer. As discussed in chapter 1 he had been a successful post-Mao entrepreneur eager to break with the iron rice bowl tradition to strike out on his own. In the fifteen years prior to our meeting, his business ventures had gone badly. Despite having stretches of paid employment in recent years working as a security guard (*bao'an*), Zhijun idled throughout the time that I knew him. While he lived with his retired, aging parents, his older sister—the serious student who had been sent down to the nearby countryside in her youth—had become a successful government official in a nearby city.

We drank tea and chatted in his living room while his mother prepared dinner in the kitchen. Then, the forty-four-year-old led me into the master bedroom in the small but tidy apartment provided by the work unit. (Zhijun slept on the couch in the living room.) "I have something I want your help with," he told me as he got on his hands and knees and began retrieving items from underneath his parents' bed.

He first emerged with a long, rectangular box containing an air rifle. He briefly paused to show me the weapon. While toys such as this one had been common in this mountainous community in his teenage years during the 1980s, the government had subsequently cracked down on weapons of all sorts, including the switchblade knife that he had once carried. The campaigns that stripped citizens of their knives and guns were part of a wider attempt in the post-Rush years to quell the violence associated with the mining boom. "We are living in a different moment," he noted before continuing his search.

He next pulled out a pair of unworn, brand-name leather shoes, a recent gift to him from his older sister. "I have no need for nice shoes," Zhijun commented, shaking his head, "but she buys them for me anyway." He went on to catalog her other recent gifts, purchased at the local mall—a belt, a new shirt—and the amount of money that she had spent on each.

With a bit more shuffling under the bed he retrieved what he had been looking for, an Atari system in its original box. This had been a highly desired consumer good back when Zhijun had been making good money running a motorcycle repair shop. He showed me the English-language instructions in the box and asked me if I could help him to figure out how to set it up. Moving to the living room, I gave up after a couple of minutes when I realized the obsolete cables would not fit the outputs on the family's flat-screen TV.

After dinner, we prepared to say goodbye. I was returning to the United States later that week, and neither of us knew when we would meet again. Zhijun sighed. The act of turning his attention toward the future visibly darkened his mood. He told me that I needed to take down a new contact number for him and recited the digits of his parents' home landline. He explained that as his employment prospects dwindled, he doubted he would keep his simple candy-bar-style cell phone activated for much longer.

Just before we parted, he noted sadly, "My life is entering its twilight."

Gejiu, many agreed, was a difficult place to start a new life after drugs. The most common complaint I heard during my fieldwork from heroin users and nonusers alike was that the densely packed urban center—"little Hong Kong" as some called it—was "too small." For people with heroin use history in recovery, the dense urban layout meant there was always the potential of running into dealers or active users who might try to encourage them to return to old habits. It also meant that hiding their pasts from potential employers and friends was difficult.

But this "smallness" potentially created other problems. Ning, a nurse who acted as the manager of Green Orchards, believed attempting to build a new life in this familiar environment made recovery more difficult. Drawing from the content of a training that she had recently attended in Beijing run by national addiction experts, Ning told me that recovering users in Gejiu had to move through spaces and interact with objects that were linked to memories of times when they were using. She took up the example of eating chocolate to explain the problem: "It happens to us all. If you grew up eating chocolate in a certain location for years and years, you may stop eating chocolate, but if you are suddenly back in that room again, the urge to eat chocolate will re-emerge." This explanation was, I realized, informed by neuroscientific understanding of relapse triggers, whereby particular environments and objects served as powerful cues predicting drug availability that could "hijack the brain" and provoke drug-using behavior (Volkow and Li 2005; see also Levy 2017).

A focus on narrative and its link to action provides an alternative way of understanding how moving through familiar environments influenced my interlocutors' orientations toward the future. David Carr, in emphasizing the "doubly practical function" (1991, 168) of narrative structure, differentiates between a *reflective* mode, occurring when an individual takes stock of her own actions or even life trajectory as the theme of her thinking, and a *pre-reflective* mode, which involves the configuration of the lived relation of past, present, and future. Exploring the interrelation of these two modes—with a focus on the future orientation in each—can help to draw attention to how the "sacrificial offerings of the Reform era" narrative affected Zhijun and others as they moved through contemporary Gejiu.

"Stock-taking" (*Besinnung*), a term that appears in the writings of Dilthey and Heidegger, refers to a reflective, cognitive stance whereby individuals break from the actions, experiences, and projects that often occupy their attention to consider the overall sense of what they are doing.[5] This includes taking up our past and future thematically; that is, we can turn our attention to evaluating how we have lived our lives and engage in "deliberation and planning" (Carr 1991, 60, 168) to achieve personal future goals. As part of this process, we guide our approach to what is yet to come through projects that define our lives by ordering them into a beginning, middle, and end. Moments when individuals discussed their thoughts about "return to society" appearing throughout this book are examples of this stock-taking stance.

Pre-reflective narrative, by contrast, refers to the temporal configuration of short-term, habitual tasks that make possible the cohesion of human experience or action. Rather than an isolated instant, our experience of a present moment extends into the past and future in what Edmund Husserl ([1928] 1964) calls "protensions and retensions." Husserl deploys the example of listening to a musical melody to reveal an underlying temporal experience: in order to hear the unity of a tune, the listener must hold on to the melody from an earlier moment and project an anticipation of what is to come. David Carr argues that this structure also applies to action. Even as protentions are not cognitive, they have "varying degrees of openness" and can leave the actor "vulnerable to surprise" when they are not met (1991, 28–29). Taking on different orientations over time, our "implicit horizon or background for the present" (114) inflects moment-to-moment experiences.[6]

My encounter with Zhijun can be interpreted through this "doubly practical" narrative structuring. While we were in his parents' bedroom, Zhijun broke from his action in the present—the search for the Atari—to narrate in a reflective stance for me (as he often does for himself) how various objects come to take meaning within his broader life trajectory. He emphasized that items associated with his youth and career—his gaming console, the air rifle (and, on another occasion, the digital watches he used to sell on the street)— were irrelevant to his life in the current moment.[7] He also argued that he was unprepared or unfit to use objects associated with the historical present: his cell phone and the unworn shoes gathering dust in his parents' apartment. The failure of our attempt to hook up his Atari seemed to give greater weight to his way of narrating his life story, which rejected the possibility of repurposing his past for the future. Zhijun's denial of an "active" form of hope in his "sacrificial" discussion about his employment prospects and growing uselessness as a human being, and the "passive" form of hope that manifested in his moment-to-moment feelings of obsolescence, reinforced each other with devastating effectiveness. His offhand comment to me that his life was entering its twilight could be understood as an expression of a suffocating feeling of inevitability that was both lived and told, actively produced and posited as already existing.

At times Zhijun spoke of how others figures around him—his sister and former classmates—were thriving. The success of other urban dwellers within a shared national time put his individual struggles into greater relief. But at other times, his bleak view of the future came to encompass other residents of this mountain community. Over the dinner table with his father and me, Zhijun noted that thousands of kilometers of tunnels in the region had never been filled in after minerals were excavated.[8] He speculated darkly that in the event of an inopportune earthquake, the hollowed out earth below us would collapse, burying the city and all of us with it.[9]

## HOLIDAY CHEER

Narratives of sacrifice and the theme of suffocating obsolescence also occurred in group settings. The fifteenth day in the Lunar Year is the Lantern Festival Holiday, an event celebrated throughout China by hanging red paper lights and gathering family members for leisurely meals. On this day in 2010, Bo invited me to a friend's house for an impromptu holiday dinner. Lan, our host, was a short man with a quick, wide smile. His parents were visiting relatives out of town, so we had their two-bedroom apartment to ourselves. While Bo and I sat on the sofa, Lan propped himself at the family dining table with the TV on in the background. He shifted between sudden and enthusiastic participation in our conversation and bouts of heroin-induced "nodding," his chin at times slowly descending to his chest before popping back up. His sporadic, enthusiastic participation in our conversation reminded me of the soporific Dormouse character from *Alice in Wonderland*'s tea party.

Yu, a handsome man with sharp cheekbones whose youthful appearance was accentuated by his propensity for wearing cotton muscle T-shirts, had disappeared into the kitchen. We could hear clanging sounds as this onetime professional chef expertly maneuvered the wok over the family's single hot plate. Eventually he brought eight dishes out from the kitchen. We gathered around the dining room table and began to eat. The regular explosions of firecrackers outside and the bountiful food contributed to a festive atmosphere.

The three men began to reminisce about their shared childhood. They had grown up in the same Yunnan Tin employee housing block and had roamed the neighborhood together as pre-teenagers. In the years before Reform-era policies and the tin Rush, large families had been crowded into tiny apartments that were sometimes enlarged by illegal additions cobbled onto roofs and courtyards. Bo's sister had slept on the narrow kitchen floor while he, his brother, and sometimes their father slept on a single mattress. Even as the conversation touched on the difficulties of those times—ration coupons, austere living conditions, an absence of two-day weekends—their stories emphasized the simplicity and communal connection they associated with their youth in pre-Rush times. Gesturing at the flat-screen TV that broadcast a news program during our meal, they talked about the eagerness with which they had sought out rare black-and-white television sets at that time, when they had packed into crowded living rooms to watch annual Chinese New

Year programming. With few doors and no locks separating family dwellings, children had flowed freely in and out of different homes.

The sound of a new round of fireworks outside caused the conversation to shift to the topic of Gejiu's development. The fireworks display was part of a broader campaign designed to highlight Gejiu's "famous international tin culture" and push forward its postindustrial identity as a "leisure destination." The three men agreed that life in Gejiu, like most of China, had dramatically improved as its citizens had become more refined, cultured, and materially wealthy. Yu noted that "development is definitely better than it used to be. If you compare now to any other time, there is no comparison. Life really is getting better one day at a time." Lan noted with pride that Gejiu was the only location in the province to have won the "civilized city" (wenming chengshi) distinction, an award given by a Beijing committee to urban destinations achieving outstanding sanitation, cleanliness, and beauty. In the days preceding the committee's most recent visit, local government representatives had come to Green Orchards drop-in center to give lectures and distribute educational information about the importance of keeping spitting and other unsanitary personal habits to a minimum.

An argument broke out among the three men about whether or not improvements to city life were benefiting people with heroin use history. Lan observed that government social welfare programs—including conditions in compulsory detoxification centers—were becoming more "humane" (renxinghua). While Bo did not directly disagree with his friends' observations, he noted that rapid development increased the challenges to recovering drug users by expanding the gap between themselves and other city dwellers.

The men then discussed the recent death of a childhood friend who had passed away suddenly due to a brain aneurism. Having found a girlfriend and repaired his relationship with his mother, he had appeared to have been thriving in recent months. They expressed their dismay at the unexpected loss.

Turning his attention to the apartment in which we found ourselves, Bo commented that while homes were far bigger than the long-ago bulldozed building they had grown up in, residents didn't know their neighbors anymore. Moreover, the increased living space that local inhabitants had gained over the previous thirty years was offset by the fact that apartments' doors were locked to outsiders. Though it was not mentioned, my gaze shifted to a padlocked door on the master bedroom; Lan's parents had shut off their portion of the house before leaving for the holiday.

Bo gestured toward the metal protective window guard (*fangdaochuang*) covering the living room window, also visible from our seats at the dining table. He commented that these guards had first appeared in the Rush years when rapid expansion of burglaries associated with a rise in consumer products stored in homes convinced residents of the need for extra protection. Yu then told a humorous story about an out-of-own thief known as "spider man" who rappelled off roofs and successfully robbed many of the metal-window-guard-free apartments on the upper stories of apartment complexes. Yu reported this talented burglar had finally been caught after a young child spotted him dangling outside a window.

Bo noted that while window guards were meant to keep out malevolent forces, they also created a potential safety hazard in the case of an emergency like a fire. He observed forlornly, "We have come to feel like prisoners in our own homes."

With the food eaten and holiday fireworks finished, we parted ways.

This holiday conversation brings together key themes of this chapter while raising questions about the nature of the shared feelings of hopelessness. At the end of the meal, Bo again invoked a collective subject—the "we" of "we have come to feel like prisoners in our own homes." Attention to how community came to be conceived of and called into being during my fieldwork connects to chapter 1's discussion about the conditions under which individual experiences come to be linked through shared understandings of historical experience.

During my fieldwork, drug users and nonusers alike observed that people with heroin use history shared far more than an unhealthy relationship to opioids. It was often remarked that this group possessed a "common language" (*gongtong yuyan*) built through years of spending time together as school classmates, early career colleagues, users of heroin, "students" (*xueyuan*) in state treatment spaces, and idlers on the margins of the contemporary economy. Some recovering drug users maintained that keeping a distance from other former users was a key part of any successful effort at recovery: "Break from drugs, break from the community" (*duandu, duanquan*) was a common piece of advice given to recovering heroin users. In practice, however, severing these deep bonds was a difficult, some even claimed impossible, task.

The Lantern Festival dinner conversation can serve as a starting point for examining the complex nature of the attachments of what might be understood as a "community of time."[10] This phrase comes from the work of Alfred Schutz, a sociologist and phenomenologist who was interested in the direct experience born of extended face-to-face contact. Intimacy that emerges from "growing old together," Schutz argues, produces "a rich, concrete We-relationship without any need to reflect on it" (1967, 195).[11] I argue that the deep connection between these old friends might be born of a set of shared experiences and also a "*sense* of sharing a collective time" that "converts my time to our time or to the times of my generation" (see Heinz Bunde's work as discussed in Corsten 1999, 258; emphasis in original). Whereas in chapter 1, I argued that young members of the Society shared intuitions about the movement of the country, opportunities associated with risk, and the value of particular temporal orientations, the "we" evoked here two decades later drew on an intimacy born of a common past, but also, increasingly, a shared sense of hopelessness in navigating the outside world.

I was acutely aware of a pronounced change that took place over the course of the dinner; playful reminiscences about youthful gatherings in the early evening gave way to a familiar heaviness that I had come to associate with those living the "sacrificial offerings" narrative structure. Themes of death and the dwindling of future possibilities emerged after a discussion of the ongoing impact of development associated with the trajectory of Reform-era history. Objects in our immediate environment—the television, the fireworks, the metal window guard, even the spacious apartment itself and its proximity to neighbors—became focal points for reflecting on the past and expressing feelings of loss and obsolescence. An understanding of the historical trajectory of Gejiu city—and by extension China—inflected the way that this group understood their individual and collective fates.

It is possible to argue that our dinner conversation was shaped by the pernicious effects of ideas about linearity and progress in a state-promoted development discourse (see the discussion Yan Hairong's claims and discussion of historicism in the introduction). A phenomenological take on historicity, however, enables a more nuanced way of understanding how a collective "we" might emerge through shared attention to the meanings of particular events. David Carr explains:

> The communal event of the present, in which we participate as subjects of experience or action, gets its sense from the background of comparable events to which it belongs. We participate in them (enjoy or suffer, act in common, and understand what we are doing) to the extent that we place the event in this context. And our

placing it there is a function of the overall story we tell, and if necessary retell, to each other about ourselves and what we are doing. (1991, 167)

A shared sense of history as an experience can be built up not just through widely disseminated state campaigns, but also through concrete interactions and situated ways of telling and retelling how elements of the past impact members of particular groups. These specific understandings of the past allow for the emergence of a "we" rooted in a common experience of time.[12]

Belonging to the "we" associated with now middle-aged, long-term heroin users discussed in this chapter can be seen as simultaneously attractive and dangerous. The connections between old friends enables a deep sense of mutual understanding, familiarity, and empathy forged from a shared set of references and a concrete We-relationship born of common experiences: a shared past and, perhaps, future. However, as the grim reflections of the trio toward the end of the dinner show, these reunions *also* potentially reproduced feelings of potentially overwhelming hopelessness and despair. The shared form of "sacrificial offerings of the Reform era" narrative intensified the tragic arc that their individual lives had taken and compounded feelings of alienation from the broader social world. I can still vividly remember the initial atmosphere of warmth and connectedness at this holiday dinner shifting to a feeling of hopelessness as the childhood friends experienced themselves as "prisoners" of the rapidly shifting world they lived in.

## HOPE AND RECOVERY

I finish the chapter by considering the relationship between feelings of obsolescence, hope, and recovery. Patricia Deegan, a clinical psychologist, offers an insightful meditation on recovery as lived experience. Drawing on her own early experiences with schizophrenia and a friend's debilitating depression after being paralyzed in a car accident, she speaks about the delicate but crucial emergence of hope as a precondition for recovery. For many months after her first schizophrenic episodes and his accident, she says, they were not recovering. "Time" she noted, "did not heal us," but instead acted as a "betrayer" as "our pasts deserted us and we could not return to who we had been. Our futures appeared to us to be barren, lifeless places in which no dream could be planted and grow into a reality." The present during this period was a "numbing succession of days and nights in which we had no place, no use and no reason to be." Recovery, by contrast, came to be associated with a "birth of hope" as Deegan and her friend each "experience[d] a peace in knowing that this pain was leading us forward into a new future" (1988, 12–15).

Deegan's writing beautifully captures the crucial importance of hope in recovery.[13] Her description of her recovery foregrounds both a shift in her pre-reflective narrative—her gradual ability to complete "simple acts" such as shopping and talking to friends—as well as reflective stock-taking in important decisions such as going back to school that helped her to restart her life. Deegan describes her feeling of "grace" in finding a sense of the future that came to replace a sensation of drifting without purpose.

Maintaining hope, I argue, is intimately linked to the work of recovery. Vincent Crapanzano has asserted that hope "always invokes an ever further horizon—a beyond of a mysterious, transcending (if not transcendental) nature" (2004, 104). Whether distinguishing between "active" and "passive" forms of hope (Zigon 2009), interrogating the societal distribution of hope (Hage 2003), keeping hope alive in seemingly impossible circumstances (Lear 2006), or exploring communal efforts to shape the future (Malkki 2001, 328), anthropologists have foregrounded the essential importance of hope in shaping individual and collective lives.[14] Addressing a particularly acute version of a shared sense of resignation that limits aspirations of marginalized Chinese citizens (cf. Lora-Wainwright 2017), this chapter has shown how Bo, Zhijun, and others' narratives of sacrifice through subtle everyday intimations and broader stock-taking reinforced the idea that they were "too late."

Writing on phenomenological understandings of time and therapeutic efficacy in clinical settings, Daniel Stern foregrounds the importance of patients achieving a particular orientation toward the lived protentional-retensional present: "The challenge is to imagine the present moment in some kind of dialogic equilibrium with the past and future. If the present moment is not well anchored in a past and future it floats off as a meaningless speck. If it is too well anchored it becomes diminished. Also the present must be able to influence, perhaps to the same extent, the past and future, just as they influence the present" (2004, 27). Patricia Deegan's victory over a barren future and Stern's "dialogic equilibrium" each describes ways in which individuals might maintain hopeful, open-ended futures in the face of potentially catastrophic loss.

Recovery requires engaging in projects that keep open the possibility of overcoming disappointments of the past and restoring to individuals what

Arjun Appadurai discusses as a cultural "capacity to aspire" (2013). From this perspective, the crucial function of any "return to society," irrespective of its specific goals, is to enable a narrative and experiences that allow for a hopeful orientation to the world. While life in the absence of some vision of "return" is possible, the psychic costs of such an existence are immense.[15]

## CODA: TABLE TENNIS TRANSFORMATIONS

As we walked to the gym, Zhou said little. More than anyone I met during my fieldwork, he seemed to embody the struggles of someone suffering from an overdetermined sense of hopelessness. Meeting him in person was difficult because he frequently canceled our scheduled appointments for a variety of excuses.

When we had first played table tennis together a few weeks earlier, we had been accompanied by Yan Jun, a mutual friend and his onetime classmate. Yan had explained to me that in his early teens, Zhou had been a star student and the best table tennis player in his class, someone other people respected and looked up to. Zhou had grudgingly acknowledged these statements to be true. Despite his friend's encouragement, our first match had been disappointing. I had brought my own paddle, while he used a simple plywood one supplied by the center attendant. It had been more than a decade since Zhou had last hit a ball, and it showed. He was clearly frustrated by his inconsistent play, and afterward he had said little.

Before the start of our second match, I presented Zhou with a tacky rubber paddle that I had brought as a gift for him. Standing on the far side of the table, he wore a faded Nike T-shirt with holes in it. A belt was wrapped around his thin waste and curled around his back, almost completing a second loop. Early on, he struggled to keep a rally. Yet as we continued to play, the transformation in his game was striking. His penhold forehand whipped frequent winners, sliced backhands skid on the table, and stealthily delivered serves spun in ways I couldn't anticipate. As we finished our warm-up and began to keep score, Zhou dominated the rallies, moving the ball as he wanted to. He quickly won several games in a row. His play had dramatically improved with proper equipment and the increasing confidence that he brought to his actions. Immediately following an especially impressive shot that I had been unable to return, I noticed his shoulders rotating in small circular movements. It was the first time I had seen him laugh.

As we walked to a restaurant for lunch after our game, Zhou appeared to be in a good mood. I suggested that we play more regularly, and he replied that it would be fun to hit again. But by the time we arrived at a nearby dumpling house for lunch, he was already returning to making his characteristically bleak pronouncements, not only on his own life, but also about the ventures of our mutual friends. Despite my frequent invitations, he refused to schedule another time to hit. When I ran into him on the street or at Green Orchards later during my stay in Gejiu, Zhou would inevitably tell me he needed to return the paddle I had given him, a gesture that would free him from any expectation that he should ever play again.

While I do not want to overemphasize what this single encounter might have meant to Zhou or minimize the significant barriers that he faced in navigating his daily life, I find myself returning to the dramatic shift that took place during our second and last table tennis meet-up. I wonder if it is possible to understand Zhou's experience of our table tennis encounter as briefly enabling him to connect with long-dormant bodily skills associated with a different time in his life, a time when he had been a top student with a bright future. The sudden familiarity and facility of moving he experienced in our table tennis match seemed to briefly allow him to challenge the overwhelmingly negative ideas and affects associated with what I have described as a "sacrificial offering" narrative. A challenged faced by Zhou and others appearing in this chapter was to find a way to link isolated experiences to more hopeful orientations that might allow them to define and pursue new projects.

# CHAPTER 4

# Idling in Mao's Shadow

*The Therapeutic Value of Socialist Labor*

## DIAGNOSING THE HISTORICAL PRESENT

Located a stone's throw from Golden Lake, the Green Orchards drop-in center was a well-known destination for people with heroin use history. On occasion, the promise of free packs of Honghe cigarettes handed out by the staff—the center employed five peer educators who were all in various stages of recovery, in addition to three other health workers—attracted a throng of recovering and active local users to trainings on public health topics. More typically, however, Green Orchards "members" (*huiyuan*) straggled in one or two at a time, with perhaps thirty or forty people passing through on an average day.[1]

The organization was an unusual government-NGO hybrid; it was registered as a nonprofit, funded by international donors, and supported by a global team of health consultants, but was managed by the local District Street Office (*jiedao banshichu*), which was located next door. Strong community and government support for the center ensured that police would not arrest drug users at or near the center.

While visitors often whiled away the afternoons playing mahjong, chatting, and interacting with dogs and children who at times accompanied visitors, my strongest memory of the Green Orchards patio was of a still silence (see figure 5). Members would sprawl out on plastic lawn chairs, tea thermoses resting on the pavement, eyes closed, limbs barely moving in the afternoon sun. The aimless lounging was referred to by this group as "idling" (*xianzhe*), a bodily state that they characterized as involuntary and debilitating.

FIGURE 5. The patio at Green Orchards. Photo by author.

Chen, a small man whose stiff, skinny frame often became obscured within the buckling folds of his crumpled suit jacket, spent many hours at Green Orchards each week. Arriving at the center in a foul mood one afternoon, he reported that he had just been in a fight with his mother, who, seeing him aimlessly lazing around the house, had told him bluntly, "As long as a person is alive, he needs something to do!" After failing to find steady work as a package deliverer, shop salesman, and street vendor, Chen was considering traveling across the country to see if distant relatives might provide him with a position in their factory. His recent feelings of helplessness were compounded by the fact he hadn't even been able to buy cigarettes since his mother had cut his pocket money the previous week.

"The government," Chen remarked offhandedly while leaning back in his plastic armchair, "really needs to take responsibility (*chengdan zeren*) and find us something to do!"

Chen's evocation of the responsibility of the Chinese state for the laboring lives of its wayward citizens was one small example of how socialist understandings of labor came to inflect conversations among those who gathered at Green Orchards. The patio at Green Orchards became a space where understandings of the country's socialist past could be deployed to defamiliarize the present and suggest other possibilities for life after addiction. Building on ethnographic accounts that have explored the rhythms and affective dimensions of lives organized around a permanent exclusion from local economies (Ralph 2008; O'Neill 2017), this chapter shows how the men and women who idled in this government-created center connected embodied experiences of their unemployment to perceived inadequacies of Chinese state policies and practices.

Two earlier government responses to addiction were frequently referenced as offering potential alternatives to their present predicament: the special care and benefits provided to employees and their families by SOEs that members of this group had directly experienced in the 1980s and the radical revolutionary power of collective "remolding through labor" (*laodong gaizao*) imagined to have existed in the first years of the People's Republic.[2] Approaching addiction as a threat to the collective life of the work unit and as a problem of idling inherited from China's feudal and semicolonial capitalist past, respectively, these programs from the country's socialist past were taken up by Green Orchards regulars as potent examples of how the state could help—and even force—drug users to "merge into" (*rongru*) society as productive workers. In reflecting on the intertwining of personal and national histories, idlers at Green Orchards unsettled recently emerging commonsense liberal understandings of the relationship between compulsion and freedom, labor and idling, and challenged ideas of the Hu-era state's role in improving idling citizens' lives.

## A "STRANGE PHENOMENON": LIFE BETWEEN IDLING AND COMPULSORY LABOR

Over several months of regularly visiting Green Orchards, I discovered that there was a continual, gradual shift in the composition of members at the center: New faces appeared while familiar characters abruptly stopped attending. Changes in who visited at the center were linked to this group's movement in and out of local compulsory labor centers.[3] One compulsory labor center located just a few kilometers away from Green Orchards held over one thousand individuals arrested for heroin use. Other institutions scattered throughout the prefecture detained several thousand additional users at any given time. Once arrested, "students" labored in these institutions under direction of the state for between one and three years.

Virtually every person with heroin use history that I met in Gejiu had experienced the laboring rhythms of these centers, most on several occasions.[4] A visitor one afternoon on the center's patio summed up the situation: "It is these same people, coming in, going out, coming in, going out. For many years it has been like this, they come out, relapse, and then move back in again." The aimless lounging at Green Orchards, then, constituted one pole in lives that swung sporadically between idling on the margins of the city and working in state compulsory laboring facilities.

This phenomenon had important implications for how recovering drug users came to understand the state's role in their working lives. Relying on "therapeutic governance" (Zhang 2017), Chinese state agents in the twenty-first century have increasingly deployed technologies that allow the party to "govern from afar" (Ong and Zhang 2008) through "affectively compelling" interventions (Yang 2015, 218) and "kindly power" (Yang 2010) rather than the coercive policing of private lives (Farrer 2002, 252). Though the very existence of the center at Green Orchards could be viewed as an example of how officials were increasingly prioritizing noncoercive interventions, my interlocutors referenced their extensive experience in compulsory labor centers to argue that the Chinese government's approach to addiction *also* continued to adhere to Maoist logics based on total subjection of the body to the party-state.

Meng, the computer enthusiast and occasional visitor to Green Orchards whom I first discussed in the introduction, was intimately familiar with the challenges of shuttling in and out of compulsory labor centers. Between the ages of sixteen and thirty-five, he had been detained for heroin use more than ten times. Miserable during his time in the centers, he had labored for approximately a decade in these total institutions, working extremely long days assembling light bulbs and engaging in other menial, quota-based tasks.[5] Often picked up by the police soon after relapsing, he described his relationship with heroin less as an intrusive constant in his life than as a series of relatively brief interludes that soon triggered new periods of compulsory laboring.

Meng offered a nuanced critique of how the *combination* of socialist and market-oriented demands on people with drug use history as laborers severely limited the possibilities for "return" among local heroin users.[6] He observed that movement between compulsory labor centers—operating continuously since their formalization in the legal system in 1957—and Green Orchards exposed beleaguered recovering workers to two contrasting state expectations about how Chinese citizens should labor. When in the laboring centers, drug users worked, whether they wanted to or not. But when released, the same individuals often found that they idled, even when they were desperate to find jobs. From Meng's perspective, idling was a symptom of this hybrid state institutional landscape, a system that instilled conflicting ideas about the role of labor in "return" into the bodies of eternally recovering workers.

Other former "students" who came to visit Green Orchards supported Meng's observation by describing what they experienced as a particular form of state-produced disorientation. They noted their struggles in grappling with the "strange phenomenon" (*qiguai de xianxiang*) of careening repeatedly between periods of laboring as "students" of socialist labor in the centers and idlers existing as "Chinese trash" on the peripheries of a market economy. The grueling, repetitive routines in compulsory labor centers taught "obedience" and instilled a capacity for working long hours. However, unlike earlier generations of detainees who received job assignments as a condition of being discharged, members of this group often had nothing to do after emerging from the centers. The sudden lack of employment and aimless rhythms of post-release life led Green Orchards attendees to report that they felt like "useless" beings (*wuyong*) or "idiots" (*shazi*) who were "unable to do anything." A "laziness" (*landuo*) and "passiveness" (*duoxing*) associated with the "long-term habit of idling" (*changqi xianguan*) prevailed—until relapse and arrest for heroin use put them back in the compulsory centers and the cycle began again.

These comments complicate arguments that have been made about the "vicious cycle" associated with the repeated institutionalization of people using drugs in other contexts (Young and Buchanan 2000). Green Orchards attendees, like users in many parts of the world where drug consumption is criminalized, found sudden arrests and subsequent institutionalizations profoundly disruptive. But their experiences diverge from North American manifestations of this phenomenon, in which the addict/offender is "dually and contradictorily marked" as "patient *and* prisoner" who must "reckon *and* recover" (Garcia 2010, 19; emphasis in original). Nor do they understand time in these state institutions as "actively preparing detainees for a 'capitalist labor culture' awaiting them upon their release" (Zigon 2011, 206).[7]

Instead, Meng and other Green Orchards regulars pointed to the harmful disjuncture that existed between the Maoist traditions of laboring that characterized their life in detention and the harsh realities of the labor market that awaited them outside the compulsory labor centers. Informed by their awareness of the inconsistent application of policies from different eras, Green Orchards idlers criticized the government for mistreatment in compulsory labor centers *and* for failing to provide socialist guidance and stable work opportunities in their post-release lives.[8]

Li, a frequent visitor at the center, explained to me that "students" leaving the compulsory labor centers already possessed "discipline" (*youjilüxing*) instilled through state laboring routines. As a result, the government "at any time could organize us, honestly."[9] Instead, after following the rhythms of the state as part of their "treatment," many former "students" were left to face the indignity of endless days without work. As another member at Green Orchards put it, the government "would rather let us have a little fun here [at Green Orchards] and then throw us back in [compulsory labor centers] again!" Having followed state mandates to prepare for a laboring life while in the centers, they believed the government was obligated to arrange "appropriate" work opportunities for idling former detainees.

## MEMORIES OF SOE CARE AND COMMUNITY

At times I struggled to reconcile the seemingly incompatible attitudes that my interlocutors' held toward socialist legacies of laboring. From their lawn chairs on the patio at Green Orchards, this group offered scathing critiques of the conditions in the nearby compulsory labor centers. Recently released detainees arriving at Green Orchards complained of feeling "beaten down and broken" (*zibaoziqi*) after being subjected to exhausting and repetitive bodily toil, poor living conditions, and occasional violence inflicted by guards and other people with drug use history. Moreover, members frequently derided these centers as ineffective; one joke I heard at Green Orchards was that the relapse rate for former detainees was 101 percent, as occasionally a non-heroin user was accidentally sent into a laboring center and inevitably ended up using alongside other former "students" after their release.

And yet regulars at Green Orchards also frequently defended Maoist traditions of laboring, including the right of the Communist Party to assign the labor power of its citizens as it saw fit. If the conditions in the existing labor centers that survived from the Maoist era were widely seen as inhumane and ineffective, what memories and imaginations of the country's history of socialist traditions of laboring led to the regulars' own complicated understandings of this past?

Since opening its doors in 2003, Green Orchards had been widely touted as an innovative model for government involvement in service delivery to drug users. While receiving international funding and technical assistance, Green Orchards staff worked under the direct supervision of the District Street Office, located next door. This office provided residents living in the area with ID cards, processed unemployment and health benefits, and facilitated access to other government social services and programs. Employees stationed in this busy building were also responsible for outreach to promote government campaigns; posters for the one-child policy hanging on the wall next to the patio were reminders of their work (see figure 6).[10]

Both Green Orchards and the community government administration it was a part of were the recent creation of the reforms started in the 1990s. Serving urban citizens based on the location of their residence, this system marked a turn away from the more comprehensive, employer-based system envisioned by Maoist reformers in the 1950s. While many recognized this reorganization as a sensible response to the realities of governing an increasingly mobile population in a market economy, Green Orchards members spoke with affection about the forms of care that had existed before the creation of Street Offices, when *danwei* or work units had been charged with overseeing the well-being of their workers and families.[11]

Previous chapters discuss the powerful loyalty that SOEs engendered among their employees, in particular older Gejiu residents. The tin capital had been a relatively rare area where the iron rice bowl promises first outlined by Mao in the 1950s were offered to a significant percentage of the urban population.[12] Yunnan Tin in particular exerted a powerful force in the city, where for decades its senior administrator enjoyed a higher political standing and wielded more power than the mayor. As the "sons and daughters" of government employees, many Green Orchards attendees as children enjoyed benefits of the *danwei*-administered "small society," which included its own police force, hospitals, nurseries, schools, and entertainment venues built for its Gejiu-based employees. In the 1980s, in addition to attending schools and hospitals

FIGURE 6. Government family planning banner at Green Orchards. Photo by author.

organized through the *danwei*, a number of my interlocutors received their first jobs by "taking over shifts" from retiring parents, worked in government-organized collectives, or attended SOE-sponsored training programs. SOEs emphasized a reciprocal dependency between employer and employees, and workers and their families were encouraged to "come to the [work unit's] party committee whenever you have a problem" (Yang 2015, 78).

When heroin flooded the region in the Rush years, local SOE leaders, acting like "village heads" displaying great "concern with employee welfare" (Walder 1989, 249), developed their own response to the growing epidemic. In total, more than a dozen "work unit pilot series rehabilitation centers" quickly opened to treat drug-using local SOE workers and family members. Operating in centrally located buildings easily accessible to visitors, these rehabilitation centers aimed to keep opioid users connected to family and friends during and after their detoxification. Green Orchards attendees remembered that some centers even allowed family members to bring their children home for meals. Other staff members occasionally bought chicken and fulfilled other special requests for detoxing patients, as long as their families promised to pay back the money at a later date. Employers in certain cases also extended loans to affected families during the treatment period.

Most crucially, these Deng-era heroin treatment centers operated on the assumption that detoxing patients would return to work as soon as their bodies had healed. Stays in the rehabilitation centers were initially limited to a month or less. Gejiu employers protected the jobs of those in treatment, with some even continuing to pay young workers' salaries while they detoxed. The primary task of the centers was to allow workers' bodies to recover.

SOE-organized treatment for addiction proved to be short-lived. Even during the years when the work unit centers were in operation, drug users arrested by city police rather than Yunnan Tin security forces (*baoweike*) were sent to overcrowded police-run jails and nearby reeducation through labor centers. National antidrug legislation created in 1990 clarified that rehabilitation was to be overseen either by hospitals, for short-course detoxification, or by the Ministries of Justice and Public Security, for more extensive rehabilitation. Between 1988 and 2001, the number of registered drug users flowing through the compulsory labor system increased from 50,000 to one million, with users in Yunnan province making up a disproportionate number of this total population.[13] By the mid-1990s, virtually all of the SOE detoxification centers in the Honghe region had closed their doors after public security and justice employees consolidated their power as custodians of recovering drug users in state care.

This shift corresponded with a deepening of market reforms that dramatically reconfigured urban social, economic, and spatial units of governance in a process colloquially known as "smashing the iron rice bowl" (*dapo tiefanwan*). Workers in the 1990s were increasingly expected to take responsibility for finding their own laboring opportunities as government agencies began to abandon the employment assignment system (*jiuye fenpei*) (Hoffman 2010).[14] Millions of state positions were converted from lifetime employment to contract labor as new labor laws overturned Maoist promises in the name of market efficiency (Lau 1997).

In Gejiu, approximately twenty-five thousand local SOE employees were laid off in efforts to "cut people and increase productivity" (*jianren zengxiao*) in preparation for Yunnan Tin's listings on the Hong Kong and Shanghai stock markets in 1999 and 2001 (*Southern China Weekly* 2013). Unlike in the 1980s, when SOE-organized collectives provided jobs for workers like Xun Wei, companies under pressure to generate short-term profits and auction off key assets were often unable to help families affected by the layoffs.[15] Meanwhile, following national directives, the prefecture and city governments began to take over local hospitals, schools, and security organizations around the city. For example, the Yunnan Tin Comprehensive Hospital, one of the best in the region, was renamed the Number Three Honghe Prefecture People's Hospital in 2003 as it moved from caring for state workers at subsidized rates to accepting any patient-consumers who could afford to pay for its services.

At Green Orchards, members displayed a nuanced understanding of the earlier SOE-run system of employment. Government-assigned jobs for young workers, including the positions offered to "students" released from compulsory labor centers, had paid low salaries and required working long hours.[16] In many instances, the city had suffered from duplicated services and inefficient practices. More specifically, the short-lived SOE drug treatment centers had many problems: staff members were poorly trained; access to medications was limited; and detoxing patients were often housed in uncomfortable, makeshift locations. By contrast, the services offered through Green Orchards and the District Street Office were professional, client-oriented, and far more equitable in offering care to those who needed it.

Nonetheless, coming to the patio to idle, Green Orchards members at times also spoke longingly about the possibilities of a stable, state-supported life in an earlier time when the Chinese government "set its heart" (*shangxin*) on overseeing "honorable" (*zhengjing*) work of its workers. This earlier investment in workers was contrasted to recent government actions, such as a series of nightly fireworks displays that were put on as part of a tourist promotion campaign during my stay. The proletariat vanguard who had built this Maoist city now watched the fireworks as part of a new urban poor (cf. Cho 2013).

While grateful to have the patio as an afternoon respite from his home life, Chen saw the creation of this drop-in center as a symptom of the state's broader abnegation of its commitments to workers. He wondered how his life might have turned out if local work units had continued their "small society" commitments and recognized him first and foremost as an employee with a duty to work rather than a patient at risk for transmitting disease. Chen wondered why instead of recommitting to past efforts to help recovering drug users labor, the government was content to build spaces for this group to idle.

## MAOIST REVOLUTION AND THE RADICAL POSSIBILITIES OF REFORM THROUGH LABOR

Just before nightfall, members pulled plastic chairs into loose circles and gathered to wash down snacks of stir-fried peanuts ordered from a nearby restaurant with swigs of cheap rice wine—the consumption of which was forbidden on a list of rules written on the drop-in center's walls but in practice grudgingly tolerated. Conversations occurred over occasional cracks and a high-pitched whirring noise emanating from whipping tops operated by retired workers at the lake's edge. Frequent topics of conversation included discussions about motorcycles, rumors concerning the whereabouts of common acquaintances, and stories from the laboring centers.

My interest in this section is to explore a tradition of socialist laboring that I came to see as separate from SOE attempts to offer care to its urban workers and family members through "small society" benefits. In occasional evocations of Maoist times, and in particular the tumult of early Revolutionary years, my interlocutors spoke of a more radical tradition of understanding how labor had helped wayward workers reintegrate into society. In the early years of the People's Republic, the government, as a Green Orchards member put it, "never would have allowed us to sit here without anything to do."

Like most Chinese citizens, this group knew about the anti-opium campaigns launched in the first years of the People's Republic. The nation's top politicians in the Reform era still boasted that the newly installed Chinese Communist Party in the early 1950s had been the only government in the history of the world to "completely destroy" opiate use among its people.[17] The Communist government had argued that the millions of Chinese citizens purported to be suffering from addiction at the time constituted a "national calamity" (*huoguo*) that had its origin in the "reactionary rule and the decadent lifestyles" of previous political regimes ("General Order" cited in Zhou 1999, 95; Wang 1996). Green Orchards regulars pointed out that the Communist Party had formulated a different relationship between opium use and labor. Performing manual labor was a crucial Maoist technology for self-transformation. The invention of a new word—"remolding" (*gaizao*)—captured the deep changes that were required of workers in a society that was itself marked by a radical rupture from the past.[18] Fostering a "habit of loving manual labor" enabled the "clearing away" of "ossified" attitudes of bourgeois, feudal, and capitalist pasts and prepared workers for a socialist future (State Council 1957; Mao 1961).[19]

Chen and others also noted that the newly created People's Republic, espousing the Maoist ideal of *fanshen* or the overturning of inherited societal hierarchies, had given even the most desperate cast-offs, including people with drug use history, the same opportunities as any other workers (cf. Cheng 2009). While unable to name a single Chinese politician or state employee in the new millennium who had publicly admitted to using illicit drugs, Green Orchards regulars could point to the redemptive revolutionary stories of Zhu De, the founder of the People's Liberation Army, and Zhang Xueliang, a former warlord turned communist hero, both of whom had successfully kicked their opium habits and subsequently achieved prominence serving the nation.[20]

Though some were skeptical of claims from this earlier era, a number of my interlocutors at Green Orchards had heard the stories of relatives or acquaintances of their grandparents' generation who had successfully broken long-term opium habits in those years.[21] A longtime Gejiu resident in his sixties I spoke with offered an example of how revolutionary spirit came to have lasting effects on the families of opioid users. He noted that his grandmother, one of seven people in her village to develop a crippling opium habit, lost her home in the early 1940s. This tragic event later provided the family with decades of preferential treatment after the household received the designation of "poor" landless peasants in the land reform campaigns.[22] This retired schoolteacher noted he never would have had his success without this opium-facilitated class status designation.

Though the Maoist language of a class-based society had largely disappeared during my time in Gejiu, socialist ideas about the citizens' labor power being a resource of the nation remained. A poster put out by the National Narcotics Control Commission in the late 2000s depicts a field of opium poppies engulfed in flames (see figure 7). The slogan reads: "Each year, 100,000 drug users die from drug use. Also, approximately 10,000,000 individuals lose their ability to labor" (*sangshi laodong nengli*). The message of the poster implies the loss of individual citizens' labor power is a loss to the state itself. Such Maoist messages could be seen as fueling my interlocutors' sense of frustration at contemporary government policies. If this were the case, how could people

另外 有约 **1000**万人
丧失劳动能力

死于吸毒

**10万人**

每年

珍爱 生命　拒绝毒品
YES TO LIFE　NO TO DRUGS

中国国家禁毒委员会　NNCC

FIGURE 7. Antidrug campaign poster.

who had successfully detoxified from the drug and shown their ability to labor be allowed to idle?

A final element of the Maoist response that appealed to recovering drug users at Green Orchards was the idea of revolutionary pressure enabling individual change. The Maoist state's willingness to mobilize decisive force in its campaign against drugs—or as one member put it, their success in "executing all the big drug smugglers and dealers"—was imagined to have radically disrupted the drug trade and thus made opiates all but impossible to obtain for most drug users. This point echoes the sentiments of an earlier generation of Maoist writers who argued that "by eradicating the previous system, the phenomena of drug dealing and drug using will be annihilated" (cited in Wang 1996).[23] The tightening of national borders, implementation of deep-seated land reforms, and development of a "social control network that could encompass every aspect of an individual's life" (Zhou 1999, 110) also helped to explain the purported effectiveness of the Communist Party's early campaigns to disrupt long-established flows of illicit drugs.

Even the specter of violent coercion in this earlier period appealed to some at Green Orchards. In contrast to the gentler forms of persuasion deployed by Yunnan Tin and its partners that many local residents as teenagers and young adults had disregarded to their own peril, my interlocutors on occasion argued that the reach and "great attacking power" (gongji lidu da) of the state in this earlier moment meant that idlers displaying destructive habits had "no choice but to change" (budebu gai). When attempting to reconcile the gap between government promises from the past and their own often negative experiences of state interventions into their laboring lives, former compulsory labor "students" contrasted the honest, demanding, and idealistic attitudes they attributed to officials in the early People's Republic—a time when Mao's words "were the truth"—to the widespread triumph of personal interest that they believed had come to hinder government projects three decades into the Reform era.[24]

Green Orchards members who felt increasingly excluded from the market economy in the twenty-first century felt many of the same grievances to the "vagrants" who had languished under the warlords and nationalists before joining the Communist Party in large numbers two generations earlier (Smith 2012). After decades of disappointment in their own inability to "return to society," individuals who saw limited future prospects in the market-driven "harmonious society" endorsed by Hu Jintao's government were more likely to welcome the idea of revolutionary projects that might collapse the post-Rush distinctions between state and society, public and private, and labor and leisure if doing so offered a way of transcending their troubled pasts.[25] The newly formed Maoist state's framing of addiction as a collective problem of political economy, the uncompromising revolutionary power imagined to have infused government projects in the country's early years, and the Communist Party's onetime commitment to conscripting all idling workers into an emerging laboring collective appealed to the most marginalized Green Orchards regulars, who longed for a radical treatment that might reconfigure the very contours of society, state, and market to make possible a new beginning and a true break from their pasts.

## CONCLUSION: IN SEARCH OF AN ADEQUATE LABORING LIFE

The criticisms that Chen and his friends leveled against contemporary state labor policies can be understood as part of a historically polarized debate about the appropriateness of state interventions into citizens' laboring lives. Hannah Arendt (1973), whose work explores the catastrophic human costs associated with compulsory laboring projects in twentieth-century totalitarian regimes, offers powerful arguments for why healing through forced labor is impossible. According to Arendt, labor is understood as the cyclical, constantly renewing activities of creation and consumption associated with the necessity of biological life. She argues that laboring without work and action, the other "fundamental human activities" of *vita activa*, dangerously ejects the laborer from the public realm while precluding the attainment of freedom (Arendt [1958] 1998, 108; Parekh 1979). Human rights researchers and public health experts have attempted to extend Arendt's critiques to advocate for an outright ban on forced labor in the People's Republic and elsewhere.[26]

Yet recovering addicts who idle in a recently liberalized economy were not always convinced by these seemingly decisive arguments. The frustrations expressed by this group in navigating the local labor market resonate with Karl Marx's writings on conditions in capitalist market economies. Marx inverted commonsense nineteenth-century European notions of "forced labor," arguing that the term best described a form of alienation intrinsic to a capitalist mode of production in which labor is "external to the worker," who does not own either the means of production or the product of his labor ([1844] 2012, 72).[27] Green Orchards members' unsuccessful efforts "to sell [themselves] of [their] own free-will" (Marx [1867] 2011, 839) highlighted the coercive aspects of a "free" market.

A long-established strategy for finding work in unfavorable labor markets is to seek dependency through subjection. James Ferguson (2013), for example, argues that the "will to dependence" he observed among marginalized black workers in southern Africa was not only an expression of severe abjection created through the legacies of colonialism and contemporary neoliberal policies but also an indication of the renewed importance of hierarchical affiliations or "work membership" long present in the region. These unequal social attachments "*created* the most important forms of free choice" for certain workers (Ferguson 2013, 226; emphasis in original). "Emancipatory liberal" narratives asserting that progress necessarily "lie(s) in the triumphant elimination or reduction of dependence" (225) are at risk of overlooking the harms created through marketization and underestimating the lingering appeal of alternate configurations of laboring for workers for whom the labor market has failed. Chen, Meng, and other Green Orchards attendees selectively turned to socialist traditions of laboring understood not as in Arendt's (1958) 1998 definition as a condition shared with animals or as a cultural resource for coping (Hollan 2013), but instead as a way of belonging to a broader collective that simultaneously made demands on and provided opportunities for its workers.[28]

Past state promises also helped my interlocutors sharpen their critical perspective on their idling in the historical present. The sting of the absence of work was particularly acute in a moment when the rise of leisure culture created new expectations about when and how urban citizens should consume. As Gejiu officials dismantled the Maoist infrastructure that had defined this SOE-run "productive city" and actively promoted its new image as a visitor-friendly "leisure city" (*shenchang chengshi*) the value of local workers' labor increasingly came to be defined by the money that they could channel into consumptive activities.[29] Whereas "idling" in the 1950s included both the aimless suffering of unemployed workers *and* bourgeois "leisure activities" such as gambling and opium use, leisure and idling in the early 2010s were considered to be distinct activities, with the latter increasingly understood as the individual problem of unemployed workers.

Despite the common wish for additional help in finding opportunities to labor, there was no consensus at Green Orchards about what constituted "appropriate," "suitable," or "honorable" jobs, or the role the state should play in determining where and how its idling citizens were to work. If given the opportunity, Green Orchards visitors undoubtedly would have preferred to be the bosses of their own companies or work for a friend's or family member's business rather than take on a state labor assignment. Moreover, they were intimately familiar with the shortcomings and criticisms of socialist projects from the recent past.[30] Yet as they careened between idling at community treatment drop-in centers and laboring in Maoist compulsory laboring centers, both iron rice bowl job assignments and the potential remolding power of revolutionary commitment to *fanshen* conjured up compelling alternatives to a demoralizing and disorienting present.

## CODA: A FUTURE FOR SOCIALIST LABOR AS TREATMENT?

Even as international health and human rights advocates increased pressure on China to close its forced labor centers arguing that they were "clearly at odds with their purported aims of treatment or rehabilitation" (Saucier et al. 2013, 85) and had "no place in a civilized society" (Wolfe 2012). Chinese state officials were actively reimagining socialist legacies of labor.[31] A much-publicized pilot project known as Yulu Community Drug Detoxification Recovery Center (Yulu shequ jiedu kangfuchangsuo; hereafter "Yulu Community") had opened less than forty kilometers away from Gejiu a couple years before my fieldwork began. Yulu center officials hoped that this new wing built on the grounds of an existing compulsory labor center would bring Maoist laboring traditions into the twenty-first century by offering material comforts and flexible rules to increase the therapeutic efficacy of the program.[32]

Locked inside the compound's imposing walls, nine hundred workers engaged in sewing, stitching shoes, and welding. Drug users could voluntarily commit themselves to stays lasting from one year to the rest of their lives. In return, this group, referred to as "community residents" (*shequ jumin*) rather than "students," worked standard hours while receiving job training and numerous guaranteed benefits, including a monthly salary and basic health care. Yulu's spacious campus offered residents access to a convenience store, a hospital clinic, an internet café, and bars.

On International Day against Drug Abuse and Trafficking in 2010, nearly a dozen couples took their vows in a group wedding at the center attended by national media outlets (see figure 8). Heterosexual couples who chose to marry inside Yulu could move into conjugal living quarters furnished with modern appliances. Yulu's director boasted that this government-mediated "island of safety" (*anquandao*) allowed residents to live comfortable, "normal lives" "no different" from citizens living outside its walls (Zhonguo Jingchawang 2010; Ding 2010).[33]

When I asked several recently released residents about life in Yulu, their initial reactions were overwhelmingly negative. Many of the activities featured

FIGURE 8. Group wedding in Yulu community treatment center. Photo from Haining Cheng, Xinhua News Agency Photo Section.

in media reports were "fake" (*jia*) or "done for show" (*fuyan*) to impress visitors. The great majority of those in Yulu had entered due to pressure from the state.[34] Moreover, the center retained reviled elements of the country's compulsory labor center system, including excessive pressures to meet production quotas, hidden fees, and the continued existence of a hierarchical and unforgiving "prison culture."

After listening to their litany of complaints, I asked the former detainees if they hoped the government would eliminate labor as treatment schemes altogether. The tone of the conversation abruptly shifted. Individuals who moments before had vigorously criticized the pilot recovery facility rallied to defend its mission. One former resident said he supported the basic principles behind Yulu and hoped the government could improve in its execution. A woman who had just been released admitted that she liked the idea that there was always the option of signing a voluntary contract if she struggled to support herself. Mirroring the complex dynamics of the conversations about state-administered laboring that took place at Green Orchards, this group's rebuke of the concrete conditions of Yulu coexisted with a tentative approval of the Communist Party's attempt to reinvent socialist traditions of laboring as treatment.

The very idea that individuals would need to commit themselves to an "island of safety" to receive a state labor assignment is, of course, anathema to the Maoist revolutionary proclamations that reeducation through labor would enable a new beginning for all committed members of the national laboring body. This partial resurrection of socialist ideals at Yulu appeared to some to be a farce. And yet the specter of socialist imaginations of collective life and laboring retained a potential power for those on the edges of the market economy as offering a secure future that even a welcoming patio at the best drop-in center in the country never could.

# CHAPTER 5

# A Wedding and Its Afterlife

*Ritual, Relationships, and Recovery*

If you used drugs, you'll always be a drug user. . . . When people bring up your name, if you haven't died yet, if you are living in this world, people will always say that you are a drug user.

—A recovering heroin user in Gejiu

I want a normal person's life.

—Su

## WEDDING DAY JITTERS

On a cool, clear Sunday morning in early October, Su and Pan leisurely strolled along the path next to Golden Lake. Su was wearing a flowing white gown and matching corsage. Pan, her fiancé, sported a handsome tan suit. Both were in their early forties. Their wedding party, made up of two groomsmen and me, trailed a few steps behind, our digital cameras out and ready to document the occasion.

In front of us on the path, a group of women and their children were playing by the lake, their headdresses and colorful embroidered clothing markers of their status as members of the Hani minority group. Su decided spontaneously that we should pose with them for a wedding photo. One of the groomsmen quickly ran to a nearby stall to buy ice cream popsicles to help to convince the group to participate. After a brief negotiation, fifteen of us posed by the lake. In the photo, another friend and I are seated nearby with mothers and their children, popsicle sticks dangling in the hands of the small children. Su and Pan stand in the center of the group.

After the pre-wedding photo session, the couple set off for the methadone clinic for their daily dose of opioid substitution therapy. Su grumbled that walking around the city in her heavy dress was exhausting. The couple made the daily trip to this clinic for close to eighteen months, always together. They knew many of the other patients from their childhood and time in compulsory detoxification centers, as well as through the part-time, volunteer outreach work that they conducted for a local harm reduction NGO. Familiar faces congratulated them. One of the staff members asked Su after she finished her dose, "So this is your *second* wedding, right?"

The couple then stopped by their home to check in on Pan's mother, who had suffered a stroke earlier that year and was partially paralyzed. His father was in even worse shape, confined to a nearby hospital bed, and would not attend the festivities that evening. Living in the guest bedroom of this aging couple's home, Su and Pan had recently taken on much of the responsibility for their care.

A couple of hours later the wedding party reconvened in my living room. Sipping *pu'er* tea poured by one of the groomsmen, Pan and Su reminisced about their early courtship. The couple had met in a compulsory detoxification center in nearby Datun when both had been part of the "management," an elite group selected from nearly a thousand "students" who received special privileges in exchange for their help in running the institution.[1] Despite strict policies designed to prevent direct contact between men and women detainees, Su and Pan had been able to see each other daily in brief, coordinated visits to the center's convenience store. In addition, they exchanged handwritten notes that were delivered by "students" who were refilling the hot water thermoses in the dorm rooms.[2] They had even, for a time, enjoyed brief intimate encounters at monthly supervised moonlit dances held on the center's basketball court.[3] When Pan learned that Su would be detained for a month longer than he was supposed to be, he had refused to leave the center without her. The two walked out on the same day, hand in hand, to begin their new life together.

Just after five o'clock on the afternoon of the wedding, the five of us gathered outside of Tin City restaurant. Stationed on the sidewalk, Su picked up a tray of "double happiness" cigarettes, lighter ready in her right hand to offer guests a smoke before going inside. Following his wife's lead in a slightly stooped, deliberate style, Pan lifted a platter laden with sweets and peanuts. The greeting of the guests through this gendered division of labor is the most public aspect of wedding celebrations in Gejiu, a ritual that attracts the attention of passersby on the street, including cheeky local hooligans, who would approach the proceedings in order to snatch free cigarettes.

Thirty feet behind us, another wedding party gathered. Pan and Su's wedding had been given the residual seating from this much larger group, a common practice among the half dozen or so banquet-style restaurants scattered around the city center. The other bride and groom, who appeared to be in their mid-twenties, stood under a ten-foot-high "marriage arch" covered in pink cloth and flowers. A seemingly endless flow of guests passed under the arch and then walked over a plush "double happy" carpet leading into the restaurant, while a videographer and a photographer documented the proceedings. Our efforts to ignore their party proved futile, as new arrivals gingerly approached us, looking puzzled, before hurrying past to join a line of well-wishers dropping off their "red envelopes" (hongbao) for the other couple.[4]

Passing time before the arrival of the guests, we shuffled around in the street, glanced at our phones, and made small talk. The maid of honor, Su's twenty-year-old niece, was late, and the bride was visibly displeased. Pan and Su had mentioned earlier in the day that in addition to family and friends, they had invited various benefactors from the local government, as well as a guard and a manager from the compulsory laboring center. Arms laden with offerings, the couple stood at attention and cast frequent, furtive glances up the street as they waited for their guests to arrive.

This chapter explores how Su pursued a "return to society" by focusing on her efforts to cultivate relationships with others. In our early conversations, Su frequently spoke about her intention of pursuing a "normal person's life" (zhengchangren de shenghuo), a phrase that she used interchangeably with "return to society." In discussing her future plans, she often foregrounded the importance of other people's support in achieving her own goals. For Su, "society" was not an abstract world of anonymous people, but instead a group of situated actors with whom she had actual or imagined future ties. In the absence of the full-time, well-paid job that she hoped for, Su spent considerable time and energy working to repair, expand, and manage ties to her family, friends, and potential work contacts. Whereas previous chapters have focused on elucidating a particular understanding of recovery set in a singular ethnographic present, this chapter traces how Su's hopes and strategies for creating a life after addiction shifted over several years.

The importance Su attached to cultivating connections might be traced to Chinese traditions of understanding personal action as inseparable from one's position in hierarchical relationships. Fei Xiaotong's concept of a "differential mode of association," for example, highlights the central importance of the Chinese individual's membership within oscillating, differential social circles that serve as the means through which egocentric desires come to be negotiated and fulfilled ([1947] 1992, 67). *Guanxixue* or the "art of relationships" refers to both a set of practices and a historically specific discourse about the importance of those practices that has shaped the way that Chinese citizens think about their interactions with others (Yang 1994). Many in Gejiu shared the sentiment that "real work happens after you leave the office," affirming the importance of relationships in realizing professional ambitions.

During my fieldwork, members of the Heroin Generation often spoke about the importance of breaking from old social circles and making new contacts. Some chose to "shut themselves away" (*ziji fengbi*) for periods of time in an effort to avoid bad influences and build trust among family members. Others spoke wistfully of the desire to "buy clean" (*maitong*) crucial relationships, a phrase implying the selective erasure of past missteps through strategic distribution of money. Su, by contrast, emphasized cultivating relationships as both a means of attaining her personal goals (including a desirable and well-paying job) *and* a part of a "healthy life" that she had not yet fully achieved. She prided herself on her ability to connect with others to overcome barriers in her life, including the gender discrimination that she had encountered while working in the male-dominated mining industry.

My relationship with this couple was in large part a product of Su's early efforts to establish a more sustained connection; the very first time we spent together socially, at a group dinner during my first week in Gejiu, she asked me if I would participate in the couple's wedding ceremony. A couple of weeks later, when I was holed up in my apartment with the flu, she and Pan brought me food. In the following months, the couple helped me in countless ways, expanding my limited cooking abilities, introducing me to research contacts, and offering advice in navigating various bureaucratic and personal struggles. When I was preparing to leave Gejiu after my first stint of fieldwork, Su and Pan insisted on storing my bike and tennis shoes in the small backyard outside their kitchen, symbolically holding a place for me in Gejiu until I returned.

From very early on in our relationship, the couple—and in particular Su—did not hesitate to ask favors of me in return. At her request, I met with her brother and his daughter to talk about strategies for learning English and preparing for college, helped make arrangements when she became sick, and supported their NGO and private sector activities. I was conscripted into disparate projects, including various events that aimed to expedite their "return to society." This type of relationship, characterized by mutual care and reciprocity, was not always easily realized, especially with those who had known Su and Pan for longer periods of time.

## Contested Nuptial Rituals

My first weeks of interacting with the couple were filled with discussions of their upcoming wedding. I became curious about this event in part because of the conflicting ways it was evoked. At times they were dismissive about the occasion and argued that they were not interested in (or able to afford) many of the trappings that had become common in urban weddings.[5] Instead, they said they thought of it as an excuse to throw what they hoped would be a fun party. However, at other times the couple referred to the upcoming ceremony as a pivotal event, a potential turning point in their lives. I came to understand their vacillating attitude toward this ceremony as the product of the particular pressures they faced as people with heroin use history, as well as their reaction to the complicated contemporary meanings of weddings in China.

Like the "ritual inflation" (Vasile 2015) seen in other postsocialist contexts, wedding celebrations in Gejiu had become increasingly elaborate in recent decades. Su and Pan's parents had wed in austere ceremonies at which eating anything fancier than local fruit and giving gifts other than Chairman Mao's Little Red Books would be considered potentially transgressive acts. By contrast, ceremonies during my fieldwork often featured photographers, videographers, a professional master of ceremonies, Western-style gowns and suits, larger-than-life photos of the bride and groom mounted dramatically outside the venue, and meals that featured an abundance of celebratory dishes.[6] Rites imported from other contexts, including the releasing of doves, the drinking of champagne, and the breaking of "happy" glass, were incorporated into other weddings in Gejiu that I attended. The most visible practices of conspicuous consumption associated with weddings were the elaborate car processions that had become common in the new millennium. Often decorated with roses, teddy bears, and other wedding themes, long lines of cars—preferably black

FIGURE 9. Wedding vehicle convoy. Photo by author.

or white luxury models—were driven by friends and family members at a snail's pace, less focused on transporting their passengers than on drawing attention to the procession (see figure 9).[7] Su and Pan noted that these rites were often performed without connection to or even knowledge of their original meaning (cf. Siu 1989).[8] The couple's downplaying of their wedding as consumptive event was a way of pushing against shifting standards that they struggled to meet.

Nevertheless, Su and Pan at other moments appeared to invest considerable hope in the prospect that the wedding might help to facilitate dramatic changes in their lives. Stigma relating to their status as drug users still frequently inflected their everyday encounters with others. Earlier that year Su had been offered a position as an assistant manager at a local hotel. However, when she had reported to work a couple of days later, she was told that she was no longer needed—a sign, she was sure, that someone had alerted this employer to her history of heroin use. An even more blatant form of workplace discrimination occurred when Su traveled to the provincial capital, representing her NGO to attend public health training. A Chinese Center for Disease Control and Prevention employee from a different city had been assigned to be her roommate for the three-day event. After meeting and chatting with Su for a couple of minutes, this government worker abruptly left their room. Su later learned that after this individual had complained about her room assignment, all CDC staff participants had been moved to a different hotel. For the rest of the training, the only contact she and other attendees with drug use history had with these government professionals was in the meeting hall itself; even meals were coordinated to keep the groups from mingling.

A couple of weeks before the wedding, Su had participated in a town hall meeting event that was attempting to foster a dialogue between public security officials and recovering drug users. Angered by testimonials that offered an unflattering picture of local policing practices, a senior policeman at the meeting declared to all present, "Those that take the white powder speak white speech [i.e., tell lies] (xibaifen, shuobaihua)!"[9] This essentializing statement purposefully erased the careful distinction that Su and other attendees had made when they had introduced themselves as "people with past drug history" (cengjing youxidu jingyan) rather than drug users.

The couple also observed that even their own relatives often doubted their ability to recover. As Pan once put it, "My family, they don't believe that I have changed for the good. Maybe I temporarily have the capability to change, but in the future, not necessarily" (buxiangxin wo gaihao, zhishi shuozanshi de nenggaihao, jinhou buyiding). Interactions with family, former colleagues, and friends exposed this couple to the anxiety and dread of being uncertain when and how their pasts would inflect others' judgments of their actions in the present.[10]

Faced with this weight of the past, the couple hoped the wedding could potentially help to demarcate their shift from "drug users" to "normal persons" in the eyes of others. Anthropological accounts of religious societies have documented wedding rituals as holding this life-altering power in helping participants move from a vulnerable, liminal status to a recognized, socially sanctioned one. Arnold van Gennep's early twentieth-century understanding of wedding rituals, for example, saw "rites of passage" as facilitating "permanent incorporation" into new social positions ([1909] 1969). Similar effects are described in Mircea Eliade's discussion of the "ontological function" of rituals associated with the supernatural (1959, 128) and in Victor Turner's (1967, 1969) elaboration of ritual as a social drama working dialectically between individual and collective to modulate the social group's experience. Though diverging in their analysis of the mechanism of ritual efficacy, these studies share an understanding of ritual activity as events that help to "reassure and help to elucidate the coordinates of participants' known futures" (Berger and Luckman 1967. 264).

Despite their own awareness that weddings in China had lost much of their symbolic importance, Su and Pan nevertheless at times indicated that they hoped their nuptials could enable two interrelated outcomes: allow them to take on the social status of a married couple "establishing a home" (*chengli jiating*) as newlyweds and, in a process similar to Turner's rite of affliction (1969), help them to overcome their lingering sick status.

## Performance, Risk, and Reward

After greeting approximately fifty guests at the door, the couple came to join our party on the ground floor of the restaurant. The majority of those present were people with heroin use history, and many were old friends. Two tables were reserved for their respective family members. Another table featured special guests, including a "teacher" from a local government office and a guard from the local compulsory labor center who was toasted throughout the evening by her former "students."

While guests were busy opening bottles of soda and rice wine and eating fish, dumplings, and stir-fried mushrooms, Su changed into an embroidered red *qipao*, and Pan rolled up the sleeves of his tan suit jacket. The couple then moved around the room, greeting and seeking the ceremonial approval of their guests table by table.

As usual, Su led the way. Her movement retained the grace of the training she had received decades earlier when she had been a student in a demanding extracurricular dance school. Her effortless elegance was tempered by her tendency to offer direct expression of her feelings when displeased. In the local dialect, Gejiu residents let out a slow, falling *ma* sound that expresses incredulous disbelief. Su frequently produced the most scornful *ma* I ever heard, a cutting rebuke that she on occasion accompanied with a clenched fist that she shook menacingly.

Pan followed a half-step behind. Often appearing as if he had just awakened from a nap, Pan was a warm and accepting soul. A guitarist and longtime Society hanger-on, he maintained a strong vocational identification as a driver, as we saw in the Introduction. Despite his past participation in violent private sector skirmishes, he instinctively gravitated toward conciliation in interpersonal encounters. In group discussions, he often waited until a consensus had been reached before enthusiastically interjecting a comment that summarized, often verbatim, the positions of other participants. Though I spent nearly as much time with Pan as with Su in the first year of our relationship, it was clear from the beginning that Su was the one making the crucial decisions that shaped our interactions. If I happened to call Pan to make plans, for example, he would inevitably hand his phone over to Su at the end of our conversation so that she would have the final word on where and when we would meet.

As Su and Pan made their way around the room, guests playfully attempted to embarrass the couple, asking them to tell stories, fulfill requests, or engage in silliness before offering their symbolic consent to the marriage by participating in a communal toast. During dinner the room echoed with laughter and raucous behavior.

Organizing a wedding involves taking risks, a fact that enters into J. L. Austin's (1962) work on language and its implications for ritual activity. In contrast to earlier studies, in which the social efficacy of ritual was often assumed, Austin referred to the officiant's phrase "I now pronounce you man and wife" as a speech act—an utterance that changes the social reality it also describes. Combining the illocutionary force based on the intentions of the speaker with perlocutionary effects that such an act has on the audience, a wedding when understood in Austin's terms runs the risk of becoming an "unhappy" performance that fails to meet the felicity conditions of appropriate participants and circumstances.[11]

While enjoying the warm, celebratory atmosphere in the restaurant, I began to wonder whether Su and Pan were mindful of the possibility of an unhappy performance—a term that took on additional complicated meanings for people with heroin use history.[12] Both bride and groom had previously sought out marriage partners. Su's first husband was a wealthy mining boss she had met early in her career on the mountain, who had introduced her to heroin. They had separated many years before, and he had recently died from complications related to heroin use. Pan had planned to marry his first serious girlfriend nearly twenty years earlier. When he asked for her parents' blessings, the father of his girlfriend had rejected Pan's request, noting, "You are a drug user; once you use, you will never quit!" (*yongyuan jiebudiao*). The proposed wedding never happened, and those harsh words to Pan, who at the time had been successfully abstaining from opioids, portended extended bouts of heroin use in the 1990s and early 2000s.

Perhaps unsurprisingly given Pan's previous unhappy performative utterance, in the weeks leading up to the wedding the couple often reminded me of lawyers carefully putting together a case for their own suitability as a married couple. For example, at a group dinner, Su looked at me and said, "Nick, you see how we take Pan's mother for a walk and how difficult she can be!" Upon encountering a neighbor who said hello as the three of us entered their house, she remarked to me that I could "check with him, or any of our neighbors, they can tell you" how diligent the couple had been in attending to their domestic duties.

The couple also attempted to differentiate themselves from other relationships started in compulsory laboring centers that occasionally resulted in "flash marriages" (*shandiansi de hunli*): brief, passionate affairs that often quickly flamed out. Their decision to wed, by contrast, was a deliberate decision made after they had lived together for eighteen months in the Pan family home. In another example of building the case for their relationship, Su liked to share a story about how a few months earlier she had been unable to sleep and suddenly felt intense cravings for heroin. Pan had stopped her before she could call their old dealer and convinced her to wait a few more hours until she could receive a dose of methadone at the clinic the next morning.

Su and Pan also argued that they "exercised themselves" (*duanlian ziji*) and showed their "good hearts" (*haoxin*) by caring for active drug users as peer educators at a local NGO, where in addition to conducting needle exchange and educational training, they had reversed dozens of overdoses with naloxone, likely saving a number of their peers' lives. Though moved by the powerful case that they made for their mutually nourishing and transforming partnership, I was acutely aware of the fact that the couple felt the constant need to perform for others that their relationship deserved to be recognized.

Another hour passed.

The wedding appeared to have gone according to plan. Toasts were finished and food was eaten. Guests from the larger gathering upstairs, as well as Pan and Su's family members and the distinguished invitees, had gone home. Two tables of people with drug use history, however, remained, and shouts rang out as a drinking game involving flashing fingers and yelling numbers grew in intensity. A couple of the men shed their shirts, revealing dragon tattoos on their backs and arms. As restaurant employees waited to leave, these revelers continued to drink and celebrate. Su and Pan sat at a nearby table looking exhausted and happy.

I left the restaurant that evening with a complex set of feelings. I had immensely enjoyed my time at the event and felt the warmth shown by many attendees. It had been a memorable and joyous party. Why, then, did I still feel an intense anxiety for the couple?

Recent writings have called into question the definitive ability to delineate event and context in a challenge to the boundedness of ritual assumed by Austin and others.[13] Without an assumption of the discrete boundaries of its status as an event, the particular drama of a wedding encounter shares "the suspense and risk in any social transition" (Crapanzano 2004, 62–63). From this perspective, the entire ritual might be viewed not as "an affair of the tremendum" but rather as "a quite ordinary mode of human social labor" (Smith 2004, 150).

Due in part to Su and Pan's frequent comments, I had perhaps become overly sensitized to others' reactions, including snide remarks from acquaintances ("your second wedding?"); dismissive looks from confused guests searching for a different, younger couple's wedding; and the meaning behind the empty chairs and uneaten food at the outer tables of Su and Pan's banquet.[14] I had, perhaps, held the hope myself that this might be a ritual event "of the tremendum," a powerful, bounded experience that would in an instant allow the couple to definitively put their past behind them. If it was instead an ordinary mode of labor, I feared that the exhausting performative quality of their interactions with others would continue indefinitely, and that the work of "return to society" might be far more arduous than the hope conveyed in their optimistic comments of looking forward to "normal people's married life."

## DOMESTIC DUTIES

The first months after the wedding did not bring the "return" the newlyweds had quietly hoped for. Still without a full-time job, Su decided to redecorate the Pan family home, pasting hearts and other cut-out figures on one wall, stock photos of romantically embracing models on another, and above the sofa, two striking photos of the couple taken in full wedding gear by Golden Lake. She and Pan also installed a computer and new speakers in the living room. These appeared as symbolic acts asserting the couple's prominence in

what had long been his parents' home. They were also a form of acknowledging that this was a space in which, in the absence of outside work, they would
be expending much of their energy as caregivers.

Feminist scholarship on "caring labor" has demonstrated how economic
studies of production often fail to capture the crucial labor associated with
reproduction, including preserving, maintaining, and sustaining workers,
families, and society (Himmelweit 1999; Weeks 2011).[15] Studies of "affective
labor" have further argued that in a post-Fordist global economy, the relationships between paid and unpaid, domestic and public labor have been eroded.[16]
The remaining pages of this chapter explore distinct projects that Su under-
took after the wedding: caring for elders in the home, cultivating a sales career,
expanding her family, and creating new social connections with "normal"
people. I suggest that each of these activities be understood as a form of labor
related to recovery.

Micaela Di Leonardo's (1987) writing on the "work of kinship" draws attention to an important aspect of labor present in Su's daily life. In discussing
the gendered activities performed by Italian American women, Di Leonardo
defines the work of kinship as the "maintenance of quasi-kin relations; decisions to neglect or intensify certain ties; the mental work of reflection about
all these activities; and the creation and communication of altering images of
family and kin vis-à-vis the images of others" (443). This emphasis on strategic communication and the deliberate managing of images captures a crucial
and consuming part of Su's daily activities throughout the time I knew her.

However, intense stigma and social challenges of navigating addiction
complicated Su's efforts in ways that Di Leonardo does not consider. While
the "work of kinship" assumes that women could speak on behalf of and manage enduring "households," Su found her own positions within both her natal
family and the Pan home topics of constant negotiation. Her and Pan's status
as people with heroin use history led others to carefully question their motives
and accounts of their activities. Lacking a steady salary for her caring activities,
Su had to constantly negotiate both the value of her labor *and* her position
within kin and broader societal networks. Overcoming feelings of liminality
required attempts to build secure attachments to others who would recognize
her status as a family member, worker, and friend.

Demands from the family defined the couple's early conjugal life in important
ways. Both their fathers died within the same year. As their siblings were busy

with work and families of their own, the newlyweds found that they were expected to shoulder many of the responsibilities of looking after their surviving elders. Part of this work was visiting and helping to coordinate the medical care for Su's mother and ninety-two-year-old grandmother, both of whom were frequently in and out of hospitals receiving treatment for health conditions.[17] The couple's primary efforts were focused on Pan's mother, who needed help navigating her daily routines because she suffered from dementia and partial paralysis after a stroke.

The two took up their caregiving roles in different ways. Pan had an apparently inexhaustible supply of patience when tending to his mother, taking her on walks, overseeing her medication, and moving her through her daily—and nightly—routines. If he was out for dinner, he filled up containers of food with leftovers and headed home at a prearranged hour to feed her. Su, who also took on significant responsibilities including cooking and cleaning, was less patient as a caregiver, frequently complaining that the old woman was intentionally torturing her by repeatedly requesting early morning assistance to go to the bathroom.

As they burned joss paper on a December evening, part of a forty-nine-day Buddhist ritual to honor Pan's father, the couple reflected on the significance of their caring labor. They noted that children in China increasingly either neglected their parents altogether or placed them in privately run convalescent homes, a situation that aging family members inevitably dreaded but were often unable to escape. Drawing a contrast with other members of his generation, who were too focused on their own careers to properly care for their aging parents, Pan noted that he felt relieved that he had recovered in time to show his mother proper filial piety (*xiaoshun*) at the end of her life. For both Su and Pan, these caring activities were a form of acknowledging past debts and paying back for the hurt that they had caused their parents in the past.

Their roles as caregivers also had openly self-interested, economic aspects. The couple relied on family members to provide them with gifts and pocket money to help supplement their paltry NGO stipends. Moreover, providing Pan's mother with late-life home-based care was, at least in part, a strategy to strengthen their claim on the family property. As the months passed, the two spoke more openly about having "earned" this apartment through the countless hours they had spent caring for Pan's aging mother. Taking over the deed after her death, they noted, would give them the financial security and space they needed to build their life together. Their focus on this economic asset intensified when they learned that the single-story work unit housing compound was slated to be destroyed in coming years to make way for a new luxury home development, and that residents would be offered cash payments if they moved out.

Other family members challenged these plans. Pan's "dark-hearted" older brother and sister, local workers with whom the couple frequently had fraught interactions, also expected a share of the family home. They pointed out they had their own significant needs, including the costs of raising children. Moreover, they had memories of Pan wasting a considerable portion of the family fortune by squandering investments his parents had made in his businesses and rehabilitation programs.

Su and Pan began to explore the country's byzantine housing laws, and at one point even contacting a lawyer to craft a new will. This plan was abandoned after they realized his mother's compromised mental state would likely invalidate any contract she signed. The couple's home life thus seemed to be an attempt to atone for the past through sustained acts of caring labor, as well as a period of grim preparation for coming battles to support themselves once the family elders were gone.

## A Community of Sales

Su refused to entertain the idea that her time was best spent in the home. In her ongoing search for well-paying work, she developed plans for opening a karaoke parlor, working in hospitality or retail, and managing friends' businesses. She also was constantly looking for and attending training courses to help reenter the workforce. A couple of months after her wedding, I happened to be with her and Pan when she learned of a new potential career. Eight of us had met for a simple year-end hotpot dinner organized by the leader of the NGO where the couple worked. One of our dining companions, a government administrator who had helped coordinate their activities, spoke enthusiastically about a facial cream she had recently begun to use. We subsequently learned that she was moonlighting as an Amway sales representative. Su expressed curiosity about the cream and opportunities for selling similar products.

In the following days, Su received multiple phone calls asking her to come to the local Amway "work room" (*gongzuoshi*) for a makeup appointment. Within a week of her first visit, she had participated in three Amway evening events and was talking excitedly about the possibility of becoming a sales leader. Also targeted by the company's vigorous recruiting efforts, I began attending Amway functions with her.

From her very first visit to the local headquarters, a converted apartment above a flower shop that could function as a cosmetics trial center or meeting room, Su saw her experiences at Amway as a new chapter in her own long-standing career as a self-made businesswoman. The daughter of a high-ranking police officer, as a teenager Su had utilized her family connections to secure a highly coveted job as a tin buyer at a government work unit. Arriving in the mountains at a time when nine out of ten owners of private businesses in China were men (Institute of Sociology report, cited in Zhang 2001, 236), Su was not allowed to travel into the mines due to a widely held superstition that women entering the tunnels would cause remaining tin deposits to disappear. Undeterred, Su set up her shop next to the road that truck drivers took on their way down from the mountains, paying cash for minerals based on prices set by her employer. With savings earned from this well-compensated position, Su opened a thriving car repair shop as well as a popular tea house that offered local patrons a place to gamble. She proved to be a savvy and well-connected entrepreneur until her escalating heroin use impaired her ability to effectively manage her businesses.[18]

Ethnographies of direct sales companies in Mexico and Thailand have documented how low-paid and unemployed workers come to be attracted to the new possibilities offered by international companies (Wilson 1999; Cahn 2006). Su, by contrast, spoke of her experiences at Amway as acts of "retrieving a former part of yourself" (*haoxiang jiushi zhaohui congqian de ni*) and took pleasure participating in events that she saw as refreshing her long-dormant entrepreneurial powers. For example, when we sat in on an information session on the intricacies of the Amway incentive payment scheme, Su noted that she had developed familiarity with this type of thinking during her time as a tin buyer. While attending talks focused on developing skills for promoting Amway cleaning products, Su reminded me that she had experience moving consumer goods including tin, car parts, tea, and most recently harm reduction supplies. She also argued that her work as a peer educator had helped her to develop presentation skills that would aid her in communicating information about Amway products to groups.

By constantly announcing upcoming sales targets, organizing new product unveilings, and promoting regional events and a year-end international trip to Australia for sales leaders, our local work room fostered a sense of an active Amway social community while turning our attention to a shared future horizon.

Su liked that expectations of sales targets and compensation at the firm were "transparent" (*touming*) and "fair" (*gongping*)—terms that were often conflated in the sales pitches we heard. She also quickly learned what top earners in our working room, region, province, and country were making and conducted various modeling exercises to imagine the amount of product she would have to move and the number of people she would have to recruit to meet these targets.

Evening programming offered educational sessions about new products, policies, and lifestyles that gave junior members opportunities to absorb stories of transformation and rehearse their own pitches while surrounded by a supportive audience.[19] A slogan we heard again and again at these events was, "Amway doesn't care about your past." The lack of a degree (*xueli*) or specific abilities (*nengli*) did not have to be a barrier to success if participants showed adequate commitment to their futures. Polished visiting traveling sales leaders offered moving examples of how personal misfortunes, failures, and regrets could be dramatically incorporated into narratives that led to later triumphs and wealth.

One evening in her second week of attending the work room, Su told Tingting, the city's number one sales leader, about her history of heroin use. Taking this revelation in stride, this Amway mentor argued that Su's past could help her to become a role model to active heroin users and encouraged her to talk about— and attempt to sell this underserved community—high-quality Amway products. Tingting also pushed Su to embrace her femininity, arguing that she was a "meticulous" (*xini*) person who could learn to unleash her "alluring spirit" (*yaojing*). With Tingting's encouragement, Su traveled 240 kilometers with other colleagues to Kunming, the provincial capital, to participate in an Amway regional meeting where, in addition to walking in the fashion show, she attended events that offered her tips to improve her marriage and live a healthier life. After returning, Su spoke in glowing terms about the successful, kind people she had met and proudly showed her friends the encouraging texts that she had received from "famous" Amway leaders. The "normal people" with whom she increasingly spent her time, she declared, were far more supportive than the bickering, drug-using peers whom she was surrounded by at her NGO job. Amway provided Su positive emotional support and a space for self-improvement that the wedding ritual and other recent career opportunities had not.

Su's initial enrapture with Amway faded quickly. She "invested" more than 2,500 yuan ($360)—the better part of a year's stipend from her NGO employer—on Amway products over the course of less than two months. Money borrowed from family members helped to purchase vitamins, protein powder shakes, toothpaste, cleaning goods, and other products for herself and Pan, as well as "samples" to give to her network of friends and kin. Unable to order more products without generating sales, Su soon acknowledged that she felt uncomfortable pushing others—sometimes individuals to whom she felt indebted from earlier periods in her life when she had been heavily using heroin—to buy her expensive household products. She also began to resent aspects of Amway's hard-driving, results-oriented culture.[20] By March, Su had stopped speaking about the company as a potential career. Her laboring to hasten a "return," however, continued.

## FAMILY TIES

In the spring of 2011, almost eighteen months after the wedding, I was in the United States on a Skype call with Su and Pan when the couple unexpectedly announced that they had adopted a two-week-old baby girl. The news surprised me, as I had been receiving regular updates about Su's worsening health. An undiagnosed malady—possibly connected to a hereditary heart condition—had caused Su to unexpectedly lose consciousness on several occasions.

When I arrived in their living room a couple of months later, Su showed me the small baby wrapped in blankets and cradled in her arms. She tended to refer to the baby girl as "mine" rather than "ours," a pattern she extended to Pan's family home and, at times, to their mutual friends. Pan took this quirk in stride. While he was always ready to fetch a bottle or bring a blanket, Pan was noticeably uncomfortable whenever he held his daughter and rarely watched the child on his own.

News of the couple's decision to adopt spread quickly through their network of friends, many of whom were openly critical of their decision. Others interpreted their actions through an attention to their past behaviors and grim assessment of their current social position. Given the couple's financial and health difficulties, these observers argued, this act was self-indulgent and potentially negligent. They pointed out that ultimately this child was likely to become a burden on the couple's extended families. One observer went so far as to argue that starting a family in this way was a sign of their failure to recover and act as responsible adults; the baby, like a bag of heroin, had been acquired in a hasty manner, without consideration of the consequences.

When I asked Sue about her decision to adopt, her wandering eyes and a slight smirk made it clear that she was sensitive to how others perceived their decision. In replying, she explained that the idea of "establishing a family" had always held a crucial importance to her.[21] Twenty years earlier, Su had given birth to a boy conceived with her first husband, but this baby had died due to complications arising during her pregnancy. Her deepening relationship with Pan convinced her that she was ready to try again to become a mother.

As she played with her daughter, Su noted that she felt she was "destined" to take on this role, a feeling that had been confirmed by the immediate bond the two had established the first time they met in the hospital. The newborn had been crying incessantly, but when Su approached, she had become silent and content. The duties of parenthood, Su argued, would be good for her and Pan. Engaging in the daily labor of caring for their child would help to extinguish feelings of "emptiness" (kongxu) that could appear if they had too much idle time.

Still not fully understanding the circumstances under which this baby girl had joined their family, I asked the couple to tell me a bit more about the child's biological parents. Su happily replied that I would soon be able to meet them: We had all been invited to their daughter's birth family's home for dinner later that week.

With the infant bundled in blankets in Su's arms, we entered a small two-room apartment in a well-worn building on the outskirts of town. The biological mother of Su and Pan's baby, a friendly woman who had grown up in a nearby village, answered the door and then quickly disappeared into the kitchen to finish preparing dinner. We sat down at a table already crowded with several stir-fried dishes. The father and paternal grandfather, migrant workers from a farming community in another province, sat silently on the other side of the table. Two small girls, aged five and three, sat at a smaller table next to ours. The older daughter watched our conversation attentively while a war drama played on the TV behind her.

Soon after we sat down, Pan commented to me that this compound had initially been built many years earlier for Yunnan Tin workers but had come to be occupied primarily by migrant communities. This part of town lacked a breeze, and older apartments like this were generally poorly constructed. It was not as good a place to raise a child as their own home, he noted gravely while the family looked on.

The food was served, and everyone began eating. The women talked about the children while the men said little. Upon learning that the husband and his father had been struggling to find construction work in Gejiu, Pan announced he would see if his sister might be able to give them a job on a renovation project she was planning for her home.

As we ate, I learned about the entanglement of money, goodwill, partial truths, and weight of history that connected these two families. Our hosts—described by Su before we arrived as "good people, but very traditional"—were eager to have a son. The mother wanted to keep her third daughter (now asleep in Su's arms) but lacked the resources to pay the heavy fines associated with violating the One Child policy.[22] Pan and Su had secretly hoped to adopt for some time, but their income level, age, and medical histories precluded them from obtaining a child through legal channels. While at the hospital seeking treatment for Su's health issues, my friends had heard about this family's difficulties and introduced themselves. Pan and Su had decided not to share their history of heroin use or the severity of Su's recent health issues with the biological parents.

After their initial meeting in the nursery at the hospital, the two families reached a tentative agreement. Su and Pan managed to find some money to pay the medical fees associated with the birth and agreed to take on the costs and most of the day-to-day responsibilities associated with raising the baby girl. They also promised to handle the paperwork that would allow this infant to become a legal resident of Gejiu.

Less than forty minutes after arriving, we had finished the meal. As we left, Su handed the baby girl over to her biological mother, who had asked if she could watch her for a few days so that visiting relatives could meet her for the first time. Su and Pan explained on the way home that they were relieved that this other family could continue to be involved in her upbringing. Su bluntly remarked, "If I die, the child can always go back to them."

Su also revealed to me that she had subsequently discovered that they were not the only ones hiding difficult pasts. In an unusual coincidence, heroin had also played a key role in this other couple's story. The construction worker with whom we had dinner was the second husband of our hostess. Her first husband, the father of her oldest daughter, had died of an overdose. Su shook her head as she spoke about this unexpected way that heroin connected the two families. She then noted, "It's a good thing that the heroin user wasn't [her adopted daughter's] father. If he had been, I wouldn't have wanted her."

In August 2011, five months after adopting the baby girl, Su again lost consciousness, and then underwent a battery of tests at the hospital. Months passed when she was too weak to walk up the sloping street outside her home. An increasingly frazzled Pan shuttled between attending to his wife and his mother as both women moved in and out of the same hospital. Upon my return in the summer of 2012, Su's health had improved significantly, but the baby girl had gone to live with relatives in a nearby province. Already able to walk, she had become too physically demanding for Su to care for.

## A NORMAL PERSON'S LIFE?

In April 2016 I knocked on the familiar door. Su let me into the family apartment.

Pan had died the previous fall. His leg, which had been swollen for years as the result of his previous heroin use, had worsened. Not wanting to incur additional medical costs, he had put off seeing a doctor and had died shortly after finally agreeing to be hospitalized. The last time we had spoken over Skype, a couple of months prior to his passing, he had excitedly told me about a job that he had found helping a friend deliver packages.

Su and I drank tea on their couch as I tried to make sense of Pan's absence. The framed wedding photos that once hung over their couch had been replaced by paper decorations and a photograph of a fruit bowl. Su told me that while she was still in the process of sorting out the paperwork, she was hopeful that she would succeed in taking ownership of the apartment. It was only in this moment, back in their home, that Pan's death felt real to me.

Not long after I arrived, there was another knock at the door. Su noted with pride that she had finally succeeded in making "normal" friends. Her new boyfriend, a divorcé in his early fifties with an adult child who worked in a nearby factory, arrived first. Several other guests—his longtime friends—also arrived, having biked more than forty kilometers from a nearby city.

Over dinner, the group talked about travel and bike clubs and the new life at university that awaited the teenage child of one of the guests. I felt confusion, even anger, at the site of these strange people who made themselves comfortable in what I still thought of as the Pan family home. I also felt sadness as I watched Su interact with this new group. Besides constantly urging me to eat more, she said little. Her sharp tongue, infectious sense of humor, and quick temper, qualities that were constantly on display when she had been around Pan and other friends and family, were conspicuously absent on this evening.

A couple of days later, a group of people associated with the NGO where Su continued to work part-time—seven of us in all—gathered to go on an overnight retreat to a nearby hot springs, a journey that I had taken with this group numerous times before, always with Pan present. To my surprise, Su announced that her boyfriend would be joining us. She added that he didn't know the details of her past, and that we shouldn't speak about heroin on the trip.

At the mountain retreat, I tried to adjust to this new situation and wondered what this newcomer made of us. I suddenly had a new awareness of the scarred skin exposed by swimwear that made individual histories of heroin use visible in the present. I found myself thinking of the last time I had been at this pool, three years earlier, when Pan had cheerfully soaked with the rest of us. That evening before I went to sleep, I found an image on my computer that I had taken of Pan on that last trip. In the photo, he is giving the camera two thumbs up while holding his swollen and discolored lower leg and foot, covered in plastic bags, just above the surface of the water.

A couple of days after the excursion, Su and I finally had a chance to have a longer conversation alone. She told me she missed Pan. She had intuited the very first time she had met him in the compulsory labor center that she could rely on him completely. This assessment had turned out to be correct; he had stayed by her side through all her extended health struggles. But as "one of us, this type of person" (*women zhezhongren*), Pan had been unable to help her change aspects of her life that she found difficult to accept. And in the end, he had left before her.

She then spoke about her current relationship, starting on an optimistic note. Her new partner helped to support her financially, was kind to her, and helped her to connect to a new circle of friends, exactly the type of people that she had been hoping to build relationships with for many years. However, much between the couple remained unspoken. She reflected that she would likely be sick again in the future. The first time she was hospitalized, she said, he would be gone. Thinking about any sort of long-term future together—let alone marriage—was unrealistic. In her labors of "return," Su had succeeded in forging new relationships and found a way to survive, even thrive, under shifting circumstances. Crucial parts of what she associated with a "normal person's life," however, continuously eluded her.

On my most recent visit to Gejiu, I again met Su and her new friends for a meal. This time, during our dinner she joined the rest of us at the table and occasionally cracked jokes, playfully scowled, and rebuked the comments of her companions. She seemed more at home with her place in the world.

When I asked about how her relationship with her boyfriend was going, she reiterated that they had no plans to wed. This time, however, she offered a different reason: "I promised Pan that I would never marry again. And that is a promise I plan to keep."

# CHAPTER 6

# "From the Community"

## Civil Society Ambitions and the Limits of Phenomenology

### A PASSIONATE CIVIL SOCIETY LEADER

"This country needs a certain type of people to lead the way!"

At a bar with his sister, a few of her friends, and me in Mengzi, the prefecture capital a half hour's drive from Gejiu, Yan Jun paused briefly. A pained expression appeared on his sister's face as she realized what was about to happen. "Not tonight, Yan Jun, not here." Her protest was less a reaction to the probable content of his impending speech than to the fact that she had endured her brother's passionate, long-winded orations many times before.

In his early forties, Yan's protruding, angular cheekbones, scholarly rectangular glasses, fashionable leather coat, and gift for verbal performance all contributed to a professorial appearance. A plastic tea thermos perpetually attached to his belt buckle knocked up against his leg as he walked. When traveling outside of Yunnan, his tea bottle—alongside the local specialties of pu'er tea cakes and Honghe cigarettes that he brought as gifts—served as markers of his provincial home.

Ignoring his sister's less than subtle protest, Yan began to speak about his work building a "grassroots" (caogen) movement of people with drug use history. He talked about blog posts he had written, cases of drug users facing abuse from the police he had taken up, and unfair government policies that he was in the process of challenging. He excitedly shared his latest idea: a salon and library that he hoped to open as a space in which similar-minded people could meet and discuss how to tackle pressing social problems.

Like his sister, I had heard Yan speak on many of these topics before. However, I found myself drawn to his passionate energy and ideas. As his sister and her friends retreated into their own conversation on one side of the table, I continued listening, enthralled, as Yan Jun spoke about the injustices drug users in China faced and his own aspirations for creating a better future for drug users and nonusers alike.

A couple of hours later, at the end of a night of eating, drinking, and singing karaoke, Yan Jun, swaying slightly from copious alcohol consumption, accompanied me to the street to find a cab. As we parted, he gave me a hug, smiled, and declared, "For the future of China, let's build a better civil society (*gongmin shehui*)!"

For some China watchers, civil society is assumed to hold a stable existence as an empirical object that might be measured through surveys of organizations, attention to the size and frequency of protests, or a sampling of blog posts of online Chinese citizens.[1] Anthropologists, by contrast, noting the "slippery equivocal quality" (Comaroff and Comaroff 1992, 2) the term has acquired over centuries of varied use, have argued that "civil society" is best understood as an unstable symbol frequently fought over by groups with situated interests.[2] In China, legacies of Maoist efforts to mobilize the people combined with multiple translations of the English term further complicate attempts to define what "civil society" might be and who might speak in its name.[3]

Yan Jun's ways of evoking and attempting to realize his civil society ambitions in China shaped my attempts to understand the significance of this term. Eventually, my relationship to this dynamic figure also led me to question the assumptions and methodology that have guided my phenomenological accounts of recovery. Introduced by mutual acquaintances in the health and human rights field, Yan and I met in person for the first time in late 2007. At the time, he was in Beijing looking for donors to fund his regional drug user network project. As a part-time consultant for the Open Society Foundations' (OSF) International Harm Reduction Development (IHRD) program, I was scrambling to find grantees who could participate in an international movement of drug users who were demanding greater roles in formulating and implementing the policies and programs that directly affected their lives (cf. Jürgens 2005). We quickly developed a close working relationship. I solicited and reviewed his OSF grant application, edited his PowerPoint presentations, helped to polish his conference abstracts, traveled with him to other provinces for training, and served as his roommate and translator at an international conference where we met and networked with other OSF grantees. Yan taught me an enormous amount about harm reduction and NGO work in China and enabled me to give positive reports to my employers about our sponsored grassroots activity in China.

When speaking to other people about his civil society work, Yan inevitably emphasized the importance of his own experiences of drug use and recovery in connecting him to a broader group of heroin users. His email handle at the time declared in both Chinese and English that he was "from the community, serving the community" (laizishequ, fuwushequ). In newspaper articles, email listserves, and his personal blog, Yan wrote frequently about themes relating to recovery that appear in this book, including the psychic costs of facing intense stigma, the difficulties of repairing relationships with family members and jump-starting one's career, the paradoxes of the compulsory laboring system, and the shortcomings of national drug regulation and health policies. He argued his outlook and position as a leader in China's nascent civil society grew out of personal experiences using and recovering from heroin. In addition to helping other people with heroin use history aspire to more ambitious and fulfilling futures, he claimed this work also helped to further his own recovery. In the next sections I elucidate two distinct visions that Yan gave of his life's work: grassroots network architect and fearless human rights defender. Each of these narratives found ways of linking his personal transformation to historical trajectories of his community and the nation.

## THE NETWORK ARCHITECT

During our initial collaborative partnership, Yan Jun spoke at length about how his early life experiences had prepared him to lead a grassroots movement of people with drug use history. After failing to find satisfaction as an iron rice bowl worker in his early career (see chapter 1), he struggled in the 1990s, a decade during which he spent long stretches in state detention and feeding his heavy heroin habit. A crucial turning point in his recovery and professional career occurred in 2002. While serving time in a compulsory labor center, Yan Jun was selected to be a peer educator, charged with conducting HIV education for other detained "students." This role gave him a sense of purpose; he relished the opportunity to learn potentially lifesaving public health knowledge and excelled in writing and performing humorous and informative skits.

After his release, Yan found a job with a recently opened government-affiliated NGO in Gejiu. For nearly three years he conducted needle exchange and outreach, organized training, and provided individuals with heroin use history referrals for HIV testing and care. The year 2006 marked another inflection point in his career and recovery. Growing increasingly lethargic in an organization that filled its management positions with "normal people" and relegated those with drug use history to entry-level positions as perpetual peer educators, Yan resigned in order to lead his own independent self-help organization, made up exclusively of people with backgrounds similar to his own.[4] In its early months, this group operated small-scale income generation projects, such as growing and selling flowers and hawking pet mice on the street.[5] Drawing on the previous NGO experience of its members, the group successfully applied for and implemented HIV prevention and care programs.[6]

While attending a provincial NGO training workshop, Yan Jun caught the attention of a prominent health and human rights organizer, who invited him to Beijing for a short-term stay as a paid visiting researcher.[7] In addition to acclimatizing to food and weather in the capital in what was his first extended stay outside of Yunnan province, Yan Jun for several months mingled with lawyers, project implementers, and activists fighting for the rights of ethnic minorities, medical patients, and LGBTQ communities. He and I met during this stay.

In early 2008 he returned to Honghe prefecture equipped with a new human rights vocabulary; a growing passion for community advocacy; and international funding to start a regional network run by and for people with drug use history, the first of its type in China. With the help of his Beijing-based human rights collaborators, Yan recruited and trained partners in Gejiu and four additional cities across Honghe prefecture. In addition to providing services to active drug users, network members collaborated to identify and attempt to change state policies and programs that negatively impacted their local communities.[8] Campaigns under Yan Jun's leadership included a public protest that helped to standardize a lower price for methadone across the prefecture and a series of actions designed to convince police to stop handcuffing suspected drug users before they had been tested for opioid use.

Various versions of Yan Jun's personal narrative were featured on blog posts, in newspaper articles, on evening television shows, and at least once in a foreign-language documentary. He also told his story to officials, national and international public health workers, NGO leaders, and other people with heroin use history. The structure of his account bore a striking resemblance to storytelling in 1950s Maoist revolutionary cinema, in which "historical narrative is integrated with the narrative of the Bildungsroman" (Wang 1997, 127). For example, *Song of Youth,* a Chen Huaikai film released in 1959, features protagonist Lin Daojing's transformation from a suicidal victim of an arranged marriage into a valiant Communist revolutionary leader protesting Japanese aggression. Yan Jun's narrative of recovery had a similar "double function" in welding personal biography to a broader collective becoming. In his telling, Yan's mastery of ever-more-complex public health professional skills in the first decade of the 2000s—running skits, formulating project reports and applications, conducting training sessions, publishing op-eds and reports, and managing large organizations—helped to enable his own "awakening" (*huanxing*) and realize his rights and responsibilities as a citizen and a person with heroin use history.

Yan's personal transformation diverged from Lin Daojing's in important ways. In the film, the Communist heroine's personal growth is enabled by her ability to sublimate her own personal desires to the collective needs of "the people." After documenting her growing political consciousness in the face of adversity, the movie ends by showing the ritual act of Lin being sworn in as a member of the Communist Party and then taking to the streets to lead a student protest movement against Japanese occupiers. In this account, the people, the Party, and the soon-to-be-realized republic converge in a revolutionary commitment embodied by this brave protagonist. This process is made possible by Lin's abandonment of her unhappy bourgeois background.

Yan, by contrast, argued that the preservation of his ties to a purportedly undesirable community of heroin users bolstered his abilities as a civil society leader. Moreover, in contrast to Lin Daojing's total commitment to the Party and incipient Communist state, Yan's vision designated NGO offices and planned salons as "spaces for growth" (*chengzhang de kongjian*) in which "his community" could develop and learn outside of the purview of the state. Unlike others in this book, Yan's plan for the future did not require that he emulate other Chinese workers in order to "catch up" to the demands of a rapidly shifting historical present. Instead, like other civil society leaders in the Reform era who spoke of their own work as an effort to "enunciate thoughts that are ahead of their time," Yan spoke of himself as a member of a pioneering vanguard and the "first generation" of people with heroin use history able to push for a voice in the policies and programs that affected their lives.[9] This was not the only civil society role that Yan imagined for himself.

## THE FEARLESS RIGHTS DEFENDER

Meeting at a teahouse in May 2011, I could immediately sense Yan's excitement. As we sipped our drinks, he eagerly took out his cell phone and began to play a recording for me. The group at the table next to us was engaged in a loud conversation over a game of mahjong. Annoyed by the noise, Yan Jun muttered about the "low quality" of the clientele at this establishment. Though it was difficult for me to make out all the words in the recording on his cell phone, his muffled voice was nevertheless recognizable: "What are you doing? Show me your identification. If you don't follow procedures, I will sue you!" I realized that we were listening to a recent encounter between Yan Jun and a policeman who was attempting to force him to submit to a urine test.

During my fieldwork, Yan increasingly identified as a peripatetic defender of the rights of people with drug use history.[10] Eschewing the bureaucratic work of running a large service organization that had once consumed him, he instead spent his time online in chat rooms for recovering drug users on QQ, a Chinese instant messaging service, where he steered conversations away from more medicalized discussions about "quitting drugs" toward the structural barriers this group encountered in their "return to society."[11] When drug users he met online needed additional help with legal problems, Yan would set out to investigate, traveling only with his laptop and a change of clothes in a small backpack.

Government drug testing policies became a focal point of Yan's struggle against state-perpetrated injustices. Operating since 2006, the Ministry of Public Security's nationwide monitoring system, known as the "dynamic database of registered drug users" (*xiduzhe dongtaiguankong jizhi*), alerted local police whenever one of the close to two million "registered" drug users used his or her identity card at a hotel or railway station. Those who tested positive were immediately detained for up to three years in a compulsory labor center, generally without a trial. Many of the people with heroin use history I knew who traveled had experienced a "summons" (*chuanhu*) instigated by this system at one point or another. Police claimed it had directly contributed to the arrests of over 120,000 active drug users in 2007 alone (National Narcotics Control Commission 2008).[12] Due to his frequent travel, Yan Jun had been stopped close to a dozen times in less than three years, most often in hotels, when in the middle of the night he would hear a knock on the door by police waiting to escort him to the station to provide a urine sample.

The intrusive testing procedures facilitated by the national database infuriated Yan Jun. He was especially incensed by the fact that people like himself who had been heroin-free for years and passed many urine checks kept being stopped and detained. In an essay he wrote on the topic, he drew on a Chinese saying, "all things are like smoke" (*wangshiruyan*), to protest how state policy unfairly targeted drug users.[13] He explained, "For us [i.e., people with heroin use history], the past is not like smoke. No! To put it correctly, society hasn't allowed our history of having used drugs to dissipate like smoke."[14]

Yan came to see his frequent encounters with police as crucial opportunities to defend his rights and expose the unfair treatment of people with drug use history in China to a broader audience. Each time he was confronted, he deployed his own understanding of Chinese law and police procedures to attempt to disrupt the request. This included recording interactions with police on his phone, insisting that officers present a warrant and show him their identification, and attempting to negotiate the conditions under which he would provide his urine sample. Though he never escaped having to take the test, on various occasions he later received both oral and written apologies in instances where police officers had failed to follow mandated procedures. Yan argued that by documenting and disseminating these encounters, petitioning to have his name removed from the database, presenting talks on his experiences at national and international conferences, and in one instance initiating a lawsuit against an officer for excessive use of force, he was helping to reform the institutional culture of the police while building support for broader policy changes. These activities also helped him to attain funding and attention from international donors.

Yan also argued that his actions in these encounters proved his own commitment to civil society principles in a way that few others in China could. Drug users and "normal people" alike, according to Yan Jun, tended to exist in what he termed a "squashed state" (*yajintang de zhuangtai*) in which "our internal psyche is not strong enough" (*neixing bu gou qiangda de*). In his analysis, this problem resulted from a "fatalism" born of "feudal" thinking and the survival of Confucian values, including the five constant relationships. The tendency "to control oneself and conform to rituals" (*kejifuli*) was a national trait that ultimately hindered the progress of Chinese society. People with drug use history needed to "become conscious" (*yishidao*) of their rights and responsibilities as citizens and learn to commit themselves to personal and collective ideals in the face of injustice.[15] Reading, talking, and attending rights-protecting (*weiquan*) training sessions that Yan occasionally organized could help members of the Heroin Generation foster awareness of their rights.[16] However, it was during encounters like those offered by urine-testing collection procedures that members of this group found out if they were capable of turning their knowledge into action. Civil society in this vision was portrayed as an ethos connected to an ability to take on risks by diverging from the expected ways of moving.

In this version of his civil society work, Yan Jun made the case for his leadership by referencing his documented history of resistance. In moments when the vast majority of Chinese citizens would remain silent, he spoke up for himself, for his community, and for others who were suffered when government actors stepped beyond their lawful authority.[17] While careful not to challenge the legitimacy of the Communist Party to rule—Yan argued that this labor constituted a patriotic act—he also insisted that the self-awareness he repeatedly displayed in these encounters had the power to transform China if only others could learn from his example.

The two types of civil society work posited different ways of diagnosing the immediate needs of his "community" and by extension demanded particular skills of Yan as a civil society leader. In his role of network architect helping to initiate recovering drug users into a bourgeoning sector of the economy, Yan exhibited his abilities as a manager, planner, and professional educator promoting the health of active drug users through service provision. As a human rights defender concerned with specific acts of injustice located in concrete encounters with state agents, Yan emphasized demonstrating and disseminating a critical consciousness and individuated sense of self capable of finding strength in conflict. Both projects explicitly aimed to help a community of people with heroin use history become leaders who could shape the future developmental trajectory of the nation.

## TROUBLING YAN JUN, TROUBLING CIVIL SOCIETY

On my second day living in Gejiu, Yan took me to meet his old boss from the government-affiliated NGO that he had worked at in the mid-2000s. Over rice noodles, this public health manager turned to me and observed, "Yan Jun is very talented, but he also has many problems!" She then shook her finger at him as if he were a naughty eight-year-old child. He smiled graciously and changed the subject, telling me what an exquisite mentor his former boss—a recent finalist in the Most Outstanding Person in Honghe Prefecture contest—had been to him.

Even before this meeting, I had heard various reports about "problems" associated with Yan Jun's career, murmurings that became more frequent and insistent as I spent more time in Gejiu. Discussions of this divisive figure often functioned like a Rorschach test through which differently positioned individuals revealed their generally unspoken attitudes about the prospects of creating diverging visions of "civil society" in China. While specific grievances and modes of interpretation differed, certain basic claims were the same: first, that Yan Jun was not who he appeared to be, and second, that the stories he told about the relationship between his life, civil society, and the future of the country were in need of revision. In this section I present three reactions to Yan Jun's narration of his own career that offer alternate diagnoses of his motivations and how his civil society ambitions could be made sense of in China's historical present.

Rui, a woman in her forties with drug use history who was frequently involved in local NGO activities, was eager to talk to me about Yan Jun. Earlier that year, she had responded to a call for submissions of first-person accounts of state urine-testing practices for a special publication Yan was editing. While her description of an encounter with police appeared as one of twelve powerful stories featured in this collection, she only received a fraction of the author's fee Yan Jun had initially promised her. Yan told Rui that the reason for this discrepancy was that he had needed to significantly rewrite her account to make it suitable for publication. Others, too, found their submissions altered, with Yan Jun pocketing a portion of their authors' fees. Rui noted bitterly that this volume purporting to convey the "heartfelt wishes" (xinsheng) of its authors had been commandeered by Yan to line his own pockets.

For Rui, this was just one episode in a disturbing pattern of conduct. Yan had also borrowed money from and failed to repay numerous friends, government employees, and even clients of his NGO under false pretenses. Before my fieldwork in the region started, he had gambled away a large portion of the grant that OSF, my former employer, had given to the Honghe drug user

FIGURE 10. Late night mahjong games. Photo by author.

network. When his collaborators learned about the extent of his deceit, he was demoted and eventually pushed out of the group.

In reflecting on the significance of these transgressions, Rui pointed out that Yan suffered from a severe gambling problem. Starting in the late 1980s, gambling had become widespread in Gejiu. The city was home to dozens of underground, semi-hidden casinos featuring slot machines and card games as well as hundreds of formal and informal mahjong venues where players could place wages on games (see figure 10). Once Yan Jun started to play slot machines, she noted, "even ghosts are afraid of him." Nevertheless, Rui maintained the root of his frequently deceitful interactions with others was less a function of his own addictive personality than the self-interested spirit that pervaded the country in the era of market reforms. She argued that Yan's transgressions revealed him to be a *typical* figure of the times. Behind his manipulations was a knowing subject openly "in pursuit of his own self-interest" (*zhengqu liyi*).

To support her point, Rui argued that corruption was present in all corners of contemporary Chinese society. Buddhist leaders who pocketed money from religious devotees, SOE executives who bought mansions in foreign countries, Red Cross employees who owned imported luxury cars: it didn't matter which organization or post, people in positions of authority enriched themselves and bent the rules in their favor whenever they could. Yan's mastery of the technical language and skills associated with civil society organizations allowed him to curry favor with the powerful. The only unusual part of this story was that a person with drug use history had been given so many resources and responsibilities in the first place. Rui's comments foregrounded the nihilistic attitude Yan Yunxiang has characterized as a "disbelief in unselfish compassion" (2009, 13) that proliferated in what he characterizes as the collapse of a collective, state-supported morality after Mao (see also Liu 2000).

At an informal dinner hosted by a friend of Yan Jun the summer before I moved to Gejiu, I met Lin, a lab researcher with a professional interest in addiction. In recent years he had partnered with recovering heroin users to organize training and other community-based activities. Drawing on his authority as a scientist and his civil society experience, Lin argued that recovering drug users were vulnerable and in need of careful mentoring, support, and oversight by authority figures who were in a position to balance the needs of these individuals with those of the broader society.[18] Over the course of the meal, he made clear that international donors—including my employer, OSF—were responsible for many of the problems in the civil society work performed by recovering drug users like Yan Jun. Donors with ample funds, limited on-the-ground commitments in China, and a tendency to valorize activist traditions associated with foreign understandings of civil society risked both endangering their grantees and destabilizing Chinese society.

Lin believed that the government needed to closely oversee civil society activities to ensure the growth of a "harmonious society."[19] One alternative to the independent "grassroots" organizing espoused by Yan Jun was expanding the services offered by venerable "government-organized NGOs" (GONGOs). Dating back at least to the Maoist period, organizations like the Chinese Red Cross and All-China Women's Federation served as loyal extensions of the state, delivering resources to underserved communities while upholding government mandates.[20] He also supported the "purchasing of services" (goumai fuwu) model pioneered in the first years of the new millennium in Shanghai,

Shenzhen, and other wealthy coastal cities. Applying neoliberal market mechanism principles to the task of service delivery, city governments contracted professional organizations—often recently formed social work "cooperatives" (*zongshe*)—to offer scalable services to neglected and stigmatized populations, including drug users (Fan 2014; Cho 2017).[21]

In Lin's view, organizations led by individuals who were also members of the marginalized communities that they advocated for were at risk of failing to show "self-restraint" (*zilü*).[22] A healthier civil society could be achieved by supporting organizations capable of delivering state-approved care understood in the tradition of *guan*, a term emphasizing both "caring for" and "managing" or "taking responsibility for" target populations (Zhu et al. 2018).[23] For Lin, both GONGOs and purchasing service implementers had the potential to *guan* marginalized groups without being overrun by their potentially destabilizing interests.

A third distinct way of questioning Yan's vision was to revisit the origins of his civil society career in exploring the history of his relationship to "his community." Long-term acquaintances who had worked in compulsory labor centers with Yan Jun drew my attention to the fact that peer educator positions, like other goods and opportunities that flowed through these state institutions, tended to be awarded to former "Big Brothers and Sisters."[24] Due to close relationships he had cultivated with senior staff members, Yan Jun had been part of the local center's "management team" charged with ensuring that other "students" under their supervision met daily labor quotas.[25] Like numerous other people participating in this form of labor, his connections to government workers helped him to jump-start his NGO career upon his release from state detention.[26]

This revised origins story complicates Yan's own way of representing his later civil society work. Rather than affirming a view of civil society as independent "social forces bubbling up from below in a stubbornly top-down state" (*Economist* 2014), former compulsory laboring "students" argued that the efforts of drug users turned NGO workers were frequently compromised by their ongoing relationships with Chinese state actors.[27] One immediate way the hierarchy in the centers impacted NGO work was in the language employed by staff members. In 2008 I was part of an online discussion in which a drug counselor and outreach worker who had previously been detained in compulsory detoxification centers made an impassioned plea to her colleagues to purge terms like *bangjiao* ("help-teach")—a phrase used by guards in the centers that she argued had coercive connotations—from their vocabulary. Yan strongly supported this attention to language.

Some observers argued the realities of recovering drug users' entanglements with state actors made a mockery of the egalitarian and ostensibly independent ethos expressed in Yan Jun's "from the community, serving the community" slogan.[28] Xu, a peer educator who worked at a respected NGO in Gejiu, did not hide the fact that he relied on his reputation as a powerful Big Brother while performing peer education work: "If you are a bit more powerful (*lihai*) inside, when you come out to work, you'll find that the work is easier. If you weren't powerful inside, you may find that the community won't listen to you, they might even attack you, and so it will become difficult to continue doing your work." The goals of civil society according to Xu consisted of making others listen, maintaining power, and "doing work"—a phrase that in practice often meant fulfilling service quotas provided by NGO or government managers. While Yan Jun was never to my knowledge accused of physical intimidation, his critics nevertheless suspected that he was likely to prioritize the interests of his state benefactors over their own.[29]

Even as critics united in challenging Yan's triumphalist narratives, they had diverging understandings of the sources of his destructive and deceitful actions. In the three critiques I have just presented, Yan appeared as a calculating, power-hungry entrepreneur of the times; a vulnerable worker in need of state care and protection; and a still partially embedded agent of the government with complicated loyalties. All three of these critiques eschewed essentializing understandings of Yan Jun as an addict and instead focused on how his status as a historical actor complicated his stated civil society ambitions.

These discussions articulated broader shared anxieties about the country's historical present. The merits of professionalism, the expanding influence of foreign ideas and funding for grassroots activities, the shifting role of state actors in overseeing the everyday lives of the Chinese public, and the very possibility of creating meaningful forms of community were at stake.[30] Maoist visions of workers striving to "serve the people"—embodied in the character of Lin Daojing and later in the martyr and model worker Lei Feng—had come to be viewed by most as impractical models for contemporary leaders. What vision of collective life should civil society be oriented toward attaining? And what type of person could help to guide civil society in China at a time when the country was swept up in self-interested practices ushered in by the reform and opening?

Reflecting on Yan Jun's complicated recent work history made me wonder how his participation in the Society during the Rush years had influenced his career. Was he, not unlike any other ambitious entrepreneur of the times, trying to make his way to a desirable spot on a recently opened mountain? Were the problems that others pointed to in Yan Jun's recent work of concern because he betrayed the trust of others, or because he had transgressed too severely and gotten caught? This line of inquiry also raised practical concerns. Given Yan Jun's complex and widely discussed past, how should others—including myself—respond to his newest ideas of a bold vision for a collective future? When, in short, should Yan Jun's past offenses be allowed to dissolve like smoke?

## A NEW BEGINNING?

Yan Jun beamed and gave me a warm hug before introducing me to Ming, his fiancée.

It was early June 2012, and the couple had returned to Gejiu for their wedding celebration. They had met during a training workshop that Yan had run in her hometown for a harm reduction organization where she worked. The pair had quickly become inseparable, traveling together for civil society work for several months before deciding to settle down near her family in another province.

Despite the dramatic reports I had heard of Yan Jun having alienated large numbers of friends and relatives, the couple's celebration in Gejiu was elaborate and well attended. The couple arrived at the wedding venue in an impressive motorcade. Guests included a number of respected government workers, including the former director of the compulsory labor center. Yan arranged for a camera crew that was filming a television special about how drug users could start new lives as "normal people" to document the proceedings.

Addressing the guests in the banquet hall, Yan gave a gracious speech reflecting on his difficult past and his hopes for the future. After thanking his various mentors and friends by name, he pledged his love for his wife and commitment to caring for their family members. Numerous people in attendance—including those who were most familiar with his shortcomings in the past—were moved to tears. I left the event elated, feeling that I had just participated in a transformative ritual that marked Yan and Ming's "return."

The following year I visited the couple in their new home. Both had lost their previous NGO jobs and had cycled through a number of different positions, taking on short-term jobs as managers at a fast-food restaurant, recruiters at a cleaning company, and briefly, as proprietors of an (unlicensed) home-based drug treatment facility. At the time of my visit, they had begun to sell life insurance. Yan noted that he had far less time to commit to his civil society work than he would have liked.

Despite his changing employment status, I saw Yan Jun's long-standing civil society commitments emerge in unexpected moments during my visit. Coincidentally, a psychologist at a compulsory labor center in another province who had met Yan in an online chatroom had made a special trip at his own expense to chat with Yan Jun to learn how he might better help recovering "students" in his care. As the four of us wandered around the city, sang karaoke, and visited a bar, Yan Jun offered passionate suggestions to this government worker about how to overhaul the education curriculum, improve daily routines in the centers, and more effectively support drug users' attempts to "return."[31]

Later during my stay, Ming, Yan, and I stopped at a supermarket to buy alcohol to take to a restaurant where we were hosting Ming's family and friends for dinner. Only a couple of hours into her first day on the job, the young woman at the cash register struggled to make change for the bill we had provided, eventually having to seek help from a manager. Ming, visibly annoyed, asked why the transaction was taking so long. I, too, felt myself becoming frustrated by the delay.

Yan Jun, by contrast, turned to the cashier with a smile, immediately dispelling our negative energy, and gently noted, "It is OK, take your time. If you don't have a space to make mistakes, how can you learn and grow?"

## ENTANGLED: THE LIMITS OF A PHENOMENOLOGY OF "RETURN"

In July 2019 I was rushing to meet a deadline to finish this book. While other chapters were taking final form, this one remained frustratingly unfinished. After spending nearly a week feeling stuck, grappling with how to proceed, I had a vivid dream:

> I am traveling in a moving vehicle—perhaps a train?—in the company of a small group of people that includes Yan Jun. Others in this gathering ask me what I have learned about the challenges of recovering from heroin use in China. To answer

their questions, I begin to relate some of the stories I have presented in this book. While talking, I am aware of Yan Jun's silent presence. I look in his direction, attempting to gauge his reaction to my characterizations of him and his community. He has a serious, unchanging expression on his face. Despite my frequent glances, I am unable to discern what he is thinking or feeling.

This dream pointed to a potential source of my struggles in writing this chapter. In our typical encounters, Yan Jun was eager to speak; he was one of the most ebullient orators I had ever met. His striking silence on the train heightens my unease as I speak in his place. While part of the discomfort in the dream undoubtedly stems from a broader history of unequal power relations that leave me rather than him writing this book (cf. Asad 1973), I also saw the train scene as highlighting a more specific challenge. My inability to read his taciturn presence in the dream revealed an uncomfortable and important truth: I did not—do not—understand him.

The phenomenological approach to recovery in this book has aimed to elucidate durable experiences, narratives, habits, and outlooks relating to individuals' efforts to "return to society." Despite occasionally registering doubts about these descriptions (e.g., wondering about how my own anxieties and projections may have shaped my interpretations of the meaning of Su and Pan's wedding), previous chapters generally presented stable understandings of recovery. Adopting a range of approaches to historicity and recovery allowed me to attend to different aspects of my interlocutors' ways of moving through the world. Nevertheless, much of the book implicitly assumed self-knowing subjects, emphasized the power of narrative in shaping experience, and drew attention to the critical capacity of observation displayed by my interlocutors. My effort to capture distinct stories of "return" by moving between individual and collective experiences of time reached a limit in my attempts to offer a definitive description of Yan Jun's dynamic, often polarizing, and unpredictable way of moving through the world.

In this chapter, I dramatized these difficulties by first presenting Yan Jun's narratives of his civil society career and then featuring voices that challenged his accounts. The controversies Yan provoked were intimately connected to broader shared questions about how to reckon with the country's past in the historical present. And yet I remained unsatisfied with my attempt to depict Yan Jun *either* as civil society hero transcending his past *or* as cunning trickster in pursuit of his own clearly defined interests. None of the perspectives featured here seems adequate to capturing the complexity of Yan Jun's ambitious and shifting life projects.

Echoing Byron Good's (2012) doubts about the adequacy of his own earlier critical phenomenological work in capturing important aspects of complex human experience, I want to return to Yan Jun's encounters with police officers to explore the possibilities of other ways of approaching recovering histories.[32] The powerful confrontation with law enforcement officers described by Yan Jun bears striking similarities to Louis Althusser's description of a mythic encounter in which a policeman hails a passerby on the street. In his exploration of the formation of the subject, the French structuralist thinker argues that the crucial moment in the encounter occurs when the figure on the street turns in response to the policeman's call: the hailed subject in this account enacts a "physical conversion" wherein he sees himself in the call of sovereign (state) power (Althusser 1971, 174). In this example of a material instance of the discursive production of a social subject, hailing stands in for a more general understanding of ideology in which individuals are "always-already subjects" (176). When compared to Yan Jun's claim of his own self-realization, this way of accounting for the subject offers starkly diverging understandings of authority, language, and possibilities for individual agency.

Yan, however, offered a second reading of this scene that avoids both Althusser's focus on social reproduction through the "clean cut" of interpellation (cf. Dolar 1993, 73) and his own self-congratulatory, voluntarist account.[33] In our conversations about the broader struggles of people with heroin use history, Yan emphasized the uncertainty that surrounded his contemporaries' encounters with the police: moments of hailing sometimes revealed a gap between narrative and self-representations (learning about and ostensibly committing to standing up for one's rights) and action (complying with unjust requests in situated encounters with state authorities). This reading's emphasis on the uncertainty pervading each meeting, combined with the failure of individual subjects to fully grasp their motivations or actions, offers a helpful corrective to my tendency to oversimply the relationship between narrative and experience or past event and present action.

This perspective can be extended to explore the constant and repeating encounters that Yan Jun and others experience as they inhabit a variety of different subject positions, including son, student, miner, Society member, person with heroin use history, "student," mentor, boss, civil society actor, grantee, friend, and husband. Psychoanalytic understandings of psychic processes could deepen attention to the particular dynamics of situated encounters with others and productively trouble my reductive attempts to render Yan

Jun and others as following clear-cut trajectories of return and hopes for the future.[34]

The emphasis on exploring the dynamics of situated encounters can also be applied to my relationship to the figures I write about in this book. George Devereux argues that knowledge produced in what he termed the "behavioral sciences" is always necessarily a product of both disinterested observation and the anxieties of the fieldworker's engagement with others (Devereux 1967). Providing additional reflections on my changing relationship with Yan Jun may begin to reveal how my own anxieties and wishes played a role in the production of this text.

As mentioned in the opening of this chapter, my early interactions with Yan Jun were shaped by our institutional positions and professional ambitions. Yan at the time already had extensive experience in recruiting others to participate in his shifting vision of a changing China. He effectively evoked a broader "we" that came to include colleagues with heroin use history in Honghe prefecture who were deeply moved by his invitation to participate in his ambitious regional network, government workers who were flattered by his manners and intelligence, and international donors, including me, whose imagination was captured by his way of presenting himself as a champion and implementer of the ideals and values that they hoped could change China (cf. Spence 1969).

Yet Yan's narrative in our early encounters also seemed to speak to a more specific part of my own longtime fascination with China that preceded our meeting and even my first visit to the country. It was not a coincidence that I came to focus on historicity in this account of recovery.[35] I was particularly taken by the way Yan conveyed his "civil society" ideals by placing himself within the country's complex past and raising his own life to the historical, or as Wang Ban puts it, bestowing "a lofty sense of [the subject's] historical mission as the maker and motor of history" (Wang 1995, 338).[36] Yan's invitation to accompany him in his work to change China thus built on shared institutional, geopolitical, and social dynamics while also speaking to my own individual fantasy.

Part of our bond also stemmed from a deep debt of gratitude and affection that I felt toward him. As we both left our previous institutions—he exited the network shortly after I left the foundation—Yan became the single most important person in helping me complete this research. Before I moved to

China, he insisted I make Gejiu a field site. When I arrived to start my research, he arranged to be in Kunming so that we could take the same bus to Tin City, accompanied me on my hunt for an apartment to rent, introduced me to friends, family members, and colleagues, and tirelessly answered the frequent questions I had for him in my new position as anthropologist. For example, one afternoon in a nearly empty restaurant, Yan responded to my interest in understanding life in compulsory labor centers by springing up out of his seat and acting out various scenes for my benefit. The theatrical talents he had developed while working as a peer educator allowed me to connect to his presentation of a part of Gejiu's recent past.

Over the years our relationship was further complicated by my participation in his various projects, which on various occasions evoked additional feelings of awe, frustration, anger, dependence, and respect. Even as Yan Jun offered captivating answers to questions I had about addiction, recovery, and the region, I struggled to understand *his* desire and the motivations behind his decisions, including his generous investment in my projects. A growing sense of not being able to grasp his vision—not being able to reach a definitive conclusion about who Yan Jun was, what he wanted, or why he pursued particular goals—corresponded with the increasing significance that he took on in my life.[37] Understanding him became increasingly futile *and* compelling, often for reasons that were difficult for me to describe. I stop here, acknowledging the central role that Yan Jun played in shaping this book while also recognizing the limits of my own ability to offer a definitive account of him, myself, or the complex dynamics of our relationship.

## MISSING YAN JUN

I miss Gejiu. I miss the rhythms of daily life, familiar places, and moments of connectedness to certain people.

One of the things I miss most of all is the pleasant feeling of surprise when I received a phone call from Yan Jun after a period when he had been out of touch. The familiar name and number would suddenly appear on my cell phone screen, and his excitable, slightly pushy voice would ring out loudly through the speaker: Did I have time to talk? Yan had a new idea for the future, his future, China's future, our future, that he wanted to discuss with me. He was already in my neighborhood, downstairs in fact, and hoped to meet right away.

His calls stirred up a complex mix of emotions as I struggled to make sense of this complicated, ambitious, talented individual whose ways of living I can neither fix nor fully understand. Despite—or perhaps precisely *because* of—the uncertainty that participation in Yan Jun's projects evoked in me, I sincerely hope to receive his call again.

# Epilogue

In June 2018 I returned to Gejiu.

Although the trip provided me with the opportunity to reconnect with a number of the individuals discussed in this book, I want to avoid providing the reader with hastily complied "updates" concerning the activities of Su, Sam, Yan Jun, Bo, and others, an exercise that seems anathema to the complexities of attending to "return to society" as lived experience. While recognizing with sadness that a number of the lives of those I knew in Gejiu—including Pan's—have ended in recent years, I also want to honor the open-endedness of the futures of members of the Heroin Generation.[1] As a result, this postscript draws on the reflections of a number of Gejiu residents—as well as my own experiences moving through the city—to explore ways of experiencing collective change in Xi Jinping's China.

In the United States in the months leading up to the trip, I increasingly had the feeling that the world was entering a different era. Embracing an "America First" ideology, Donald Trump was in the news for making tariffs threats that seemed designed to stoke a trade war. A few months earlier Xi Jinping had succeeded in abolishing presidential term limits from the country's constitution, a move that sparked intense conversations about the state of the Communist Party, the fate of Chinese workers, and the future of the nation. Recent growth of the Chinese economy and expanding overseas influence through the Belt and Road Initiative led media commentators to speculate that the "tectonic plates" of the geopolitical order were shifting, and that the "passing of the torch" of global leadership from the United States to the

People's Republic was at hand (Haas 2018). Dai Jinhua argues that China has recently entered what she calls a post-post–Cold War. The country, she claims, "is no longer out of joint with Time. Conversely, it has finally entered into the time corridor of world history or Euro-American Western history" (2018, 13). For Dai, this moment posed new dangers by diminishing the promises of alternate imagined socialist futures.

Arriving ten years to the month after my first visit to the region, my time in Gejiu reinforced my feeling that, while shaped by circulating national narratives, historicity takes on a variety of embodied forms. Residents during my stay expressed conflicting opinions about the future of the city. Some complained that the collective outlook was grim in this "aging" (laolinghuan) mountain community. New waves of corruption scandals, layoffs, and rumors about additional cutbacks contributed to low morale among the state workers who remained employed at Yunnan Tin. Friends with children lamented that local public schools had recently fallen behind others in the region, a sign of the city's changing stature in the prefecture. Hani laborers from nearby counties who came to work downtown or in the nearby mountains during my fieldwork now passed through on the way to more attractive opportunities in southern coastal cities. Young local residents, too, continued to flock to larger urban centers for better career prospects, a development that led some of my interlocutors to claim that the city had already begun what would soon be a precipitous decline in population. Ten years after receiving designation as a "resource-depleted city," Gejiu was struggling to find a path to a postindustrial future.

Others I spoke with expressed a far more sanguine perspective on the collective future of this longtime mining outpost. Gejiu's natural beauty, capable local government leadership, and ability to benefit from the country's growth were among the reasons offered for this optimism. Investments made by the Communist Party in recent years had resulted in the encouraging expansion of new industries. Condos recently carved into the foothills of Gejiu, some noted, were luring wealthy retirees, who could help support the local economy. Nearby Mengzi, the city that had replaced Gejiu as the prefecture seat in 2003, was now a dynamic regional hub. Collaborations with partners in Vietnam and Myanmar also contributed to new business opportunities. I was struck by the fact that both dyspeptic and optimistic visions tied local futures to intimations of a dynamic, historical trajectory for the nation.

A three-year absence increased my sensitivity to the rapid changes taking place in the region. Traveling from the capital to Gejiu in 2018 involved navigating a subway system in the provincial capital, highways, and a high-speed railway option that had not existed during my initial fieldwork. Next to the lake in downtown Gejiu, a massive construction project was creating thousands of underground parking spots to accommodate the expansion of car ownership among city residents. The government had also recently completed a state-of-the-art drainage system to divert stormwater and avoid the flooding that had on occasion plagued the city in the past.

Outside the city center, new water parks had sprung up in nearby farmland. Featuring giant tidal pools and waterslides, these weekend destinations felt like a different type of establishment from the simple soaking pools at the hot springs I had visited on previous trips. WeChat, a social media, messaging, and mobile payment program, had taken over cell phones, replacing an earlier generation of popular chat applications that I was more comfortable using. In addition to constantly communicating with others on this new platform, my friends now paid for parking, meals, and even vegetables with their phones.

As I struggled to find my way to the city, installed confusing apps, and wandered around a massive waterpark in search of the friends I had arrived with, I felt disoriented, uncomfortable with changes to spaces that I had once felt comfortable moving through, and wary of the people who appeared to have embraced them. I thought of Meng's complaints of being left behind and wondered if my visceral reaction to these changes in some small way mirrored his own earlier complaints of "lagging behind" the historical present.

Unexpected absences during the trip contributed to my own feeling that China had entered a different historical moment. Green Orchards, the drop-in center, had shut its doors more than a year before my arrival. This closure could be interpreted as good news. Competent and proactive state policies and programs—including the government's ongoing provision of methadone maintenance and antiretroviral treatments—had helped prevent the looming peril of an overwhelming HIV epidemic predicted more than fifteen years earlier.[2] In the meantime, the country had outgrown its status as a recipient of international public health aid. Nevertheless, standing alone on the concrete patio next to the overgrown garden and fading signs, I felt a profound sadness. I thought of the dynamic energy that this and other now-disbanded NGOs in the region had brought to their work in Hu's China. Smaller in number and diminished in influence, the surviving grassroots groups run by people with heroin use history received official recognition as "social organizations" (shehui zuzhi) and participated in the state-led "purchasing service" model discussed in chapter 6. However, the passionate possibilities of network build-ing and independent advocacy championed by Yan Jun a decade earlier seemed impossible in the more restrictive atmosphere of this later moment.

Part of the sting of Green Orchards' closing was how it compounded my difficulties in reconnecting to a community of people with heroin use history in the city. Some members of the Heroin Generation, including a couple of friends I had hoped to see, were detained in the compulsory laboring center in nearby Datun. The total number of heroin users in local and national state detention centers, however, was shrinking over time. These institutions now increasingly focused their efforts on younger "new style" drug users.[3] Illnesses and drug-related mortality also continued to take a toll on this group. Cumu-latively, these trends contributed to my own fears that Bo's dramatic predic-tion of the Heroin Generation's premature disappearance might still come to pass.

A second troubling absence was the Uighurs who had once worked in the city. During my initial fieldwork in Gejiu, I occasionally spent time in the evenings chatting with young men from Xinjiang who sold food in downtown night markets. In response to perceived threats from religious extremism, the Chinese government had forced migrant workers residing in Honghe prefec-ture and other parts of Yunnan back to Xinjiang (Nan 2014).[4] Starting in 2016, the government detained an estimated one million Uighurs in "vocational training centers." The government justified the operation of the newly con-structed centers by evoking the therapeutic value of laboring in language that closely resembled that of compulsory laboring centers. State media outlets reported that wayward Uighur workers sent to these centers would "return to society" by becoming "useful" and "professional" "laboring devotees" (laod-aoren) (Xinjiang Ribao 2018). The massive scale of these detentions and the threat that this project presented to the transmission of Uighur culture, religion, and language lent new urgency to questions about the future of compulsory labor and extrajudicial detention in Xi's China.

My time in Gejiu left me feeling that the country under Xi Jinping was growing at once more confident and less open. I worried about those who might be less willing or able to follow the paths the state forged for its citizens.

On my last day in Gejiu, I met with Xun Wei. He agreed to take me to his original mining site, a spot on a nearby mountain he himself had not visited in more than twenty years. We boarded a well-worn minibus, the same model,

FIGURE 11. Entering Laochang mining area. Photo by author.

he noted, as those that once roamed these hills when he was a teenager. An hour later, walking on the dusty Laochang streets that Old Passout had introduced me to eight years earlier, Xun pointed to an apartment where a previous girlfriend's family had lived and gestured toward a dilapidated building that had once hosted dance parties he had attended with friends. At the outskirts of the residential district, a recently erected sign announced "mountain area closed." A combination of environmental concerns, depleted minerals, and the low international price for tin had led local authorities to institute a temporary ban on most mining activity in the region.[5]

We stepped over a locked gate that prevented motor traffic from accessing nearby mines. Ahead of us we could see massive dumps and slag heaps (see figure 11). Xun marveled at how much the area had changed over the past two decades. Capital-intensive surface mining relying on explosives had transformed majestic peaks into rubble. Continuing along an empty road, we ducked our heads into abandoned "tents" (zhangpeng)—they seemed to me more like barracks—erected by private mine owners for migrant miners. On occasion we heard barking dogs announcing our presence. Having listened to stories emphasizing how this area had teemed with mining outfits in the Rush years, I was struck on this day by the absence of other people.

FIGURE 12. Abandoned building on the Laochang mountainside. Photo by author.

Just before noon, we reached a hilltop that Xun identified as his former mining site. Less than one hundred meters below us, we could see the shuttered entrance to an impressive, concrete-reinforced tunnel once run by a well-known boss who had made tens of millions of yuan from his investments in the 1990s. Train tracks ran from the sealed entrance to a nearby loading area that had berths for several trucks to cart away tin ore.

It began to drizzle. Though his tunnel had been filled in many years before, Xun lingered for a time on the outcropping where he had once worked.

As we slowly walked back through the desolate landscape (see figure 12), Xun Wei began to talk about the future. Xun noted that much of the area could eventually be reclaimed for farming. "You'd be surprised to see what grows up here," he commented hopefully. He then added that he thought some of the abandoned tunnels and extracting and sorting stations could be turned into a museum for tourists.

Sitting in the front row on the bus back to Gejiu, Xun started a conversation with the driver, who, as it turned out, had also participated in private sector mining as a young worker in the Rush years. The two chatted happily about various aspects of the trade, including the challenges of securing access to water needed for sorting, and gossiped about well-known figures from those earlier times. The shared past of these two onetime miners facilitated an immediate connection between them.

As I listened to their easy banter, I found myself thinking about Xun's idea to build a new museum and wondered how he and other members of the Heroin Generation might curate the recent history of the region. Two other regional museums presented powerful stories of the changing way that the city had come to *kao* the mountains. Less than ten kilometers from Laochang on another mountain, government officials during the Cultural Revolution had opened The Recollect Bitterness Center, an institution that had welcomed over one million visitors during the first decade of Xun's life. Utilizing the remnants of pre-Liberation mining sites, "recollectors" (*yikuren*)—former laborers turned tour guides—helped visitors experience what they presented as the harsh realities of mining life before the founding of the People's Republic by sharing songs, traversing narrow tunnels, and even eating the unpalatable food associated with the country's recent past. By contrasting the past with the present (*jin-xi duibi*), this museum aimed to assure visitors that they were part of a "golden age" of technological advancement that had vanquished the exploitation and cruelty of an earlier capitalist approach to mining and delivered them to a comfortable and equitable socialist future (Kusnetzky 2011, 209–23).[6]

The Yunnan Tin Museum, by contrast, offered a government perspective on mining from the first decade of the new millennium. In tracing the vicissitudes of tin extraction in the region, its exhibits recorded the violence and waste of the Rush years, noting "negative effects of non-government mining and ahead-of-time exhaustion [of] earth surface tin resources."[7] Other displays praised an increase in efficiency and expansion of production associated with privatization, market discipline, and the "Gejiu model" of SOE-led extraction.

Xun was unlikely to ever become involved in creating his own museum. He did, however, keep detailed records of the past. This included a set of notes—he wouldn't go as far as calling them a memoir—about key events in his own life, including his role in the mining industry. He also had a notebook in his office with an expanding list of the names of people with heroin use history who had died prematurely. Xun recognized that the policies on the mountain had contributed to violence, waste, and the suffering of many, including himself. And yet these experiences also provided him with a distinctive way of moving through the world that continued to define him.

During this visit, Xun also expressed his admiration for Xi Jinping, a leader who he argued possessed a strength and vision that the country had not seen since Mao himself. Xun was especially taken by Xi's commitment to eradicating poverty by 2020, a goal that he believed the country would achieve. There were still many problems, Xun noted, but he had faith that Xi's government was guiding the nation in the right direction.

We continued our descent back to Gejiu mostly in silence. Our bus made a number of sharp zigs and zags on its downward descent. Soon the familiar clamor of construction from the city center was audible. We turned a corner, and a clear view of the dense network of high-rise buildings surrounding Golden Lake opened up below us. The city appeared, humming with activity, familiar and beautiful. To the east, Old Yin Mountain silently loomed.

# Appendix: Events Impacting the Heroin Generation

| Leader | Nation | Gejiu | Heroin Generation |
|---|---|---|---|
| Mao Zedong 1949–1976 | 1953: Country is declared drug free. 1957: Law formalizes reeducation through labor centers. | 1979: Special economic zones pilot reforms. 1986: Mineral resources law accelerates privatization of mines. 1992: War on drugs begins; first PRC drug law passes. | 2004: Methadone maintenance scale-up begins. 2006: Dynamic database starts tracking drug users. 2008: New drug law retains compulsory labor as treatment. |
| Deng Xiaoping 1978–1992 | 1950: Gejiu is designated a city with prefectural status. 1958: Yunnan Tin, a state-owned enterprise, quadruples in size. | 1983: Entrepreneurs arrested in government crackdown. 1986: First local drug treatment centers open. 1992: SOE-run drug treatment centers begin to close. | 1997: Yunnan Tin lays off workers, prepares for public stock offering. 2003: Prefecture capital moves to Mengzi. 2004: Local government takes over Yunnan Tin hospital; Green Orchards opens. 2008: City receives resource-depleted designation. 2011: Notorious Society boss Ma Zhibao is arrested. |
| Jiang Zeming 1992–2003 Hu Jintao 2003–2012 Xi Jinping 2012–2020 | 1952–1970: Parents are assigned jobs in state work units. 1965–1978: Members of the Heroin Generation are born. | 1985–1995: Private sector mining boom; "the Society" flourishes. 1985–1992: Heroin, primarily inhaled, rapidly spreads in the city. | 1993–2000: Use of heroin, now primarily injected, peaks. 2000–present: Heroin use decreases, cohort of users shrinks. |

# NOTES

INTRODUCTION: TOWARD A PHENOMENOLOGY OF RECOVERY

1. Names and, in a small number of instances, identifying details of individuals in this account have been changed to protect privacy.

2. This is the term I use throughout the book to refer to a national network of government-run centers that forced detainees to engage in laboring activities for up to three years. See chapter 4 for a history of these centers.

3. Steve Brady, the narrator in Susan Isaacs's *Magic Hour*, offers a similar evaluation, arguing that the heroin he encountered in Southeast Asia "takes you out of time" (1992, 19), as opposed to marijuana, which he describes as slowing down the passing of time.

4. At the time, more than half of all detected HIV infections in the country were traced to intravenous drug use. HIV/AIDS played an important part in the lives of many people with heroin use history in Gejiu; approximately half of my interlocutors were HIV positive and receiving state-provided antiretroviral treatment. In order to keep a focus on the shared problems of recovery, I do not discuss the HIV status of individuals here. Instead, my focus is on the general way that members of this group grappled with the immense toll that a variety of health conditions, as well as overdoses, took on this group. For more on the HIV epidemic and government response in China, see Hyde (2007), Liu (2011) and Uretsky (2016).

5. I ended my formal affiliation with international health organizations in the summer of 2009. For my dissertation research, I lived in Gejiu for just over a year between 2009 and 2011. I also made shorter visits in 2012, 2013, 2016, and 2018. Previous experiences conducting public health work in China, as well as six months of fieldwork in Beijing and Ningbo, also inform the arguments made in this book.

6. My estimate is based on conversations with employees at two harm reduction organizations that conducted extensive mapping activities as part of their outreach work.

7. Scholars in this tradition have explored the temporal experiences of everyday risks of illegality faced by migrants in Tel Aviv and documented the rhythms of life on the fringes of postindustrial American cities among shelter dwellers (Willen 2007; Desjarlais 1997). Other important work documents the experiences of Chilean families whose lives are shaped by a "temporality of credit" characterized by waiting and uncertainty (Han 2011) and Eastern Congolese cobalt miners whose lives lack an incremental flow of time due to the collapse of social institutions, widespread violence, and "temporal dispossession" (Smith 2011). While not directly addressing historicity, this body of critical phenomenological scholarship shares an interest in how individual experiences of past, present, and future come to be shaped by social forces.

8. The term *historical present* initially appeared in Husserl's writings. I use it to refer to the way that individuals feel, intuit, or reflect on the way that their lived present relates to a public sense of inhabiting a shared time and events. Karl Mannheim observed that "human beings do not theorize about the actual situations in which they live as long as they are well adjusted to them" ([1936] 1952, 299). I contend that vicissitudes in the life trajectories of heroin users in Gejiu contribute to this group's frequently perspicacious attention to the historical present.

9. Anthropologists have argued for the importance of distinguishing between Western history as paradigm on the one hand, and "Western history as nonhomogeneous social field, on the other" (Palmié and Stewart 2016, 210). The messy plurality of a "nonhomogeneous social field" in my reading allows for the shifting perspectives future chapters take on this topic.

10. Marshall Sahlins's (1985) pithy formulation "other cultures, other historicities" indicates a division between European and Polynesian modes of historical production that is typical of culturalist formulations.

11. *Kangfu* is a third term associated with recovery that emphasizes bodily rejuvenation. Recent ethnographic explorations of the temporality of cure, remedy, and recovery include Meyers (2013), Raikhel and Garriot (2013), Venkat (2016), and Wolf-Meyer (2014). Attention to the extra/ordinary in her study of returned American soldiers severely injured in war offers a nuanced approach to the temporal politics of recovery.

12. Methadone, an opioid substituted for heroin, complicates this "quitting drugs" distinction. Nevertheless, patients and clinicians alike still referred to the amount of time they had accumulated without using heroin as a key indicator of the program's success.

13. While working at the foundation before starting my fieldwork, I found that prospective Chinese grantees were eager to pitch proposals—opening a waste disposal company, for example—with the primary goal of employing recovering drug users, sometimes even after I had explained that such programs did not fit within IHRD's funding mandate. These advocates expressed surprise at my employer's circumscribed health and advocacy agenda; it seemed obvious to them that any serious intervention to improve the lives of long-term heroin users required putting chronically underemployed people to work.

14. They also referenced "old society" (*jiushehui*), the Communist Party's term for the time before the founding of the People's Republic in 1949 when this part of Yunnan had been flooded by French colonial and Chinese private sector business owners.

15. The language of historicism appears frequently in ethnographic accounts of China. See, for example, Yan (2003, 213) on how *sui daliu* (following the big trend) serves as rationale for making a particular fertility choice. Chu (2010) also foregrounds the importance of particular orientations toward the future in her documentation of Fuzhounese migrants' attitudes toward their impending illicit journey to the United States. For an exploration of temporal reasoning among struggling workers in post-socialist Sarajevo expressed in a similar language, see Jansen (2014b.)

16. Tropes of progress, development, and the pursuit of the promises of modernity took root in China in the early twentieth century in response to the collapse of the Qing empire (Duara 1996). These themes continued to play a central part in Communist campaigns, most famously through the Great Leap Forward's revolutionary ideal of "catching up to America, surpassing England" (*ganmei, chaoying*). While Buddhist and other traditions of understandings of time provide alternatives to the assumptions of historicism in certain communities (e.g., Yang 2020), scholars have noted how campaigns in Maoist and reform and opening China operated according to a shared historicist rhetoric focusing on a "fantasy destiny of the future perfect" (Harootunian 2007, 489; see also, Anagnost 1997; Hershatter 2014, 83; Rofel and Yanagisako 2018, 145).

17. Even as "social order (is) organized around national development" in Nepal, Stacey Pigg (1996, 17) emphasizes the role of dialogue and iterative processes of negotiation in mediating between state messages and situated individual understandings of development.

18. Following my interlocutors to broaden what constitutes the problem of addiction builds on a long tradition of medical anthropologists who push against biomedical logics that reduce complex, socially embedded conditions to diseases treated in the clinic (Kleinman 1980; Lock 1986; Young 1982).

19. For an insightful mapping of the assumptions of biomedical and other discourses on addiction, see Keane (2002). Sandra Hyde (2011) explores the migration of Western treatment modalities and understandings of addiction to Yunnan.

20. This concern echoes Lauren Berlant's reservations about the tendency of certain cultural Marxists—including Harry Harootunian and others representing the first mode of historicity previously presented—to see the present as "an effect of historical forces that cannot be known fully by the presently living, who require scholarly and political education toward comprehending the structural and the systemic" (2011, 65).

21. What Garcia refers to as Hispano "tradition" or "ethos" could be interpreted as a challenge to the linearity of the historicism latent in dominant North American modes of historical time.

22. A team of medical experts declared heroin had the highest potential for abuse among more than a dozen commonly abused drugs (Nutt et al. 2007).

CHAPTER I. MAYHEM ON THE MOUNTAINS: THE RUSH
OF HEROIN'S ARRIVAL

1. Jing Jun writes that illicit drug use among young people "always occurs after a chain of deviant conduct" and constitutes part of a shift from "minor deviant behavior to more serious deviant behavior" (2008, 83; author's translation). On "deviant" behavior and heroin initiation in China see also Li, Zhou, and Stanton (2002).

2. The company was founded in 1883 as the Gejiu Tin Industry Stock Corporation and became Yunnan Tin Company Limited in 1940 after merging with a local smelting company under Chiang Kaisheck's nationalist government. The Communists greatly increased its size in the 1950s by merging it with other mining businesses (Yunnan Tin Museum 2011).

3. "Iron rice bowl" (tiefanwan) refers to the Maoist aspiration of offering workers in SOEs benefits that included lifetime job security, steady income, medical benefits, state housing, and a retirement pension.

4. Experiences in the intervening two-plus decades have undoubtedly influenced the ways in which the individuals in this chapter remembered and structured their accounts in important ways (cf. Crapanzano 1984). While I examine the situated politics of narrative and experience in later chapters, here I emphasize what I take to have been broadly shared experiences of the cohort of young workers who entered the Society in the Rush years.

5. The full name of this SOE is the "Southwest non-ferrous geological prospect office, Team 308" (Xinan youse dizhen kanchaju 308), though it is referred to by local residents as "three zero eight."

6. Besides bookselling and tin mining ventures, 308 also owned a chemical factory, a construction company, a supervision company, a tin refining plant, and many other businesses. Yunnan Tin oversaw a far greater sprawling business empire that included collectives and affiliated enterprises.

7. The "replacement with sons and daughters system" (zinü dingti zhidu) had been a widespread feature of SOE employment since the founding of the People's Republic. Referred to colloquially as "holding up" (jieban) or "taking over" (diban) a shift, the transfer of workers' jobs to their children was a common rite of passage and an important privilege that families in this mining community enjoyed for more than three decades.

8. Following policy directives from Beijing, regional government officials began to "release" the local mountains to private sector mining outfits. The Chinese slogan associated with this policy, and in some sources attributed to Hu Yaobang, was dakuang dakai, xiaokuang fangkai, qianghua kaicai, youshui kuailiu.

9. Members of this 308 collective were paid the low monthly wages of iron rice bowl workers, but without the guarantee of lifelong gainful employment, housing, health care, and other lifetime benefits. Theoretically, when the collective was disbanded, profits were to be distributed among workers through bonuses and payouts based on length of service, though in practice workers did not always see this money. See Mueggler (1991) for more on money, mining, and state power in these years.

10. Na Qi cited in Gray (n.d., 32). For more on the history of Hui-Han relations, see Gladney (2004).

11. Locally, Hui-Han relations were tense. In 1975, after escalating conflicts about the unauthorized reopening of a local mosque, the People's Republic deployed army forces to subdue growing rebellion in nearby Shadian. Hundreds of Hui residents and dozens of People's Liberation Army (PLA) soldiers were killed in the brief conflict (Gray n.d.). I learned about the complex relationship between Han and Hui when a local NGO run by people with drug use history—all Han—attempted to expand their needle exchange and naloxone interventions into nearby Jijie and Shadian, a Hui-dominated area a few miles outside of the city. Though eventually able to recruit a Hui peer outreach worker, this organization found building trust in these communities extremely difficult.

12. Xun believed he took after his mother, who also had never received an iron rice bowl job and instead had taken a leadership position in founding and running a local collective.

13. Throughout the book, dollar estimates are converted based on the exchange rate at the time in question ("approximately $100"). The Hani are a minority group who live in rural counties in Honghe prefecture. Guizhou is a nearby province that is home to a number of different minority groups, though Gejiu locals referred to workers from this region by their province of origin rather than ethnicity. These two groups made up a significant proportion of the seasonal migrant laborers who came to Gejiu in ever-increasing numbers beginning in the 1980s.

14. Xun returned to the city center to participate in a hastily assembled training program aimed at preparing 308 family members for medical positions in a soon-to-be-opened hospital. After plans to open the facility stalled and an internship at a nearby health clinic did not go well, Xun Wei returned to the mountains. During this second round of exploration, he encountered an older 308 engineer and his son preparing to dig. Following a hunch that a professional responsible for state survey work was likely to be familiar with where high-grade tin might be found, Xun successfully chased them off the mountain by showing a permit he had obtained through his work unit connections and a willingness to fight.

15. "Hundred-thousand-aire" is used in a similar sense to "millionaire" in America. In the early 1980s, "ten-thousand-aires" were a small group. By the late 1980s, hundred-thousandaires began to proliferate in the mining industry. In the early 1990s, millionaires were becoming more common. During my stay, Sam and other long-term heroin users could identify the local wealthy elite, now including ten- and even hundred-millionaires, by their imported luxury cars. On the complex moral discourse on wealth in China in the 1980s, see Anagnost (1989). For additional description of Gejiu during the Rush years, see Bartlett (2018b).

16. At the start of the 1990s, Xun was staying in the city when a longtime worker whom he had given permission to sleep in his bed was severely injured in a competing mining party's nighttime raid.

17. Renato Rosaldo's "cohort analysis" takes up similar themes in exploring how Ilongot youth became "self-conscious about their identity as a group in the face of life chances terribly different in appearance from those of their elders" (1980, 110–111).

18. The tradition of giving Yunnan Tin workers distinctive uniforms started in 1953, when each received a Wool Sun Zhongsan suit (Kusnetzky 2011, 23). Though this practice had ended well before I arrived in Gejiu, my interlocutors remembered that in the 1980s Yunnan Tin employees still wore their standard-issue uniforms with pride.

19. In total, approximately sixteen million young urban dwellers from around the country were sent to rural areas between 1968 and 1978.

20. It is important to emphasize how Li's understanding of the importance of the opportunities of the period shaped his outlook instead of reading his antiauthoritarian behavior as part of the process of "learning to labor" fueling a reproduction of long-standing societal class divisions (Willis 1977).

21. Mannheim ([1927] 1952) draws on Wilhem Pinder's formulation of the "non-contemporaneity of the contemporaneous" to explore qualitatively different generational times. See also Harootunian's (2007) discussion of "noncontemporaneous contemporaneity."

22. These feelings were broadly shared. Cultural critic Wang Ban has commented that the post-Mao period in general and "especially the late 1980s" was a period "of widespread disenchantment with Communist ideology, with the Party, with history as teleological and inevitable progression led by sublime heroes" (1995, 341). Grappling with the emergence of particular forms of experience in literature rather than field-work encounters, Raymond Williams uses the phrase "structure of feeling" to char-acterize the emergent *quality* of a social experience or relationship taking shape in a generation or period—he uses the two terms interchangeably—in an effort to better capture what earlier scholars formulated as ideology or worldview (Williams 1977, 129, 133).

23. The government's violent response to the Tiananmen protests at the end of the decade added to the disillusionment of certain members of this generational cohort, though by that point, Xun Wei was already on his Society path.

24. In the 1970s and early 1980s, tin could only be bought and sold by state-affiliated agents. As a result, it was worth next to nothing to private citizens, a fact clearly demonstrated by the once-common practice of leaving piles of high-grade tin products stacked in public places unattended. By the late 1980s, pilfering had become common.

25. It is worth noting that Yan Jun partially disagreed with the way that I have come to characterize Gejiu's Society in the Rush years. He argued that there were three groups: "normal people," private sector workers, and the unemployed people who became involved in crime. Having talked to many people whose lives moved between these activities, I believe my own emphasis on the split between the Society—which includes wealthy bosses as well as under- and unemployed drifters seeking opportu-nistic income—and the regularized work schedule of state enterprises captures the instability and a sense of possibility associated with nonstate activity during this period. Some, like Yan Jun himself, "mixed in Society" while they continued to hold down SOE jobs. By contrast, after the mining boom subsided, extrastate sector economic activity increasingly became divided between legal private sector economy and much-

diminished Society activities, primarily understood as criminal activity. In this recon-figured economic and social division of labor, heroin users were increasingly isolated and discriminated against, even by Society workers (see chapter 2 for a discussion of these dynamics.)

26. This colleague continued to describe what he characterized as an education that espoused Maoist ideals to students in a moment before the confusion and oppor-tunity of the Rush years had arrived: "Teachers taught us to warmly love our country, and humanity. The social world also had this type of thought consciousness, right? So in school you receive an education that relates to the environment that exists in the social world. So our belief was strong." The correspondence between transmitted knowledge and realities of the social world no longer held when this generational cohort entered the workforce. Yan Jun agreed, noting that his own struggles occurred with the growing feeling that "earlier things [we learned] had been negated" (*beiquan-pan faudingdiao*).

27. Opium in the first post-Mao years continued to serve as a crucial symbol for China's past humiliation and the dangers of the corrosive influence of outsiders. Chinese politicians referred to emerging Western influence—in particular new forms of con-spicuous consumption—as "spiritual opium" (*jingshen yapian*) (Reaves 1983).

28. Despite state claims to the contrary, opium was never completely eliminated in Yunnan under Mao. Nearby Weishan county, for example, operated drug treatment centers throughout the 1970s (Gray n.d., 24). These centers treated a small number of patients made up primarily of opium users. Treatment centers for heroin users opened on a much larger scale throughout the province in the late 1980s and early 1990s.

29. This contrasts with Yi minority users in Liangshan, who referred to heroin and opium by the same word (Liu 2011, 63).

30. Like cigarettes, heroin enabled a "fusion of commodity and relationality" among men sharing a common occupation in China (Kohrman 2007, 107).

31. The name derives from a four-step purification process that produces a white powder-based, injectable form of the drug.

32. Scholars have demonstrated the ways in which individual and group experiences of the effects of ingested pharmacological substances are intimately connected to con-texts of use and symbolic meaning ascribed to particular drugs (cf. Becker 1953; Mey-erhoff 1975).

33. My use of this term focuses on the particular dynamics surrounding the tin mining boom in Gejiu and nearby communities. However, I found that certain attri-butes and attitudes described here were also present among individuals born in the same years whom I met in other parts of the country.

34. One of my interlocutors described a distinct period of time as a teenager when classmates staying in school or preparing to take SOE jobs and those pursuing Society opportunities "separated into groups" (*chengfen yiba yiba*). Mannheim [1927] 1952 noted that "generational units" occur within, and at times display antagonistic relationships to, other units of a broader generational cohort.

## CHAPTER 2. RECOVERY AS ADAPTATION: CATCHING UP
## TO THE PRIVATE SECTOR

1. Completed in 1936 after sustained fund-raising by Yunnan-based Chinese businesspeople, the *cungui* railway operated in Gejiu until the 1980s.

2. The Communist Party recognized large-scale "private firms" (*siying* or *siren qiye*) at the end of the 1980s; private businesspeople were able to join the Communist Party in 2001; and in 2012 the country's wealthiest businessman was selected as a representative to the prestigious Central Committee of the Communist Party.

3. Others speak of the increasing importance of later-arriving "bureau-preneurs" (Lü 2000) and a "cadre-capitalist" class (So 2003; see also Hsu 2006).

4. Entrepreneurs around the country in the first decades of reform thrived on "the frontiers of capitalism where centralized state control has been weak" (Chen 1999, 287) but found their sources of competitive advantages eroded with time. In Hangzhou, for example, "budding entrepreneurs" in the 1980s, initially envied for their high salaries, "a few years hence . . . would be pushed aside by government cadres who become keen on their own abilities to turn power into money" (Rofel 1999, 35).

5. Gejiu locals proudly told me that their city had residents hailing from every province in the country, a legacy of the socialist labor allocation system. When comparing themselves to natives of the provincial capital (whom they called "Kun bugs" (*kunchong*)—a pun based on the fact that the same character *kun* is used in both the word "insect" and the name of the city) my interlocutors argued that they were open and welcoming to outsiders, while Kunming residents were provincial, narrow-minded, and discriminatory.

6. Similar shifts in other parts of the country have caused complex conflicts between poor urban residents and recent waves of migrants (Cho 2013).

7. Fifteen years before my arrival, crimes committed in the city were often attributed to Han heroin-using residents. During my fieldwork, ethnic minority migrant workers had replaced addicts in the local imagination as dangerous threats who menaced law-abiding residents.

8. The city government also employed thousands of workers in its own mining operations before an internal reorganization in the 1990s.

9. Work unit policies differed by year, employer, and geographic area. In the 1980s, in order to keep workers from leaving their jobs in droves, Laochang government officials threated to permanently cut state workers' iron rice bowl privileges if they engaged in private mining ventures.

10. Tunnels dug less than two hundred meters below the earth's surface were hired out to private bosses, while Yunnan Tin's own workers mined the deepest of the more than twenty thousand kilometers of tunnels that crisscrossed the region.

11. Two of China's largest asset management companies made close to a 300 percent return on their investment after offering Yunnan Tin debt-to-equity conversions in the first years of the new millennium (Wu and Wang 2016).

12. Anthropologists have explored the challenges facing entrepreneurs in the informal economy who attempt to "go legit" in "mainstream" culture (Bourgois [1995] 2003;

Ralph 2014). This process was complicated in Gejiu as distinctions between public and private and legal and illegal forms of laboring shifted throughout Sam's career.

13. Pierre Bourdieu has been criticized for ahistorical sociological abstractions of hypostatized, synchronic, structural dynamics of the field and for offering an inadequate account of reflexive agency (Born 2015, 361–62, 380–81). While Bourdieu's analyses tended to assume historical actors failed to recognize the sources of their marginalization, Sam's diagnosis of his own feelings of obsolescence perform much of the work the former assumed would be unearthed in the analysis of the social scientist.

14. Others—in particular martial arts practitioners and dancers—also told me that bodily training that they took up in their youth helped them to find success in the Society during the Rush years.

15. The Society, of course, nurtured different types of workers; a T-shirt seller would have a different outlook and work habits than Sam did as a tin buyer and later hired fighter. Nevertheless, shared time spent in consumptive evening venues and frequent short-term movement of city-based workers onto the mountainside helped to produce shared characteristics among this group.

16. Sam's descriptions at times reminded me of Max Weber's "capitalist adventurer," who acted as a "speculator[] in chances for pecuniary gain of all kinds" ([1905] 1987, 20), though vicissitudes of local economic and social changes contributed to distinct experiences of local speculators

17. Sam for several years kept his position at Yunnan Tin through the national "taking leave without pay" (tingxinliuzhi) policy, a practice that symbolically and materially preserved a tenuous link to the Maoist ways of living of his parents. At a time when the great majority of China's housing stock was owned and controlled by work units (Dittmer and Lü 1996, 253), part of his consideration had been that his former employer could furnish him with an apartment when he married.

18. Sam was arrested and served time in prison for a robbery conviction and later in compulsory labor centers for heroin use.

19. Sam acknowledged behaviors associated with mining bosses *also* created much suffering and loss in this earlier moment. His point was that there were once significant incentives to following these routines that had since disappeared.

20. In the Deng years, locally consumed heroin was generally inhaled. By the 2010s, virtually every heroin user I knew reported injecting the drug. Moreover, in an effort to reduce cost, most local heroin users added copious amounts of benzodiazepines and antihistamines to their solutions before injecting them.

21. "Scary and pathetic" (youkelian youkepa) was a phrase that a non-heroin-using friend used to describe the people she had observed congregating at Green Orchards.

22. It was in these settings that extended contact with nonfamily "normal" people was at times possible. For example, Ms. Cao, a finance worker and government employee who had once been involved in HIV programming, was an enthusiastic gambler who on occasion hosted games at her home for people with drug use history. Sam and others spoke respectfully of her nonstigmatizing attitude and noted that they often felt comfortable in the casual conversations occurring around mahjong tables.

23. A saying among Gejiu businesspeople at that time was "Doing business isn't as good as opening a factory, opening a factory isn't as good as getting a loan, getting a loan isn't as good as not repaying it" (*zuomaoyi buru banchang, banchang buru daikuang, daikuan buru buhuan*).

24. I took this to be a reference to the various practices that supported the "spontaneous privatization" undertaken by self-enterprising citizens, including the valorization of profit-oriented logics and state-sanctioned job training strategies that encouraged and helped young workers to navigate competitive labor markets (cf. Hoffman 2010).

25. Bourdieu was interested in how "objective structures" of a newly implemented capitalist economy rationalized Algerian workers' daily routines.

26. Ann Anagnost makes use of a slightly different version of the pun in her exploration of the play of interpretations surrounding Zhang Longquan's infamous impersonation of an official's son in the early Reform period (1997, 55–56). Elisabeth Croll offers another modification on this theme, arguing that in Maoist China there was a massive gap between "rhetorical representation and experience," whereas the introduction of the reform "led to the demise of the collective dream with the substitution of experience for image and of present for future as the focal points of attention, policy and aspiration" (1993, 4). See also Yang (1994) for another take on this pun.

27. Thomas Gold's description of private sector actors in the 1980s parallels Sam's observations: "Many *getihu* do not take a long-term view or plan to expand operations. Their objective is to make a lot of money as quickly as possible, consume grandly, then extemporize" (Gold 1989, 188).

28. Others puns popular in the 1980s emphasize this same shift from the collective to individual, from distance to immediate: from "serve the people" (*weirenmin fuwu*) to "serve the people's currency" (*wei renmingbei fuwu*) and "to have potential" (*youqiantou*) to "if there is money, then go for it" (*youqianjiutu*).

29. Sam's anxieties extended to his tendencies to make *and* spend money. These themes also appear prominently in Jon Osburg's study of self-made entrepreneurs in Chengdu. See in particular the conflicting ideals of consumption embraced by Mr. Pan and Mr. Wang (Osburg 2013, 113–21).

30. Pundits have asserted that the pace and scope of reform and opening policies created new temporal dispositions among local residents. The Chinese public is said to have an "eye towards the horizon," a new "faith in the future" (Brooks 2009), and a "different experience and expectation of change" (Jacques 2009, 107). Sam's reflections on the diverging ways that private sector actors in different decades came to be oriented both affirm and complicate these observations.

31. There are many examples of obsolescence of this sort. See, for example, Yan Yunxiang's description of how fathers of families who no longer perform the role of family manager (*dangjia*) find not just their farming and ritual skills devalued, but also their basic ability to manage the family (2003, 104).

32. Thanks to Alex Beliaev for pointing out the term and for translating. For an account detailing Soviet narcology practices, see (Raikhel 2016).

33. HIV-infected blood donors who tragically entered into the 1990s "plasma economy" might be another group who became caught in a similar eddy (Shao 2006).

## CHAPTER 3. ABSENCE OF A FUTURE: NARRATIVE, OBSOLESCENCE, AND COMMUNITY

1. The newer meanings associated with the term most likely emerged in the late Qing revolutionary period in anarchist and feminist writings drawing from Japanese and Chinese translations of texts from the West (Lydia Liu, personal communication with author, October 2017); on "super-sign," see Liu (2004).

2. See Rofel (2007, 111–134) for a discussion of "sacrifice" in Reform-era narratives of Maoist China.

3. Workers more commonly designated as "sacrificial offerings of the Reform era" were the victims of the economic decline in the Northeast rust belt region. In Gejiu, hundreds of state employees who had developed lung cancer as a result of decades spent in the mines were also candidates for this label. On more than one occasion, when I introduced myself as a medical anthropologist, doctors in Gejiu assumed I was part of a group of foreign oncology researchers who had come to the city to study this other cohort of waylaid workers.

4. One of my interlocutors told me that young drug users had often been referred to by this term in the first years of widespread heroin use in Gejiu. However, after years of witnessing relapsing and the criminal activity that came to be associated with heroin use, local residents were unlikely to refer to this group as "sacrificial offerings."

5. While Ricoeur and Mattingly speak of "emplotment" as the distinctive form-giving of narrative action, Carr argues that this term is more suitable for literary narrative than action and instead prefers "stock-taking" and "configuring" (1991, 64–65).

6. Explorations of similar themes include Koselleck's "horizons of expectation" (2004), Hartog's "regimes of historicity" (2015), and Adams, Murphy, and Clarke's "regimes of anticipation" (2009).

7. Rebecca Bryant (2014) offers an incisive discussion of the temporal dynamism of historical objects.

8. To my great discomfort, Zhijun's mother did not sit with us during meals when I visited. Instead, she filled her bowl at the table and retreated to the kitchen to eat her supper alone.

9. This story takes on an added salience given that the city's most distinctive geographical feature, Golden Lake, had been created in 1957 in a mining accident when a drilling project had hit an underground water aqueduct.

10. Throughout my fieldwork, I struggled with the potential ambiguities of various instances in which a "we" was evoked. On this occasion, was I included in the "we"? Could this final "we" have been residents of Gejiu—or even a far greater collective of Chinese people who had suffered feelings of isolation and anomie during the post-Mao decades? For the purpose of this analysis, I understand it to be a more intimate community of longtime friends.

11. For Schutz, a sense of the historical world can be obtained by moving from the intimacy of a We-relationship with another, to consociates—those sharing space as well as time—to contemporaries (who, when they become increasingly anonymous, come to

be represented by ideal types), to predecessors and successors, people with whom we do not live in the same space or time.

12. Carr notes: "In a naive and prescientific way the historical past is there for all of us, that it *figures* in our ordinary view of things. . . . We have what the phenomenologists call a *nonthematic* or *pre-thematic* awareness of the historical past which functions as background for our present experience, or our experience of the present" (1991, 3).

13. While evoking here a "we" that refers to herself and another patient struggling with the effects of a devastating injury, Deegan generally speaks about catastrophic illnesses and disabilities as *personal* devastating events and talks of life in the aftermath of these afflictions as an *individual* journey.

14. For Zigon active hope is "the temporal orientation of conscious and intentional action" activated in crucial moments, while passive hope acts as a "temporal structure of the background attitude that allows one to keep going or persevere through one's life" (2009, 258). With minor modification, Zigon's distinction maps onto the reflect-prereflective forms of narrative derived from Carr that I have developed here. Though Zigon sees his intervention as a corrective to an excessive focus on the "future-orientation towards the good" (2009, 257), in my reading his "passive" hope articulated in the protensional-retensional structure of temporality includes the possibility of variable future orientations.

15. My argument applies specifically to long-term heroin users who had come to embody the sacrificial offerings narrative. International activists in recent years have forcefully argued that it is possible to lead a highly meaningful and productive life while using heroin and other illicit drugs. Even potentially self-destructive narratives, including the pursuit of dangerous illicit activities, could still have the forward-facing function I am attributing to "recovery." For example, a "righteous dopefiend" committed to the hustle of sustaining drug use might also maintain a future-oriented horizon—if, perhaps, often a short-term future—in a way that Bo and others in this chapter did not (cf. Preble and Casey 1969; Bourgois and Schonberg 2009.)

## CHAPTER 4. IDLING IN MAO'S SHADOW: THE THERAPEUTIC VALUE OF SOCIALIST LABOR

1. For several months, I offered English classes two times a week in one of the center's three patio-facing rooms. Two peer educators were my most consistent students, though others, including the children of members, also occasionally participated.

2. My interest here is in this group's imagination of Maoist state power in treating addiction (cf. Ferguson and Gupta 2002; Aretxaga 2003; Gammeltoft 2014) rather than asking whether their representations corresponded to the historical realities of the Communist Party's antidrug efforts.

3. I use the phrase "compulsory labor center" to refer to three types of institutions that supervised the labor of detained drug users. "Reeducation through labor centers" (*laodong jiaoyusuo*) were first opened by the Ministry of Justice in 1957 and began detaining drug users in large numbers in the late 1980s. "Compulsory detoxification centers"

(*qiangzhi jiedusuo*), specifically designated to house drug users, were run by the Ministry of Public Security, and opened throughout the country at the start of the 1990s. The two formerly separate parallel systems merged into newly named "isolated compulsory detoxification centers" (*geli qiangzhi jiedusuo*) at the end of the first decade of the twenty-first century (State Council of the People's Republic 1957, 1990, 2007, 2011).

4. This change was representative of a nationwide trend. In a particularly intense period of police crackdowns, 40 percent of Chinese people who had been previously detained by the state spent time in a state compulsory labor center within a single calendar year (State Council 2000, 20).

5. My interlocutors spoke of two types of labor performed in the centers: "indoor" (*nei*) and "outdoor" (*wai*). The latter could include work on farms, construction sites, and even mining on the nearby mountains. In the 2010s, "indoor" work, such as assembling handbags, sewing sneakers, welding, and wrapping chopsticks, had become more common. Former detainees complained that these repetitive, menial tasks failed to teach them marketable job skills.

6. He credited these bitter experiences with awakening his interest in the law and inspiring his (often unpaid) work as a paralegal defending the rights of local drug users.

7. In his study of Russian Orthodox detention centers, Jarret Zigon (2011) argues that the moral mandates and temporal rhythms of laboring routines in a drug treatment program run by the Church discipline and prepare recovering Russian addicts for low-status jobs in the post-Soviet economy.

8. Meng's work as a paralegal exposed him to the contradictions produced by this system. After aiding one client who claimed to have been unjustly detained in a local compulsory labor center, he helped another drug user appeal the government's decision to deny his application to be moved to the voluntary wing of the same center due to a preexisting health condition.

9. The wish for state employment was thus in part a product of the "desires to establish rhythms and trajectories" that workers frequently attributed to former socialist state projects (Jansen 2014a, 253).

10. Among their many other tasks, Street Office government workers under the new drug law promulgated in 2008 were charged with coordinating "community treatment" (*shequ jiedu*) for drug addicts. Theoretically, this involved tracking down recovering drug users and coordinating regular urine testing. In practice, however, implementation of this widely touted program was minimal in the areas I visited.

11. For an investigation into how legacies of *danwei* modes of organizing influenced expectations of care held by patients with schizophrenia and their families, see Sevigny, Chen, and Che (2009). For an account of Cuban patients whose expectations are also inflected by memories of previous state commitments, see (Brotherton 2012).

12. While most urban workers in Maoist China belonged to a *danwei*, their ability to enjoy iron rice bowl benefits depended on the prestige and financial health of their employer. Labor insurance, for example, covered only 7 percent of workers when it was initiated in 1952 and reached an all-time high of 30 percent coverage in 1958 (Perry 1996, 67).

13. In the 1980s, reeducation through labor centers began to take in increasing numbers of sex workers, religious dissidents, arsonists, accomplices to serious crimes, and other offenders as numbers of political detainees diminished (Williams and Wu 2004). By the early 1990s, heroin users made up the largest constituency of detainees in those centers.

14. Yang Jie (2015) shows how state actors responding to layoffs at state enterprises organized mental health interventions that aimed to psychologize problems that many workers saw as the direct consequence of structural reforms to work units.

15. This included the local bus station and many of the regional bus routes.

16. Those released locally from prison and compulsory labor centers were offered jobs in mountain-based enterprises in the early 1980s. However, see Williams and Wu (2004) for a cautionary tale about the nature of these postcompulsory labor job assignments in the Maoist period.

17. For example, Deng Xiaoping argued, "After the founding of the People's Republic of China, the country needed just three years to clear up [problems in inherited from the past]. Smoking opium, using heroin, who in the world has the ability to completely destroy them? Capitalism couldn't do it. Facts provide proof; the Communist party has the ability to destroy this horrible thing" (Deng 1992; author's translation).

18. Instead of following earlier Chinese rulers' understanding of "making oneself anew" (zixin), evoking a Confucian ideal of an enduring social order, Communist leaders popularized "remolding" to emphasize a more radical, deep-seated transformation (Williams and Wu 2004, 40, 47).

19. Labor directives were part of a government campaign strategy that promoted a "cordoning off of pre-1949 past 'before Liberation' and measuring the present by state initiatives and popular participation in them" (Hershatter 2014, 44; see also Dutton, Lo, and Wu 2008, 16–17).

20. The North American present, like the Chinese socialist past, also became a site for imagining alternatives to their laboring struggles. Green Orchards regulars marveled at the fact that Barack Obama, the president of the world's most powerful country, had openly discussed his own drug use history in a widely read autobiography before successfully running for office. As he was preparing to leave office with soaring approval ratings, Obama publicly joked, "The last time I was this high, I was trying to decide my major" (Eagen 2016). My interlocutors could not imagine a senior official in China ever making this sort of lighthearted quip about recreational drug use.

21. In Yunnan, illicit drug consumption was greatly curtailed but never completely eradicated. For details, see footnote 28 on page 163.

22. William Hinton also documented how loss of property due to opioid addiction figured in designation of class status during the mid-1940s ([1966] 1997, 140). On the enduring effects of the "class status" system, see Billeter (1985).

23. For a laudatory account of Maoist anti-opioid measures, see Lowinger (1977).

24. Others frustrated by a sense of moral loss, ineffective government, and corruption in the Reform era trace these changes to the death of Chairman Mao (Ng 2020).

25. These sentiments echo historians of the early Maoist period, who argue that urban work units at that time served as "politicized affective communities" that effectively "blurred the lines between state and civil society as well as life and economy" (Dutton 2008, 107).

26. These debates are not isolated to China. Summerson Carr (2010) documents how board members at a treatment facility in the United States struggled to reconcile their voluntarist ethos with the fact that many of their successful clients were coerced, often by mandating their participation in order to access housing and other services. This service organization ultimately "verbally finessed" language in its reports, substituting the less offensive "externally motivated" for "coercion" (323). For a more extended discussion of international debates about compulsory labor as treatment, see Bartlett (2018a).

27. A Marxist economic critique of the efforts of international labor activists to demarcate "free" from "forced" labor notes that such a distinction makes little sense without taking into account the broader dynamics generating the development of all labor relations (Lerche 2007, 447).

28. Arendt observed that "forced labor is the normal condition of all" (1973, 444) in the Soviet Union. My interlocutors at times voiced a wish to join this broader imagined laboring collective, even if this required certain forms of submission.

29. Cultural theorist Wang Jing argues that the Communist Party's policies promoting leisure activities in the 1990s ultimately disciplined production, since "naming and administering leisure consumption as such" increases the pursuit of "a lifestyle that can spare no time for unproductive labor" (2001, 78).

30. Even the most ardent defenders of abandoned Communist Party projects could speak at length about personal suffering in the state compulsory labor centers that had been created under Mao as well as the hardships that members of their parents' and grandparents' generations had endured. Moreover, many harbored deep mistrust of the Chinese state. One member, articulating a position that resonated with the country's more ardent human rights critics, declared, "The government and us, we are eternal enemies (diduide)! They will always attack us!"

31. Declaring forced labor unscientific, ineffective, and in violation of the human rights of those detained, twelve UN agencies in 2012 issued a historic joint statement urging governments to find alternative methods to aid people with problem drug use (United Nations 2012). International human rights campaigners targeted Chinese officials, who oversaw the largest network of compulsory labor centers in the world, for "tortur[ing] in the name of treatment" (Human Rights Watch 2012).

32. Despite announcing that it was closing reeducation through labor centers in 2013, the government reported that 264,000 drug users continued to labor in recently renamed "isolated compulsory detoxification centers" the following year (Narcotics Control Commission 2015). Concerned human rights groups worried that the government had "changed the soup but not the medicine" (Amnesty International 2013).

33. The director of Yulu explained, "If you provide drug users with an institutional environment that is even better than what they find outside, they will be able to give up drugs with a peaceful heart" (Remin gonganbao 2007; author's translation).

34. Similar projects opening in Beijing and just outside of Gejiu struggled to recruit voluntary participants, even after offering salaries and spacious rooms in newly constructed living spaces. One recovering drug user offered a simple analysis of these programs' struggles to recruit: "No one likes to be 'locked up' (*jiya*)."

## CHAPTER 5. A WEDDING AND ITS AFTERLIFE:
## RITUAL, RELATIONSHIPS, AND RECOVERY

1. Pan had obtained this position after serving time in a state prison for stealing state resources. Su, who had avoided detention for years by using her family connections, obtained her position in the management team at least in part because the prison guards knew she was the daughter of a prominent public security figure.

2. Su had learned to write Chinese characters backward in bold motions that could be read by suitors in the men's dorms located across the courtyards, in a practice known as "surfing the web" (*shangwang*). She stopped her correspondence with other suitors soon after she met Pan.

3. The evenings were canceled by the management after "students" attempted to escape during the proceedings.

4. "Red envelope" refers to celebratory cards stuffed with cash that guests give to couples at weddings and to family members at Chinese New Year's celebrations. The term has also become synonymous with government bribes.

5. Despite their emphasis on the simplicity of the occasion, the couple noted proudly at another wedding we later attended together that their own celebration had been a "four hundred yuan" ($60) spread—a reference to the price that they had paid for each table reserved—an expense that they maintained bought some of the tastiest banquet food in the city.

6. A musician friend of mine had made extra money for years by acting as a master of ceremonies. On days when she officiated multiple weddings, she would write the names of each bride and groom on an inconspicuous place on her hand to make sure she was prepared during the service.

7. On Sunday afternoons, two or three of these motorcades (*chedui*) could often be seen parked next to each other by the lake as competing wedding parties took pictures with the same shared backgrounds. Assembling the wedding convoys was a coveted opportunity to display social capital generally organized by the groom's family; I attended one ceremony at which the mother of the groom boasted about the cars she had been able to assemble at no expense to the family. Once, while sitting in a café on one of Gejiu's narrower side streets, I looked out of the window to see a particularly impressive procession of wedding cars covered with roses and teddy bears that included a massive camper that barely avoided banging into cars parked on each side of the narrow road. The hood of the lead vehicle in the parade, a Hummer, was covered in flowers, a grass-like material, and dozens of pairs of animals—a menagerie fit for Noah's ark.

8. Their wedding did not include a *koutou* to the parents, presentation of the couple's room (*dongfang*), or stirring up of the new couple's residence (*naofang*), rites that were

still performed in and around Gejiu (cf. Kipnis 1997, 86–96). While weddings in the nearby Honghe countryside could still last for three or more days, once-elaborate Confucian rituals attached to the propriety (*li*) of rural reproduction were disappearing (Yan 2003). In the city, even full-day wedding celebrations were becoming less common. I attended one wedding at which a number of guests came, ate, and left before the bride and groom had even had the opportunity to come in from the street where they were greeting their guests.

9. I heard about this encounter afterward but did not attend the meeting.

10. A mutual acquaintance expressed a particularity powerful characterization of his experience of heroin addiction by contrasting his experience of addiction with another deeply stigmatized part of his past. As a teenager, he had killed another man during a fight in a local holding cell; he served eight years in a high-security prison for manslaughter. Upon his return to Gejiu, he found that his past heroin use history followed him in ways that this much more serious crime did not. He gave the example of time when his seven-year-old daughter had come home from school one day and asked him if he was a drug user. Taken by surprise at the comment, he lost his temper. Standing in front of his apartment complex, he screamed at the top of his lungs that whoever had told his daughter that he was a drug user should make themselves known and confront him about it. No one did, and he was denied the opportunity he desperately desired to confront and move beyond his long history of heroin use. "Unlike other crimes," he remarked, "addiction stays with you."

11. The perlocutionary effects of particular utterances can be understood as taking on meanings through the audiences' understanding of a particular utterance within a broader set of conventions.

12. The Chinese term *biaoxian*—often translated as "performance" or "presentation" (*biao*, to show or display, and *xian*, to become visible or manifest)—describes an individual's behavior at work, comportment in interpersonal relationships, and mood. Someone with a good *biaoxian* at a company might be expected to receive a promotion. But when applied to drug users, *biaoxian* often referred to a person's state of recovery. If someone had recently missed a number of engagements and looked unhealthy, others in her circle might note a "poor performance," an understated way of implying the person had likely resumed using heroin. For an exploration of performativity of gender, ethnicity, and modernity in wedding rituals in China, see (Schein 2000).

13. Jacques Derrida deconstructs Austin's understanding of ritual by arguing that a speech act requires a clear delineation between event and context that can never, in fact, exist ([1971] 1998); cf. Morris 2007 for a helpful exploration of implications for anthropologists' writing on ritual.

14. Some of our mutual acquaintances told me that couples with heroin use history did not need to have wedding celebrations, while others argued that these unions should not be given the same weight as those organized by "normal" couples.

15. Work on "caring labor" in the late twentieth century undermined the dichotomized understandings of Euro-American gendered division of labor. These divisions are themselves historically particular and do not map onto the *nei/wai* (inside/outside)

gendered laboring practices that were common in "Old Society" and Maoist China (cf. Rofel 1999).

16. On affective labor see Hardt and Negri (2000). Scholars have pointed out that feminist critiques anticipated the conceptual questions this work raises (Weeks 2007) and argue that gendered divisions of labor under empire remain underexplored (Rofel 2001).

17. Due to their frequent absence from the labor force, recovering drug users—and especially women—were frequently pressured into performing reproductive labor in relatives' homes.

18. Her "daring" sprit and resourcefulness extended even to her heroin use career. When the drug supply dried up after a local crackdown, Su volunteered to go down to the border to buy the opioid in larger quantities. Ingeniously, she put the heroin in a ball of thread and calmly knitted all the way back on the bus, to the great admiration of her friends.

19. The sales leaders and regulars in the working room helped to institute an enthusiastic culture of responding to sales pitches, frequently clapping energetically and interjecting encouraging words such as *dui, tai bangle, waooaa, wo de tian, tai ganjing le!,* and *bu de liao!* ("correct," "that's too great," "wow," "my heavens," "it's so clean," and "unbelievable!").

20. Su one evening agreed to attend an event that was an hour's drive away in a nearby city. She was suffering from the flu and had to excuse herself several times to go to the bathroom. Tingting's assistant Wu, a tall woman who possessed Tingting's inflections and speech patterns but lacked the professional charm and polish of her boss, kept finding reasons to delay our return to Gejiu. While she was able to maintain a pleasant demeanor for the earlier part of the evening, Su by the end of the night increasingly struggled to control her temper.

21. Sons and daughters spanning in age from babies to teenagers sometimes came with their parents to Green Orchards. However, a significant percentage of the Heroin Generation did not have children. Over time, I learned of a number of complicated and traumatic stories of unsuccessful attempts to start families. Relatives and state agencies at times discouraged these efforts; certain methadone clinics, for example, had actively advised women patients not to have children. The longing for children became especially strong among those whose recovery had brought them to a more stable place in life but who felt it was too late or financially impractical to have their own biological children.

22. The policy was amended in 2015 to allow families to have two children. In practice, local guidelines and enforcement throughout the country in previous years had varied.

## CHAPTER 6. "FROM THE COMMUNITY": CIVIL SOCIETY AMBITIONS AND THE LIMITS OF PHENOMENOLOGY

1. Research on civil society in China has included categorizing NGOs (Hildebrandt 2013), analyzing the changing legal environment (Simon 2013), and providing histories

of service organizations (Huang et al. 2013). Other scholars have provided helpful histories of the emergence of *minjian* (grassroots) intellectual traditions (Veg 2019) and nonconfrontational, internet-based activist movements (Wang 2019).

2. Katherine Verdery, for example, has documented how in Romania after the collapse of the Soviet Union the term came to be linked to a historically particular political program of "returning to Europe" and reestablishing a range of institutions that socialism had repressed (1996, 104).

3. The English phrase corresponds to at least four different renderings into Chinese (Madsen 2002). "Civilized society" (*wenmin shehui*) is an alternate rendering that appeared in government documents. Historians engaged in an influential post-Tiananmen discussion of whether European genealogies of civil society and notions of a public sphere could be applied to the China context (Madsen 1993; Wakeman 1993). Phillip Huang (1993), for instance, argued for the emergence of a particularly Chinese intermediate space between state and society he termed the "third realm." In examining the legacies of Japanese empire, Yukiko Koga explores complex negotiations between civil society actors about who could speak as the legitimate inheritors of Chinese victimhood (2016, 189).

4. Regarding "an organization that filled its management positions," organizational charts that hung in prominent locations in many of these institutions, including Green Orchards, provided evidence of this hierarchy. Government leaders and "normal people" with medical training or administrative backgrounds occupied the upper and middle rungs. The lowest rung was perpetually reserved for "peers" or "volunteers" with heroin use history. One government-run organization that I visited prohibited "peer" employees from using the office landline. Though promoting its "peer" credentials, even the name of this particular organization had been chosen by senior government officials. Regarding "made up exclusively of people with heroin use history," in the first decade of the twenty-first century, groups run by people with drug use history, sex workers, gay men, and other "vulnerable populations" often struggled to register as NGOs and thus existed as "self-help groups" (*zizhu xiaozu*), "working rooms" (*gongzuoshi*), or "companies" (*gongsi*), which paid tax.

5. The street-based pet selling business took a tragic turn when a shipment of mice Yan Jun and his colleagues bought in the provincial capital suffocated on the five-hour bus ride back to Gejiu.

6. Yan made a strong case that this group's "alternative basis of expertise" derived from their experiences as heroin users made them particularly qualified to run harm reduction interventions (cf. Epstein 1998).

7. In part due to its hospitable climate, its natural beauty, and the charm of the provincial capital, Yunnan during the first decade of the 2000s attracted significant international funding and foreign technical support, leading some to informally call it the "Republic of NGOs."

8. As "activist" (*jiji fenzi*) in China had strong negative connotations for many, my interlocutors generally framed their work as "doing advocacy" (*zuo changdao*) or "offering suggestions" (*ti jianyi*) to the government.

9. The quotation "enunciate thoughts that are ahead of their time" is taken from the writings of Liu Xiaobo, the late activist and Nobel Peace Prize winner (quoted in Johnson 2017). Chinese state media responded with a different deployment of historicism in efforts to discredit the activist, noting that Liu was "almost an outsider to China's development" who had become "marginalized by Chinese society" (*Global Times* 2017). The phrase "first generation" appeared in the utterances of a mutual friend—"We are the first generation of drug user civil society builders" and "the first generation of harm reduction innovators"—with such compulsive frequency that others started mockingly repeating what he said whenever he mentioned "generation."

10. Yan at times became critical of what he saw as the apolitical and distancing work of NGO workers exclusively focused on implementing "programs" (*xiangmu*). Grassroots NGO workers who spent their time in offices, he argued, could become complacent, bureaucratic, and spoiled, expecting a donor-funded life of cabs, hotels, and restaurant food. His criticisms echoed anarchists in the former Yugoslavia who complained about money-seeking, government-collaborating "NGOnicks" (Razsa 2015). Yan Jun's shift from network architect to rights defender echoed Mao Zedong's vascillation between endorsing "expert" and "red" approaches to realizing Communist ideals. The Great Helmsman at various points promoted competent technical experts and managers before becoming "bitterly critical of party cadres who, he charged, had abandoned their revolutionary ideals and become conservative bureaucrats, seeking only power, social status and luxuries" (Meisner 1988, 101).

11. One of Yan's civil society protégés explained to me that a commitment to work would be classified as either *shiye* and *zhiye*. *Shiye* was about following one's "ideals" (*lixiang*), while *zhiye* was simply the attempt to "make a living" (*mousheng shouduan*). A true civil society spirit required embracing this work as a *shiye* and persevering irrespective of donors' funding priorities.

12. This policy created problems when I attempted to check into a hotel in another city in Honghe that was not permitted to accept foreigners. Trying to help us circumvent the restriction, the receptionist suggested my friend with heroin use history provide his identity card instead of using my passport to register. He sheepishly replied that this would create even more problems, and we left to find a different hotel.

13. While the government eventually issued regulations that clarified how individuals could move from "active" to "passive" status in the dynamic database, during my fieldwork, if and how one could have one's name removed from the database were important unresolved questions that advocates like Yan Jun were actively exploring.

14. It could be argued that in Maoist times, class backgrounds, like heroin addiction, refused to disappear like smoke for many of the same reasons (cf. Billeter 1985).

15. This characterization of Chinese people bears a resemblance to Hegel's China as "unhistorical History," a place where the state operates rationally but the people obey without self-conscious reflection (Hegel [1802] 1956, 123). Yan's characterizations of the limits of Chinese society also resonate with the contrast drawn by Fei Xiaotong between rural China and the West. Whereas the organizational mode of association existing in the West purportedly relies on the actions of an agent free to move into and

break from distinct voluntary organizational units, Chinese actors in Fei's account operate in a differential mode of association understood as overlapping webs of concentric circles. In this latter system, distinctions between public and private spaces and voluntary and involuntary forms of association become murky as individuals move within ripples of social relations (Fei [1947] 1992, 70,78; cf. Madsen 2002). The West in these accounts offers a model for a more individuated—and in Yan's telling, more fully realized—way of relating to the state and other citizens.

16. I attended one of Yan Jun's trainings on this topic. He offered advice on everything from operating the recording device on cell phones to important statutes of the law they should be familiar with to how to address the police; he suggested people with heroin use history refer to officers by the term *minjing* rather than *ganjing* in order to put the police on a more equal footing.

17. One complicating factor is that Yan Jun's advocacy efforts were contingent on abstaining from heroin use. Anyone who had recently used the opioid could be sent away to a compulsory laboring center at any moment. This policy helped to explain the absence of organizing by active drug users (or "people who use drugs," PUD) visible in many other countries (cf. Zigon 2018).

18. For example, Wu Zunyou, the head of the Chinese Center for Disease Control and Prevention (CDC) and internationally recognized architect of the country's methadone program, published a letter in the *Bulletin* of the WHO that defended the continued operation of China's compulsory labor centers by pointing to the country's long-standing tradition of prioritizing the interests of the "broader community" over those of the individual (Wu 2013).

19. Harmonious society (*hexie shehui*) was a key policy promoted by Hu Jintao emphasizing national stability by encouraging equitable growth and diminishing social conflict.

20. The Chinese government and GONGOs implemented the great majority of activities funded by international donors. Of almost $500 million sent by foundations in the United States to Chinese grantees between 2002 and 2009, less than 6 percent went directly to "grassroots" organizations (Spires 2011).

21. At the start of my fieldwork, Shanghai's Strive for Self-Improvement Cooperative (*Ziqiang shehui fuwu zongshe*), for example, had mobilized hundreds of social workers to provide a range of community-based services to more than ten thousand local recovering drug users.

22. For those with strong prejudices against people with drug use history, the shortcomings Yan Jun displayed in his civil society work could be traced to his ontological status as a drug user. People with drug use history were considered by some to be a *type* of person who at any moment could revert to antisocial, irrational, or dangerous actions. Proponents of this viewpoint—sometimes hailing from organizations that claimed to empower drug users—opined to me in informal conversations that individuals with heroin use history like Yan Jun should never be allowed to assume management positions or be trusted with money. Lin's view is not based on this dichotomy. Instead, recovering drug users are understood to belong to a broader group of "vulnerable

populations"—including sex workers and men having sex with men, to name other groups often involved in HIV-prevention focused NGO work—who were purportedly also at risk of running into problems if organizing on behalf of their communities.

23. This ideal of care filtered into government-implemented public health work. For example, during the Olympics in Beijing in 2008, district public health officials were asked to *guan* (control and care for) people with heroin use history who also had a history of antisocial behavior to minimize the possibility of public disruption.

24. International human rights activists in the early 2010s criticized the US government for funding the training that had jump-started Yan Jun's civil society career. As a Human Rights Watch advocate succinctly put it, "you can't have peer education in a forced labor camp" (Amon 2011).

25. While not fitting the stereotype of an intimidating boss, Yan had worked his way into management in part due to his skills as a financial assistant and bookkeeper and, some speculated, his ability to provide useful information about his peers to guards.

26. Programs run by CDC government employees offered another avenue for Big Brothers and Sisters from compulsory labor centers later to become involved in public health activities. Without existing connections to people with drug use history, government health workers often turned to public security contacts for help in recruiting peers. In certain cities, this created a situation wherein former members of the "management" in compulsory laboring centers helped local CDC programs reach their harm reduction outreach targets while they also were helping police meet their drug user arrest quotas.

27. Ralph Litzinger makes a similar critique of state-society distinctions in discussing technologies of rule "where government happens from above, and below" (2001, 264).

28. In a nearby city, a Society boss with heroin use history and longtime criminal connections started an NGO that was part of Yan's network. From the start of involvement in the network, this widely respected leader had rejected certain aspects of "civil society" pushed on him by Yan Jun and his colleagues, most notably in his initial refusal to sign a statement that he would not resort to violence to resolve disagreements.

29. Yan spoke with pride about the ties he had created with government officials. These relationships frequently turned out to be useful in both his advocacy campaigns and the negotiation of his personal affairs. His connections helped me at various points in my fieldwork.

30. These tensions also surfaced among NGO workers who vacillated between understanding their participation in civil society as a professional career and as a lifelong passion. One of Yan's civil society protégés explained to me that the disagreement was captured in the difference between *shiye* and *zhiye*. *Shiye* was about following one's ideals (*lixiang*), while *zhiye* was simply the attempt to "make a living" (*mousheng shouduan*). A "civil society" spirit for this figure meant embracing helping drug users as *shiye* and persevering irrespective of donors' funding priorities.

31. Outraged by the prices on the menu of the venue selected by Yan Jun, this visitor insisted that the only drink he would order at the bar was a glass of boiled water.

32. Expressing a growing discomfort with the limitations of the critical phenomeno-logical approach that defined his career, Byron Good argues that drawing on writings in psychoanalysis can help to focus "genuine attention to crucial aspects of psycho-logical experiences of authority and authority relations, both individual and collective; to the dynamics of 'subjection' and anxiety; to the real force of loss as it reverberates through ones being; to the power of desire and the chaos it may loose; to the sources of ambivalence and self deception, and how these play out in social life" (2012, 27). Anthropologists whose work productively explores these themes include Borneman (2007), Crapanzano (1980), and Ewing (1997).

33. In revisiting Althusser's scene of hailing, Dolar argues for the richness of psy-choanalytic insistence on the remainder in considerations of human subjectivity over the structuralist focus on reproduction through the clean cut (Dolar 1993). Discussions of interpellation and subjection lead in other productive directions. Linking hailing to Austinian speech acts, Judith Butler emphasizes the reiterative convention of interpel-lative naming to show how such hailing continues to function without a speaker—for example in the way drug user status comes to be linked to identity cards in China (Butler 1998, 34).

34. Lacanian critiques of ego psychology disrupt claims made by Yan or me that posit an enduring self-knowing "I" produced through the narrative acts of an autonomous ego (cf. Lacan 1991). Though difficult to explore ethnographically, a Lacanian understanding of desire as operating through a lack and founded on narcissistic misrecognition poten-tially better captures aspects of the discontinuous nature of psychic reality.

35. On my most recent visit to China, a longtime friend in the harm reduction world made a passing comment that reflected back to me how she saw my tendencies as a fieldworker. She noted that she could tell when something in a conversation caught my interest: I had a different focus and level of attunement in these discrete moments. The idea of China expressed through tropes of historicism—as moving according to Mao's will or rushing forward through reform polices to change the world—has cap-tured my attention since I was a teenager. Life in China, I imagined and then felt, possessed a dynamic movement that the United States lacked.

36. Žižek offers a Lacanian reading of the psychic power of historicism noting, "the Stalinist politician [and perhaps also certain post-Maoist subjects] exerts his power in as far as he recognizes himself as interpellated by the big Other of History, serving as its Progress" (1999, 260).

37. Todd McGowan writes, "The desire of the Other appears as a puzzle that one might solve, but this is its great lure" (2016, 35).

## EPILOGUE

1. I follow Gananath Obeyesekere, who, in writing about Sri Lankan Hindu-Buddhist religious devotees, notes, "There is no terminal point to my interviews, since the lives of my informants haven't ended. This essay perforce must be open-ended" (1981, 10).

2. With a national prevalence rate under 0.1 percent of the general population, many in the public health field hailed the country's response to HIV/AIDS as a success story (*China Daily* 2015).

3. National figures also followed this trend. In 2009 heroin users made up 78 percent of the nation's 1.2 million registered individuals. By 2017 more than 60 percent of the country's two-million-plus registered drug users were primarily using methamphetamines, ecstasy, and other nonopioid drugs (National Narcotics Control Commission 2009, 2018).

4. Bedside tables in Gejiu hotel rooms during my visit displayed terrorism prevention booklets alongside tourist pamphlets about the region's attractions. One reason for the noticeable state of vigilance in Honghe prefecture was the aftereffects of an attack at the Kunming train station in 2014, in which thirty-one bystanders had been killed by Uighur separatists. The perpetrators had connections to Shadian, a predominantly Muslim community located a few kilometers down the road from Gejiu.

5. I later learned that Gejiu had recently begun sorting and smelting tin imported from nearby Myanmar.

6. This paragraph draws from a fascinating chapter in Lara Kusnetzky's dissertation (2011), "Class Education: Bodies of Evidence and Living History in the Socialist Education Movement (1962–1965) and the Cultural Revolution (1966–1976)."

7. This English-language sign from the museum continues, "as well as the difficulties brought on from long-term planned economy system in state-owned enterprise, the operation and business of YTC (Yunnan Tin Company) were once again slumped into the low ebb" (Yunnan Tin Museum 2011). The phrase "once again" encourages the reader to link the excesses of the Rush years with those of Maoist mining. Both are portrayed as inefficient and wasteful compared to the market discipline instilled by Yunnan Tin and its partners.

# REFERENCES

Acker, Caroline. 2002. *Creating the American Junkie: Addiction Research in the Classic Era of Narcotic Control*. Baltimore, MD: Johns Hopkins University Press.

Adams, Vincanne, Michelle Murphy, and Adele Clarke. 2009. "Anticipation: Technoscience, Life, Affect, Temporality." *Subjectivity* 28, no. 1: 246–65.

Agar, Michael. 1973. *Ripping and Running: A Formal Ethnography of Urban Heroin Addicts*. New York: Academic Press.

Ahmed, Sara. 2006. *Queer Phenomenology: Orientations, Objects, Others*. Durham, NC: Duke University Press.

Althusser, Louis. (1967) 1971. "Ideology and Ideological State Apparatuses (Notes towards an Investigation)." In *Lenin and Philosophy and Other Essays*. New York: Monthly Review Press.

Amnesty International. 2013. *Changing the Soup but Not the Medicine? Abolishing Re-education through Labour in China*. London: Amnesty International Publications.

Amon, Joe. 2011. "'Utterly Irresponsible': Donor Funding in Drug 'Treatment' Centers." *Huffington Post*, September 14. www.huffpost.com/entry/vietnam-drug-treatment -centers_b_960272.

Anagnost, Ann. 1989. "Prosperity and Counterprosperity: The Moral Discourse on Wealth in Post-Mao China." In *Marxism and the Chinese Experience*, edited by Arif Dirlik and Maurice Meisner, 210–34. New York: Routledge Press.

———. 1997. *National Past-times: Narrative, Representation, and Power in Modern China*. Durham, NC: Duke University Press.

Anderson, Benedict. 1983. *Imagined Communities: Reflections on the Origin and Spread of Nationalism*. New York: Verso.

Appadurai, Arjun. 2013. *The Future as Cultural Fact: Essays on the Global Condition*. London: Verso.

Arendt, Hannah. (1958) 1998. *The Human Condition*. Chicago: University of Chicago Press.

————. 1973. *The Origins of Totalitarianism*. San Diego, CA: Harvest Press.

Aretxaga, Begoña. 2003. "Maddening States." *Annual Review of Anthropology* 32, no. 1: 393–410.

Asad, Talal, ed. 1973. *Anthropology & the Colonial Encounter*. London: Ithaca Press.

Austin, John. 1962. *How to Do Things with Words*. Oxford: Clarendon Press.

Baer, Hans, Merrill Singer, and Ida Susser. 2004. *Medical Anthropology and the World System*. Westport, CT: Greenwood Publishing Group.

Bambach, Charles. 1995. *Heidegger, Dilthey, and the Crisis of Historicism*. Ithaca, NY: Cornell University Press.

Bartlett, Nicholas. 2018a. "Idling in Mao's Shadow: Heroin Addiction and the Contested Therapeutic Value of Socialist Traditions of Laboring." *Culture, Medicine, and Psychiatry* 42, no. 1: 49–68.

————. 2018b. "The Ones Who Struck Out: Entrepreneurialism, Heroin Addiction, and Historical Obsolescence in Reform Era China." *positions asia critique* 26, no. 3: 423–49.

Becker, Howard. 1953. "Becoming a Marihuana User." *American Journal of Sociology* 59 no. 3: 235–42.

Berger, Peter, and Thomas Luckmann. 1967. *The Social Construction of Reality*. London: Allen Lane.

Bergmann, Luke. 2008. *Getting Ghost: Two Young Lives and the Struggle for the Soul of an American City*. New York: New Press.

Berlant, Lauren. 2011. *Cruel Optimism*. Durham, NC: Duke University Press.

Beyrer, Chris, Myat Htoo Razak, Khomdon Lisam, Jie Chen, Wei Lui, and Xiao-Fang Yu. 2000. "Overland Heroin Trafficking Routes and HIV-1 Spread in South and South-east Asia." *AIDS* 14, no. 1: 75–83.

Billeter, Jean-Francois. 1985. "The System of Class Status." *The Scope of State Power in China*, edited by Stuart Schram, 127–69. Hong Kong: Chinese University of Hong Kong Press.

Born, Georgina. 2015. "Making Time: Temporality, History, and the Cultural Object." *New Literary History* 46 no. 3: 361–86.

Borneman, John. 2007. *Syrian Episodes: Sons, Fathers, and an Anthropologist in Aleppo*. Princeton, NJ: Princeton University Press.

Bourdieu, Pierre. (1960) 1979. *Algeria*. Translated by Richard Nice. Cambridge, UK: Cambridge University Press.

————. (1962) 2008. *The Bachelors' Ball: The Crisis of Peasant Society in Béarn*. Chicago: University of Chicago Press.

————. 1990. *The Logic of Practice*. Stanford, CA: Stanford University Press.

Bourgois, Philippe. (1995) 2003. *In Search of Respect: Selling Crack in El Barrio*. New York: Cambridge University Press.

Bourgois, Philippe, and Jeffrey Schonberg. 2009. *Righteous Dopefiend*. Berkeley: University of California Press.

Bray, David. 2005. *Social Space and Governance in Urban China: The Danwei System from Origins to Reform*. Stanford, CA: Stanford University Press.

Brooks, David. 2009. "The Nation of Futurity." *New York Times*, November 16.

Brotherton, Sean. 2012. *Revolutionary Medicine: Health and the Body in Post-Soviet Cuba*. Durham, NC: Duke University Press.

Brown, Jeremy. 2012. *City versus Countryside in Mao's China: Negotiating the Divide*. New York: Cambridge University Press.

Browne, Victoria. 2014. *Feminism, Time, and Nonlinear History*. New York: Palgrave Macmillan.

Bryant, Rebecca. 2014. "History's Remainders: On Time and Objects after Conflict in Cyprus." *American Ethnologist* 41, no. 4: 681–97.

Burawoy, Michael, and Katherine Verdery. 1999. *Uncertain Transition: Ethnographies of Change in the Postsocialist World*. Lanham, MD: Rowman & Littlefield.

Burraway, Joshua. 2019. "'Not Enough': Killing Time in London's Itchy Park." *Ethnos*. doi:10.1080/00141844.2019.1641536.

Burroughs, William. (1953) 1977. *Junky*. New York: Viking Penguin.

Butler, Judith. 1997. *Excitable Speech: A Politics of the Performative*. New York: Routledge.

Buyandelgeriyn, Manduhai. 2008. "Post-Post-Transition Theories: Walking on Multiple Paths." *Annual Review of Anthropology* 37, no. 1: 235–50.

Cahn, Peter. 2006. "Building Down and Dreaming Up." *American Ethnologist* 33, no. 1: 126–42.

Carr, David. 1991. *Time, Narrative, and History*. Bloomington: Indiana University Press. First published by Midland Books, 1986.

———. 2014. *Experience and History: Phenomenological Perspectives on the Historical World*. New York: Oxford University Press.

Carr, Summerson. 2010. *Scripting Addiction: The Politics of Therapeutic Talk and American Sobriety*. Princeton, NJ: Princeton University Press.

Chakrabarty, Dipesh. 2000. *Provincializing Europe: Postcolonial Thought and Historical Difference*. Princeton, NJ: Princeton University Press.

Chen, Chih-Jou Jay. 1999. "Local Institutions and the Transformation of Property Rights in Southern Fujian." In *Property Rights and Economic Reform in China*, edited by Jean C. Oi and Andrew Walder, 49–70. Stanford, CA: Stanford University Press.

Cheng, Yinghong. 2009. *Creating the "New Man": From Enlightenment Ideals to Socialist Realities*. Honolulu: University of Hawaii Press.

*China Daily*. 2015. "China among 'Success Stories' in Global HIV/AIDS Fight: UNAIDS Chief." July 15.

Cho, Mun Young. 2013. *The Specter of "the People": Urban Poverty in Northeast China*. Ithaca, NY: Cornell University Press.

———. 2017. "Unveiling Neoliberal Dynamics: Government Purchase (goumai) of Social Work Services in Shenzhen's Urban Periphery." *China Quarterly* 230: 269–88.

Chu, Julie. 2010. *Cosmologies of Credit: Transnational Mobility and the Politics of Destination in China*. Durham, NC: Duke University Press.

Cohen, Myron. 1993. "Cultural and Political Inventions in Modern China: The Case of the Chinese Peasant." *Daedalus* 122, no. 2: 151–70.

Comaroff, John, and Jean Comaroff. 1987. "The Madman and the Migrant: Work and Labor in the Historical Consciousness of a South African People." *American Ethnologist* 14, no. 2: 191–209.

———. 1992. *Ethnography and the Historical Imagination.* Boulder, CO: Westview Press.

Corsten, Michael. 1999. "The Time of Generations." *Time & Society* 8, nos. 2–3: 249–72.

Crapanzano, Vincent. 1980. *Tuhami: Portrait of a Moroccan.* Chicago: University of Chicago Press.

———. 1984. "Life-Histories: Lives: An Anthropological Approach to Biography." *American Anthropologist* 86, no. 4: 953–60.

———. 2004. *Imaginative Horizons: An Essay in Literary-Philosophical Anthropology.* Chicago: University of Chicago Press.

Croll, Elizabeth. 1993. *From Heaven to Earth: Images and Experiences of Development in China.* New York: Routledge.

Dai, Jinhua. 2018. *After the Post–Cold War: The Future of Chinese History.* Durham. NC: Duke University Press.

Deegan, Patricia. 1988. "Recovery: The Lived Experience of Rehabilitation." *Psychosocial Rehabilitation Journal* 11, no. 4: 11–19.

Deng, Xiaoping. 1992. *Deng Xiaoping nanxun jianghua* [The Nanxun talks]. http://finance.ifeng.com/opinion/zjgc/20111231/5390024.shtml.

Derrida, Jacques. (1971) 1988. "Signature Event Context." In *Limited Inc.* Evanston, IL: Northwestern University Press.

Desjarlais, Robert. 1997. *Shelter Blues: Sanity and Selfhood among the Homeless.* Philadelphia, PA: University of Pennsylvania Press, 1997.

Desjarlais, Robert, and Jason Throop. 2011. "Phenomenological Approaches in Anthropology." *Annual Review of Anthropology* 40: 87–102.

Devereux, George. 1967. *From Anxiety to Method in the Behavioral Sciences.* The Hague: Mouton.

Di Leonardo, Micaela. 1987. "The Female World of Cards and Holidays: Women, Families, and the Work of Kinship." *Signs: Journal of Women in Culture and Society* 12, no. 3: 440–53.

Ding, Shuyong. 2010. "Pingan Kaiyuan, Guanai Gongcheng Nuan Minxin" [Safe and sound Kaiyuan: Caring project warms popular sentiment]. *Wen Wei Poi* [newspaper], June 4.

Dittmer, Lowell, and Lü Xiaobo. 1996. "Personal Politics in the Chinese Danwei under Reform." *Asian Survey* 36, no. 3: 246–67.

Dolar, Mladen. 1993. "Beyond Interpellation." *Qui Parle* 6 no.2: 75–96.

Duara, Prasenjit. 1996. *Rescuing History from the Nation: Questioning Narratives of Modern China.* Chicago: University of Chicago Press.

Dunn, Elizabeth. 2004. *Privatizing Poland: Baby Food, Big Business, and the Remaking of Labor.* Ithaca, NY: Cornell University Press.

Dupont, Robert, Howard Josepher, Sally Satel, and Maia Szalavitz. 2015. "Room for Debate: Should Drug Addicts Be Forced into Treatment?" *New York Times*, November 11.

Dutton, Michael. 2008. "Passionately Governmental: Maoism and the Structured Intensities of Revolutionary Governmentality." *Postcolonial Studies* 11, no. 1: 99–112.

Dutton, Michael, Hsiu-ju Stacy Lo, and Dong Dong Wu. 2008. *Beijing Time*. Cambridge, MA: Harvard University Press.

Eagen, Timothy. 2016. "A Farewell to the Comedian in Chief." *New York Times*, November 25.

Eagleton, Terry, and Pierre Bourdieu. 1992. "Doxa and Common Life." *New Left Review* 191: 120.

*Economist.* 2011. "Entrepreneurship in China: Let a Million Flowers Bloom." March 10.
———. 2014. "Beneath the Glacier." April 12.

Eliade, Mircea. 1959. *The Sacred and the Profane: The Nature of Religion*. Vol. 144. Boston: Houghton Mifflin Harcourt.

Epstein, Steven. 1998. *Impure Science: AIDS, Activism and the Politics of Knowledge*. Berkeley, CA: University of California Press.

Ewing, Katherine Pratt. 1997. *Arguing Sainthood: Modernity, Psychoanalysis, and Islam*. Durham, NC: Duke University Press.

Fabian, Johannes. 1983. *Time and the Other: How Anthropology Makes Its Object*. New York: Columbia University Press.

Fan, Elsa. 2014. "HIV Testing as Prevention among MSM in China: The Business of Scaling-Up." *Global Public Health* 9, nos. 1–2: 85–97.

Farquhar, Judith. 2002. *Appetites: Food and Sex in Post-Socialist China*. Durham, NC: Duke University Press.

Farrer, James. 1999. "Disco 'Super-Culture': Consuming Foreign Sex in the Chinese Disco; Cosmopolitan Dance Culture and Cosmopolitan Sexual Culture." *Sexualities* 2, no. 2: 147–65.
———. 2002. *Opening Up: Youth Sex Culture and Market Reform in Shanghai*. Chicago: University of Chicago Press.

Fearnley, Lyle. 2020. *Virulent Zones: Animal Disease and Global Health at China's Pandemic Epicenter*. Durham, NC: Duke University Press.

Fei, Xiaotong. (1947) 1992. *From the Soil, the Foundations of Chinese Society*. Translated by Gary G. Hamilton, and Zheng Wang. Berkeley: University of California Press.

Ferguson, James. 1999. *Expectations of Modernity: Myths and Meanings of Urban Life on the Zambian Copperbelt*. Berkeley: University of California Press.
———. 2006. *Global Shadows: Africa in the Neoliberal World Order*. Durham, NC: Duke University Press.
———. 2013. "Declarations of Dependence: Labour, Personhood, and Welfare in Southern Africa." *Journal of the Royal Anthropological Institute* 19, no. 2: 223–42.

Ferguson, James, and Akhil Gupta. 2002. "Spatializing States: Toward an Ethnography of Neoliberal Governmentality." *American Ethnologist* 29, no. 4: 981–1002.

Gammeltoft, Tine. 2014. "Toward an Anthropology of the Imaginary: Specters of Disability in Vietnam." *Ethos* 42, no. 2: 153–74.

Garcia, Angela. 2010. *The Pastoral Clinic: Addiction and Dispossession along the Rio Grande*. Berkeley: University of California Press.

Garro, Linda. 1994. "Narrative Representations of Chronic Illness Experience: Cultural Models of Illness, Mind, and Body in Stories Concerning the Temporomandibular Joint (TMJ)." *Social Science & Medicine* 38, no. 6: 775–88.

Geertz, Clifford. 1973. *The Interpretation of Cultures*. New York: Basic Books.

Geertz, Hildred. 1968. "Latah in Java: A theoretical paradox." *Indonesia* 5: 93–104.

"Gejiu Moshi Chengjiu Shijie Xiye Longtou Laiyuan" [Gejiu model: World success of the tin industry leader's origin]. 2008. *Jingji Cankaobao* [Economic reference paper].

*Gejiushi Shimin Duben.* [Gejiu city citizen's reader]. 2011. Gejiu: Gejiushi jingshen wenmingjianshe weiyuanhui.

Gladney, Dru. 2004. *Dislocating China: Reflections on Muslims, Minorities, and Other Subaltern Subjects*. Chicago: University of Chicago Press.

*Global Times*. 2017. "Lu Xiaobo's Medical Treatment Arouses Clamour from the West." June 26. www.globaltimes.cn/content/1053833.shtml.

Gold, Thomas. 1989. "Guerrilla Interviewing among the Getihu." In *Unofficial China: Popular Culture and Thought in the People's Republic*, edited by Perry Link, Richard Madsen, and Paul Pickowicz, 175–92. Boulder, CO: Westview Press.

Golub, Andrew, Bruce Johnson, and Eloise Dunlap. 2005. "Subcultural Evolution and Illicit Drug Use." *Addiction Research & Theory* 13, no. 3: 217–29.

Good, Byron. 2012. "Phenomenology, Psychoanalysis, and Subjectivity in Java." *Ethos* 40, no. 1: 24–36.

Good, Byron, and Mary-Jo Good. 2000. "'Fiction' and 'Historicity': Doctors' Stories; Social and Narrative Dimensions of Learning Medicine." In *Narrative and the Cultural Construction of Illness and Healing*, edited by Cheryl Mattingly and Linda Garro, 50–69. Berkeley: University of California Press.

Gray, Robert. n.d. "Chapter Four: Heroin, the Hui, and Historical Conflict in Yunnan: The Independent Kingdom of Pingyuan Township." Unpublished manuscript.

Greenhalgh, Susan. 2003. "Planned Births, Unplanned Persons: Population in the Making of Chinese Modernity." *American Ethnologist* 30, no. 2: 196–215.

Gruber, Jacob. 1970. "Ethnographic Salvage and the Shaping of Anthropology." *American Anthropologist* 72, no. 6: 1289–99.

Gu, Gong. (1980) 1985. "The Two Generations." In *Mao's Harvest: Voices from China's New Generation*, edited and translated by Helen Siu and Zelda Stern, 9–15. New York: Oxford University Press.

Haas, Lawrence. 2018. "Passing the Torch to China?" *U.S. News and World Report*, March 6.

Hacking, Ian. 2006. "Making People Up." *London Review of Books*, August 17.

Hage, Ghassan. 2003. *Searching for Hope in a Shrinking Society*. London: Pluto Press.

Han, Clara. 2012. *Life in Debt: Times of Care and Violence in Neoliberal Chile*. Berkeley: University of California Press.

Hansen, Helena. 2018. *Addicted to Christ: Remaking Men in Puerto Rican Pentecostal Drug Ministries*. Berkeley: University of California Press.

Hardt, Michael, and Antonio Negri. 2000. *Empire*. Cambridge, MA: Harvard University Press.

Harootunian, Harry. 2007. "Remembering the Historical Present." *Critical Inquiry* 33, no. 3: 471–94.

Harrell, Stevan. 1985. "Why Do the Chinese Work So Hard? Reflections on an Entrepreneurial Ethic." *Modern China* 11, no. 2: 203–26.

Hartog, François. (2003) 2015. *Regimes of Historicity: Presentism and Experiences of Time*. Translated by Saskia Brown. New York: Columbia University Press.

Hegel, Georg W. F. (1802) 1956. *The Philosophy of History*. Translated by J. Sibree. Mineola, NY: Dover Books.

Hellbeck, Jochen. 2009. *Revolution on My Mind: Writing a Diary under Stalin*. Cambridge, MA: Harvard University Press.

Hershatter, Gail. 2014. *The Gender of Memory: Rural Women and China's Collective Past*. Berkeley: University of California Press.

Hildebrandt, Timothy. 2013. *Social Organizations and the Authoritarian State in China*. New York: Cambridge University Press.

Himmelweit, Susan. 1999. "Caring Labor." *Annals of the American Academy of Political and Social Science* 561, no. 1: 27–38.

Hinton, William. (1966) 1997. *Fanshen: A Documentary of Revolution in a Chinese Village*. Berkeley: University of California Press.

Hirsch, Eric, and Charles Stewart. 2005. "Introduction: Ethnographies of Historicity." *History and Anthropology* 16, no. 3: 261–74.

Hodges, Matt. 2019. "History's Impasse: Radical Historiography, Leftist Elites, and the Anthropology of Historicism in Southern France." *Current Anthropology* 60, no. 3: 391–413.

Hoffman, Lisa. 2010. *Patriotic Professionalism in Urban China: Fostering Talent*. Philadelphia: Temple University Press.

Hollan, Douglas. 2013. "Coping in Plain Sight: Work as a Local Response to Event-Related Emotional Distress in Contemporary US Society." *Transcultural Psychiatry* 50, no. 5: 726–43.

Honghezhou Shiweixuanchuan [Honghe Prefecture Publicity Committee]. 2009. "Honghe Fenjin 60 Zhounian" [Honghe prefecture's 60 year determined entry].

Hsu, Carolyn. 2006. "Cadres, Getihu, and Good Businesspeople: Making Sense of Entrepreneurs in Early Post-Socialist China." *Urban Anthropology and Studies of Cultural Systems and World Economic Development* 35 no. 1: 1–38.

Huang, Chien-Chung, Guosheng Deng, Zhenyao Wang, and Richard Edwards, eds. 2013. *China's Nonprofit Sector: Progress and Challenges*. Piscataway, NJ: Transaction.

Huang, Philip. 1993. "'Public Sphere'/'Civil Society' in China? The Third Realm between State and Society." *Modern China* 19, no. 2: 216–40.

Human Rights Watch. 2012. "Torture in the Name of Treatment: Human Rights Abuses in Vietnam, China, Cambodia and Lao PDR." www.hrw.org/report/2012 /07/24/torture-name-treatment/human-rights-abuses-vietnam-china-cambodia -and-lao-pdr.

Humphrey, Caroline. 2002. *The Unmaking of Soviet Life: Everyday Economies after Socialism*. Ithaca, NY: Cornell University Press.

Hunt, Linda. 2000. "Strategic Suffering: Illness Narratives as Social Empowerment among Mexican Cancer Patients." *Narrative and the Cultural Construction of Illness and Healing*, edited by Cheryl Mattingly and Linda Garro, 88–107. Berkeley: University of California Press.

Husserl, Emund. (1928) 1964. *Phenomenology of Internal Time Consciousness*, edited by Martin Heidegger. Translated by James Churchill. Bloomington: Indiana University Press.

Hyde, Sandra. 2007. *Eating Spring Rice: The Cultural Politics of AIDS in Southwest China*. Berkeley: University of California Press.

———. 2011. "Migrations in Humanistic Therapy: Turning Drug Users into Patients and Patients into Healthy Citizens in Southwest China." *Body & Society* 17, nos. 2–3: 183–204.

Iggers, Georg. 1995. "Historicism: The History and Meaning of the Term." *Journal of the History of Ideas* 56, no. 1: 129–52.

Isaacs, Susan. 1992. *Magic Hour*. New York: HarperCollins.

Jackson, Michael. 2012. *Lifeworlds: Essays in Existential Anthropology*. Chicago: University of Chicago Press.

Jacques, Martin. 2009. *When China Rules the world: The End of the Western World and the Birth of a New Global Order*. New York: Penguin Press.

Jameson, Fredric. 1990. *Postmodernism, or, The Cultural Logic of Late Capitalism*. Durham, NC: Duke University Press Books.

Jansen, Stef. 2014a. "Hope for/against the State: Gridding in a Besieged Sarajevo Suburb." *Ethnos* 79, no. 2: 238–60.

———. 2014b. "On Not Moving Well Enough: Temporal Reasoning in Sarajevo Yearnings for 'Normal Lives.'" *Current Anthropology* 55, no. S9: S74–S84.

Jeffery, Lyn. 2001. "Placing Practices: Transnational Network Marketing in Mainland China." In *China Urban: Ethnographies of Contemporary Culture*, edited by Nancy Chen, Constance Clark, Suzzanne Gottschang, and Lyn Jeffery, 23–42. Durham, NC: Duke University Press.

Johnson, Ian. 2017. "Lu Xiaobo: The Man Who Stayed." *New York Review of Books*, July 14.

Jürgens, Ralf. 2005. *"Nothing about Us without Us"—Greater, Meaningful Involvement of People Who Use Illegal Drugs: A Public Health, Ethical, and Human Rights Imperative*. Toronto: Canadian HIV/AIDS Legal Network.

Keane, Helen. 2002. *What's Wrong with Addiction?* New York: New York University Press.

Kipnis, Andrew B. 1997. *Producing Guanxi: Sentiment, Self, and Subculture in a North China Village*. Durham, NC: Duke University Press, 1997.

Kleinman, Arthur. 1980. *Patients and Healers in the Context of Culture: An Exploration of the Borderland between Anthropology, Medicine, and Psychiatry.* Berkeley: University of California Press.

———. 1982. "Neurasthenia and Depression: A Study of Somatization and Culture in China." *Culture, Medicine and Psychiatry* 6, no. 2: 117–90.

Kleinman, Arthur, and Joan Kleinman. 1994. "How Bodies Remember: Social Memory and Bodily Experience of Criticism, Resistance, and Delegitimation Following China's Cultural Revolution." *New Literary History* 25, no. 3: 707–23.

Knight, Kelly Ray. 2015. *Addicted. Pregnant. Poor.* Durham, NC: Duke University Press.

Kohrman, Matthew. 2007. "Depoliticizing Tobacco's Exceptionality: Male Sociality, Death and Memory-making Among Chinese Cigarette Smokers." *The China Journal* 58: 85–109.

Koselleck, Reinhart. 2004. *Futures Past: On the Semantics of Historical Time.* New York: Columbia University Press.

Kusnetzky, Lara. 2011. "Stories of Tin City: Narrative Identity and the Histories of Gejiu, Yunnan Province." PhD diss., City University of New York.

Lacan, Jacques. (1975) 1991. *The Seminar of Jacques Lacan: Book I, Freud's Papers on Technique, 1953–1954,* edited by Jacques-Alan Miller. Translated by Jon Forrester. New York: Norton.

Lambek, Michael. 2002. *The Weight of the Past: Living with History in Mahajanga, Madagascar.* Basingstoke, UK: Palgrave Macmillan.

Lardy, Nicholas. 2016. "The Changing Role of the Private Sector in China." *Structural Change in China: Implications for Australia World,* edited by Iris Day and John Simon, 37–50. Sydney, Australia: Proceedings of a Conference.

Lau, Raymond 1997. "China: Labor Reform and the Challenge of Facing the Working Class." *Capital and Class* 21, no. 1: 45–80.

Lear, Jonathan. 2006. *Radical Hope: Ethics in the Face of Cultural Devastation.* Cambridge, MA: Harvard University Press.

Lerche, Jens. 2007. "A Global Alliance against Forced Labour? Unfree Labour, Neo-Liberal Globalization and the International Labour Organization." *Journal of Agrarian Change* 7, no. 4: 425–52.

Levy, Neil. 2017. "Hijacking Addiction." *Philosophy, Psychiatry, & Psychology* 24, no. 1: 97–99.

Li, Deming, and Changdong Xu, eds. 2009. *Zhuanxing: Xidu Gejiukexuefazhanshixian* [Transformation: The Tin Gejiu realizes scientific development]. Beijing: Renmin ribao Press.

Li, Jianhua. 2009. Interview with author, Kunming, China, August.

Li, Jianhua, and Ruimin Zhang. 2003. *Hailuoyinyilairenqun Guifan Guji Fangfa Yanjiu Baogao.* [A report on the formal research method of estimating heroin dependent individuals]. Kunming: Yunnan Institute of Drug Abuse.

Li, Xiaoming, Yong Zhou, and Bonita Stanton. 2002. "Illicit Drug Initiation among Institutionalized Drug Users in China." *Addiction* 97, no. 5: 575–82.

Lindesmith, Alfred. 1938. "A Sociological Theory of Drug Addiction." *American Journal of Sociology* 43, no. 4: 593–613.

Litzinger, Ralph. 2001. "Government from Below: The State, the Popular, and the Illusion of Autonomy." *positions: east asia cultures critique* 9, no. 1: 253–66.

Liu, Lydia. 2004. *The Clash of Empires*. Cambridge, MA: Harvard University Press.

Liu, Shao-hua. 2011. *Passage to Manhood: Youth Migration, Heroin, and AIDS in Southwest China*. Stanford, CA: Stanford University Press.

Liu, Xin. 2000. *In One's Own Shadow: An Ethnographic Account of the Condition of Post-Reform Rural China*. Berkeley: University of California Press.

Lock, Margaret. 1986. "Ambiguities of Aging: Japanese Experience and Perceptions of Menopause." *Culture, Medicine, and Psychiatry: An International Journal of Cross-Cultural Health Research* 10, no. 1: 23–46.

Lora-Wainwright, Anna. 2017. *Resigned Activism: Living with Pollution in Rural China*. Cambridge, MA: MIT Press.

Lowinger, Paul. 1977. "The Solution to Narcotic Addiction in the People's Republic of China." *American Journal of Drug and Alcohol Abuse* 4, no. 2: 165–78.

Lü, Xiaobo. 2000. "Booty Socialism, Bureau-preneurs, and the State in Transition: Organizational Corruption in China." *Comparative Politics* 32, no. 3: 273–94.

Luhrmann, Tanya. 2007. "Social Defeat and the Culture of Chronicity; or, Why Schizophrenia Does So Well Over There and So Badly Here." *Culture, Medicine and Psychiatry* 31, no. 2: 135–72.

Madsen, Richard. 1993. "The Public Sphere, Civil Society and Moral Community: A Research Agenda for Contemporary China Studies." *Modern China* 19, no. 2: 183–98.

———. 2002. "Confucian Conceptions of Civil Society." In *Alternative Conceptions of Civil Society*, 190–204. Princeton NJ: Princeton University Press.

Malkki, Liisa. 2001. "Figures of the Future: Dystopia and Subjectivity in the Social Imagination of the Future." In *History in Person*, edited by D. Holland and J. Lave, 325–48. Santa Fe, NM: School for Advanced Research Press.

Mannheim, Karl. (1936) 1997. "The Problem of Generations." In *Karl Mannheim: Essays*, edited by Paul Kecskemeti, 206. London: Routledge.

———. (1936) 1997. *Ideology and Utopia*. Vol. 1. New York: Routledge Press.

Mao, Zedong. 1961. *Introducing a Cooperative in Selected Works of Mao Tse-tung*. Beijing: Foreign Languages Press.

Marx, Karl. (1867) 2011. *Capital*. Vol. 1. New York: Dover Press.

———. (1844) 2012. *Economic and Philosophic Manuscripts of 1844*. New York: Dover Press.

Mason, Katherine. 2016. *Infectious Change: Reinventing Chinese Public Health after an Epidemic*. Stanford, CA: Stanford University Press.

Mattingly, Cheryl. 1994. "The Concept of Therapeutic 'Emplotment.'" *Social Science & Medicine* 38. no. 6: 811–22.

———. 1998. *Healing Dramas and Clinical Plots: The Narrative Structure of Experience*. New York: Cambridge University Press.

———. 2000. "Emergent narratives" in *Narrative and the Cultural Construction of Illness and Healing*, edited by Cheryl Mattingly and Linda Garro, 181–211. Berkeley: University of California Press.

———. 2010. *The Paradox of Hope: Journeys through a Clinical Borderland*. Berkeley: University of California Press.

Mauss, Marcel. (1934) 1973. "Techniques of the Body." *Economy and Society* 2, no. 1: 70–88.

McGowan, Todd. 2016. *Capitalism and Desire: The Psychic Cost of Free Markets*. New York: Columbia University Press.

Meisner, Maurice. 1988. "Marx, Mao, and Deng on the Division of Labor in History." In *Marxism and the Chinese Experience*, edited by Arif Dirlik and Maurice Meisner, 79–116. New York: Routledge.

Meyerhoff, Barbara. 1975. "Peyote and Huichol Worldview: The Structure of a Mystic Vision." In *Cannabis and Culture*, edited by Vera Rubin, 417–38. Berlin: Walter de Gruyter.

Meyers, Todd. 2013. *The Clinic and Elsewhere: Addiction, Adolescents, and the Afterlife of Therapy*. Seattle, WA: University of Washington Press.

Morris, Rosalind. 2007. "Legacies of Derrida: Anthropology." *Annual Review of Anthropology* 36: 355–89.

Mueggler, Erik. 1991. "Money, the Mountain, and State Power in a Naxi Village." *Modern China* 17, no. 2: 188–226.

Nan, Hai. 2014. "China Deports Hundreds of Uyghur Residents from Yunnan." *Radio Free Asia*, March 12.

Nash, June. (1979) 1993. *We Eat the Mines and the Mines Eat Us: Dependency and Exploitation in Bolivian Tin Mines*. New York: Columbia University Press.

National Narcotics Control Commission [Zhongguo guoji jindu weiyuanhui]. 2008. *2008 Nian zhongguo jindu baogao* [2008 annual drug prohibition report].

———. 2009. *2009 Nian zhongguo jindu baogao* [2009 annual drug prohibition report].

———. 2015. *2015 Nian zhongguo jindu baogao* [2015 Annual drug prohibition report].

———. 2018. *2018 Nian zhongguo dupin xingshi baogao* [2018 annual drug situation report].

Ng, Emily. 2009. "Heartache of the State, Enemy of the Self: Bipolar Disorder and Cultural Change in Urban China." *Culture, Medicine, and Psychiatry* 33, no. 3: 421.

———. 2020. *A Time of Lost Gods: Mediumship, Madness, and the Ghost after Mao*. Berkeley: University of California.

Nutt, David, Leslie King, William Saulsbury, and Colin Blakemore. 2007. "Development of a Rational Scale to Assess the Harm of Drugs of Potential Misuse." *The Lancet* 369, no. 9566: 1047–53.

Obeyesekere, Gananath. 1981. *Medusa's Hair: An Essay on Personal Symbols and Religious Experience*. Chicago: University of Chicago Press.

———. 1985. "Depression, Buddhism, and the Work of Culture in Sri Lanka." In *Culture and Depression: Studies in the Anthropology of Cross-Cultural Psychiatry of Affect and Disorder*, edited by Arthur Kleinman and Byron Good, 134–52. Berkeley: University of California Press.

O'Brien, Charles P., Dennis Charney, Lydia Lewis, et al. 2004. "Priority Actions to Improve the Care of Persons with Co-occurring Substance Abuse and Other Mental Disorders: A Call to Action." *Biological Psychiatry* 56, no. 10: 703–13.

O'Neill, Bruce. 2017. *The Space of Boredom: Homelessness in the Slowing Global Order.* Durham, NC: Duke University Press.

Ong, Aihwa, and Li Zhang. 2008. "Introduction: Privatizing China; Powers of the Self, Socialism from Afar." In *Privatizing China: Socialism from Afar,* edited by Li Zhang and Aihwa Ong, 1–20. Ithaca, NY: Cornell University Press.

Osburg, John. 2013. *Anxious Wealth: Money and Morality Among China's New Rich.* Stanford, CA: Stanford University Press.

Palmié, Stephan. 2013. "Historicist Knowledge and Its Conditions of Impossibility." In *The Social Life of Spirits,* edited by Ruy Blanes and Diana Espírito Santo, 218–39. Chicago: University of Chicago Press.

Palmié, Stephan, and Charles Stewart. 2016. "Introduction: For an Anthropology of History." *HAU: Journal of Ethnographic Theory* 6, no. 1: 207–36.

Parekh, Bikh. 1979. "Hannah Arendt's Critique of Marx." In *Hannah Arendt: The Recovery of the Public World,* edited by Melvyn Hill, 67–100. New York: St. Martin's Press.

"Perezhitki proshlogo" [Remnants of the past]. 1981. In *Dictionary of Philosophy,* 4th ed., edited by I. T. Frolova. Moscow: Politizdat.

Perry, Elizabeth. 1996. "Labor's Love Lost: Worker Militancy in Communist China." *International Labor and Working-Class History* 50: 64–76.

Pigg, Stacy Leigh. 1996. "The Credible and the Credulous: The Question of 'Villagers' Beliefs' in Nepal." *Cultural Anthropology* 11, no. 2: 160–201.

Preble, Edward, and John Casey. 1969. "Taking Care of Business-the Heroin User's Life on the Street." *Substance Use & Misuse* 4, no. 1: 1–24.

Pun, Ngai. 2005. *Made in China: Women Factory Workers in a Global Workplace.* Durham, NC: Duke University Press.

Pun, Ngai, and Huilin Lu. 2010. "Unfinished Proletarianization: Self, Anger, and Class Action among the Second Generation of Peasant-Workers in Present-Day China." *Modern China* 36, no. 5: 493–519.

Pursley, Sara. 2019. *Familiar Futures: Time, Selfhood, and Sovereignty in Iraq.* Stanford CA: Stanford University Press.

Raikhel, Eugene. 2016. *Governing Habits: Treating Alcoholism in the Post-Soviet Clinic.* Ithaca, NY: Cornell University Press, 2016.

Raikhel, Eugene, and William Garriott, eds. 2013. *Addiction Trajectories.* Durham, NC: Duke University Press Books.

Ralph, Laurence. 2014. *Renegade Dreams: Living through Injury in Gangland Chicago.* Chicago: University of Chicago Press.

Ralph, Michael. 2008. "Killing Time." *Social Text* 26, no. 4: 1–29.

Razsa, Maple. 2015. *Bastards of Utopia: Living Radical Politics after Socialism.* Bloomington: Indiana University Press.

Reaves, Joseph. 1985. "China Smacks 'Spiritual Opium.'" *Chicago Tribune,* October 17.

*Renmin gonganbao.* [The people's public security paper]. 2007. "Kaiyuan Jiedu 'Yulu-shequ': Chongxin Qifei Shengmin.": Kaiyuan's Yulu drug detoxification center: Allowing life to take off again. January 4.

Ricoeur, Paul. 1990. *Time and Narrative.* Vol. 3. Chicago: University of Chicago Press.

Rofel, Lisa. 1999. *Other Modernities: Gendered Yearnings in China After Socialism.* Berkeley: University of California Press.

————. 2001. "Discrepant Modernities and Their Discontents." *positions: east asia cultures critique* 9, no. 3: 637–49.

————. 2007. *Desiring China: Experiments in Neoliberalism, Sexuality, and Public Culture.* Durham, NC: Duke University Press.

Rofel, Lisa, and Sylvia Yanagisako. 2018. *Fabricating Transnational Capitalism: A Collaborative Ethnography of Italian-Chinese Global Fashion.* Durham, NC: Duke University Press.

Rojas, Carlos. 2016. "Introduction: Specters of Marx, Shades of Mao, and the Ghosts of Global Capital." In *Ghost Protocol: Development and Displacement in Global China,* edited by Carlos Rojas, and Ralph A. Litzinger, 1–12. Durham, NC: Duke University Press.

Rosaldo, Renato. 1980. *Ilongot Headhunting, 1883–1974: A Study in Society and History.* Stanford, CA: Stanford University Press.

Sahlins, Marshall. 1985. *Islands of History.* Chicago: University of Chicago Press.

————. 1990. "China Reconstructing or Vice Versa: Humiliation as a Stage of Economic 'Development,' with Comments on Cultural Diversity in the Modern World System." In *Toward One World Beyond All Barriers,* 78–96. Seoul, Korea: Poong Nam Press.

Saucier, Roxanne, Nancy Berlinger, Nicholas Thomson, Michael Gusmano, and Daniel Wolfe. 2010. "The limits of equivalence: ethical dilemmas in providing care in drug detention centers." *International Journal of Prisoner Health* 6(2): 81–87.

Schein, Louisa. 2000. *Minority Rules: The Miao and the Feminine in China's Cultural Politics.* Durham, NC: Duke University Press.

Scheper-Hughes, Nancy, and Margaret Lock. 1987. "The Mindful Body: A Prolegomenon to Future Work in Medical Anthropology." *Medical Anthropology Quarterly* 1: 6–41.

Schutz, Alfred. 1967. *Phenomenology of the Social World.* Evanston, IL: Northwestern University Press.

Scott, David. 1999. *Refashioning Futures: Criticism after Postcoloniality.* Princeton, NJ: Princeton University Press.

————. 2014. "The Temporality of Generations: Dialogue, Tradition, Criticism." *New Literary History* 45, no. 2: 157–81.

Sevigny, Robert, Sheying Chen, and Elaina Che. 2009. "Personal Experience of Schizophrenia and the Role of Danwei: A Case Study in 1990s Beijing." *Culture, Medicine and Psychiatry* 33: 86–111.

Shao, Jing. 2006. "Fluid Labor and Blood Money: The Economy of HIV/AIDS in Rural Central China." *Cultural Anthropology* 21, no. 4: 535–69.

Simon, Karla. 2013. *Civil Society in China: The Legal Framework from Ancient Times to the New Reform Era*. New York: Oxford University Press, 2013.

Smith, Aminda. 2012. *Thought Reform and China's Dangerous Classes: Reeducation, Resistance, and the People*. Lanham, MD: Rowman & Littlefield Press.

Smith, James. 2011. "Tantalus in the Digital Age: Coltan Ore, Temporal Dispossession, and 'Movement' in the Eastern Democratic Republic of the Congo." *American Ethnologist* 38, no. 1: 17–35.

Smith, Jonathan. 2004. *Relating Religion: Essays in the Study of Religion*. Chicago: University of Chicago Press.

Siu, Helen. 1989. *Agents and Victims in South China: Accomplices in Rural Revolution*. New Haven, CT: Yale University Press.

So, Alvin. 2003. "The Making of a Cadre-Capitalist Class in China." In *China's Challenges in the Twenty-First Century*. Peaceworks no. 21. United Institute of Peace. www.usip.org/sites/default/files/pwks21.pdf.

Solinger, Dorothy. 2013. "Temporality as Trope in Delineating Inequality: Progress for the Prosperous, Time Warp for the Poor." In *Unequal China*, edited by Wanning Sun and Yingjie Guo, 75–92. New York: Routledge.

Song, Yusheng. 2000. *Wo de 28sui he baise emo* [My 28th year with the White Devil] Beijing: China Youth Press. 2000

*Southern China Weekly (Nanfang zhoumo)*. 2013. "Ziyuan kujiu mozhou" [Resources dry up under spell]. April 18.

Spence, Jonathan. (1969) 1980. *To Change China: Western Advisers in China 1620–1960*. New York: Penguin.

Spires, Anthony J. 2011. "Contingent Symbiosis and Civil Society in an Authoritarian State: Understanding the Survival of China's Grassroots NGOs." *American Journal of Sociology* 117, no. 1: 1–45.

State Council of the People's Republic [Zhonghua renmin gongheguo guowuyuan]. 1957. "Guowuyuan Guanyu Laodongjaoyang Wenti de Jueding" [Decision regarding the problem of reeducation through labor]. Beijing.

———. 1986. "Kuangchan Ziyuan Fa" [Regulations concerning mineral production]. Beijing.

———. 1990. "Guanyu Jindufa de Jueding" [Decision regarding anti-drug laws]. December 28. Beijing.

———. 2000. "Zhongguo de Jindu" [Narcotics control in China]. June. Beijing.

———. 2007. "Zhonghua Renmin Gongheguo Jindufa" [The People's Republic of China's anti-drug laws]. December 29. Beijing.

———. 2011. "Jiedu Tiaoli" [Drug detoxification regulations]. June 22. Beijing.

Stern, Daniel. 2004. *The Present Moment in Psychotherapy and Everyday Life*. New York: W. W. Norton.

Stewart, Charles. 2016. "Historicity and Anthropology." *Annual Review of Anthropology* 45: 79–94.

———. 2017. *Dreaming and Historical Consciousness in Island Greece*. Chicago: University of Chicago Press.

Stewart, Pamela, and Andrew Strathern, eds. 2003. *Landscape, Memory and History: Anthropological Perspectives*. London: Pluto Press.

Summerfield, Derek. 2002. "Effects of War: Moral Knowledge, Revenge, Reconciliation, and Medicalised Concepts of 'Recovery.'" *BMJ: British Medical Journal* 325, no. 7372: 1105.

Turner, Victor. 1967. *The Forest of Symbols: Aspects of Ndembu Ritual*. Ithaca, NY: Cornell University Press.

———. 1968. *The Ritual Process: Structure and Anti-structure*. New York: Routledge.

UNAIDS. 2002. "AIDS: China's Titanic Peril." The UN Theme Group on HIV/AIDS in China.

*United Nations Joint Statement: Compulsory Drug Detention and Rehabilitation Centres*. 2012. www.hivpolicy.org/Library/HPP000056.pdf.

Uretsky, Elanah. 2016. *Occupational Hazards: Sex, Business, and HIV in Post-Mao China*. Stanford, CA: Stanford University Press.

Van Gennep, Arnold. (1909) 1969. *The Rites of Passage*. Translated by Monika B. Vizedom and Gabrielle L. Caffee. Chicago: University of Chicago Press.

Vasile, Monica. 2015. "The Trader's Wedding: Ritual Inflation and Money Gifts in Transylvania." In *Economy and Ritual: Studies of Postsocialist Transformations*, edited by Stephen Gudeman and Chris Hann, 137–65. New York: Berghahn.

Veg, Sebastian. 2019. *Minjian: The Rise of China's Grassroots Intellectuals*. New York: Columbia University Press.

Venkat, Bharat. 2016. "Cures." *Public Culture* 28, no. 3: 475–97.

Verdery, Katherine. 1996. *What Was Socialism, and What Comes Next?* New York: Cambridge University Press.

Vogelsang, Kai. 2012. "Chinese 'Society': History of a Troublesome Concept." *Oriens Extremus* 51: 155–92.

Volkow, Nora, and Ting-Kai Li. 2005. "The Neuroscience of Addiction." *Nature Neuroscience* 8, no. 11: 1429–30.

Wakeman, Frederic, Jr. 1993. "The Civil Society and Public Sphere Debate: Western Reflections on Chinese Political Culture." *Modern China* 19, no. 2: 108–38.

Walder, Andrew. 1989. "Factory and Manager in an Era of Reform." *The China Quarterly* 118: 242–64.

Waldram, James. 2012. *Hound Pound Narrative: Sexual Offender Habilitation and the Anthropology of Therapeutic Intervention*. Berkeley: University of California Press.

Wang, Ban. 1995. "The Sublime Subject of History and Desublimation in Contemporary Chinese Fiction." *Comparative Literature* 47, no. 4: 330–53.

———. 1997. *The Sublime Figure of History: Aesthetics and Politics in Twentieth-Century China*. Stanford, CA: Stanford University Press.

Wang, Jing. 2001. "Culture as Leisure and Culture as Capital." *positions: east asia cultures critique* 9, no. 1: 69–104.

——— 2019. *The Other Digital China: Nonconfrontational Activism on the Social Web*. Cambridge, MA: Harvard University Press.

Wang, Jinxiang. 1996. *Zhongguo Jindushi* [China's anti-drugs history]. Shanghai: Shanghai People's University Press.

Wang, Xiaomin. 2003. "China on the Brink of a 'Momentous Era.'" *positions: east asia cultures critique* 11, no. 3: 585–611.

Wang, Yunxiang. 2004. *Diyu Tiantang: Yi Ge Xiduzhe De Xueyansushuo* [Heaven and hell: A drug use's blood and tears account]. Beijing: Qunzhong chubanshe.

Wank, David. 1999. *Commodifying Communism: Business, Trust, and Politics in a Chinese City*. Cambridge, UK: Cambridge University Press.

Weber, Max. (1905) 1987. *The Protestant Ethic and the Spirit of Capitalism*. Translated by Talcott Parsons. New York: Routledge.

Weeks, Kathi. 2007. "Life Within and Against Work: Affective Labor, Feminist Critique, and Post-Fordist Politics." *Ephemera: Theory and Politics in Organization* 7, no. 1: 233–49.

———. 2011. *The Problem with Work: Feminism, Marxism, Antiwork Politics, and Postwork Imaginaries*. Durham, NC: Duke University Press.

Willen, Sarah. 2007. "Toward a Critical Phenomenology of 'Illegality': State Power, Criminalization, and Abjectivity among Undocumented Migrant Workers in Tel Aviv, Israel." *International Migration* 45, no. 3: 8–38.

Williams, Philip, and Yenna Wu. 2004. *The Great Wall of Confinement: The Chinese Prison Camp through Contemporary Fiction and Reportage*. Berkeley: University of California Press.

Williams, Raymond. 1977. *Marxism and Literature*. New York: Oxford University Press.

Willis, Paul. 1977. *Learning to Labour: How Working Class Kids Get Working Class Jobs*. New York: Columbia University Press. First published by Saxon House Press.

Wilson, Ara. 1999. "The Empire of Direct Sales and the Making of Thai Entrepreneurs." *Critique of Anthropology* 19, no. 4: 401–22.

Wolf, Charles, J. K. C. Yeh, Benjamin Zycher, Nicholas Eberstadt, and Sungho Lee. 2003. *Fault Lines in China's Economic Terrain*. Santa Monica, CA: Rand Corporation.

Wolfe, Daniel. 2012. "UN on Drug Detention: Ineffective. Illegal. Close It Down." *Blog Open Society*, March 12. www.opensocietyfoundations.org/voices/un-drug-detention-ineffective-illegal-close-it-down.

Wolf-Meyer, Matthew. 2014. "Therapy, Remedy, Cure: Disorder and the Spatiotemporality of Medicine and Everyday Life." *Medical Anthropology* 33, no. 2: 144–59.

Wool, Zoë. 2015. *After War: The Weight of Life at Walter Reed*. Durham, NC: Duke University Press.

World Health Organization. 1993. *The ICD-10 Classification of Mental and Behavioural Disorders: Diagnostic Criteria for Research*. Geneva: WHO.

Wu, Fushui. 2011. "Yunnan Honghe 43ren Sheheian Tingshen Zhufan Burenzui" [43 individuals from Honghe Yunnan in court hearing implicated in organized crime activity maintain do not admit to guilt]. *Yunnan Wang*, June 30.

Wu, Hongyuran, and Yuqian Wang. 2016. "Yunnan Tin Strikes Debt-For-Equity Swap Deal." *Caixin*. October 17.

Wu, Xiaobo. 2007. *Jidangsanshinian: Zhongguo Qiye 1978–2008, Shang* [Surging 30 years: Chinese business from 1978–2008, part one]. Beijing: Zhongxin chubanshe.

Wu, Zunyou. 2013. "Arguments in Favour of Compulsory Treatment of Opioid Dependence." *Bulletin of the World Health Organization* 91, no. 2: 142–45.

*Xinjiang Ribao* [Xinjiang daily]. 2018. "Weizhiye Peixun Jiaoshenghao" [Occupational training sounds good]. November 11.

*Xinlan Lishi* [Xinlan History]. 2015. "466 gongli dianyuetielushangde5wantiaoxing-ming" [The 70,000 lives taken for the 466 kilometer Yunnan-Vietnam railway]. *Tianshitiandi*, no. 160. March 31. http://history.sina.com.cn/bk/jds/2015-03-31/1439118161.shtml.

Yan, Hairong. 2003. "Neoliberal Governmentality and Neohumanism: Organizing Suzhi/Value Flow through Labor Recruitment Networks." *Cultural Anthropology* 18, no. 4: 493–523.

———. 2008. *New Masters, New Servants: Migration, Development, and Women Workers in China.* Durham, NC: Duke University Press.

Yan, Yunxiang. 2003. *Private Life under Socialism: Love, Intimacy, and Family Change in a Chinese Village, 1949–1999.* Stanford, CA: Stanford University Press.

———. 2009. "The Good Samaritan's New Trouble: A Study of the Changing Moral Landscape in Contemporary China." *Social Anthropology* 17, no. 1: 9–24.

Yang, Jie. 2010. "The Crisis of Masculinity: Class, Gender, and Kindly Power in Post-Mao China." *American Ethnologist* 37, no. 3: 550–62.

———. 2015. *Unknotting the Heart: Unemployment and Therapeutic Governance in China.* Ithaca, NY: Cornell University Press.

Yang, Mayfair Mei-hui. 1994. *Gifts, Favors, and Banquets: The Art of Social Relationships in China.* Ithaca, NY: Cornell University Press.

———. 2020. *Re-enchanting Modernity: Ritual Economy and Society in Wenzhou, China.* Durham, NC: Duke University Press.

Yardley, Jim. 2005. "Chinese City Emerges as Model in AIDS Fight." *New York Times,* June 16, 27.

Young, Allan. 1982. "The Anthropologies of Illness and Sickness." *Annual Review of Anthropology* 11, no. 1: 257–85.

Young, Julian, and Lee Buchanan. 2000. "The War between Drugs and a War on Drug Users?" *Drugs: Education, Prevention, and Policy* 7, no. 4: 409–22.

Young, Robert. 1990. *White Mythologies: Writing History and the West.* London: Routledge.

Yunnan Tin Museum. 2011. *The Course of One Hundred Years of Vicissitudes Has Built Yunnan Tin* [museum exhibit]. August.

Yunnan Wang [Yunnan Net]. 2011. "Yunnan 43ren Shehei'an Jie Minjian Kuanye Ziyuan Zhengduo Luanxiang." [Yunnan's 43 person gang-related case exposes chaos in fights over private mining resources]. June 28.

Zhang, Everett Yuehong. 2001. "Goudui and the State: Constructing Entrepreneurial Masculinity in Two Cosmopolitan Areas of Post-Socialist China." In *Gendered Modernities*, edited by Dorothy Hodges, 235–65. New York: Palgrave Macmillan.

Zhang, Li. 2001. *Strangers in the City: Reconfigurations of Space, Power, and Social Networks within China's Floating Population*. Stanford, CA: Stanford University Press.

———. 2006. "Contesting Spatial Modernity in Late-Socialist China." *Current Anthropology* 47, no. 3: 461–84.

———. 2017. "The Rise of Therapeutic Governing in Postsocialist China." *Medical Anthropology* 36, no. 1: 6–18.

Zhang, Zhen. 2000. "Mediating Time: The 'Rice Bowl of Youth' in Fin de Siecle Urban China." *Public Culture* 12, no. 1: 93–113.

Zhao, Junfeng. 2008. "Xidu 370wanyuan: Shanyi de 'Zhenshi Huangyan'" [3,700,000 yuan using drugs: Goodwill behind a white lie]. *Gejiu Daily*. In the author's possession.

Zhonguo Jingchawang [Chinese police net]. 2010. "Kaiyuan Yulu Shequ Jiedu Moshi Hui Quanguo Tuiguang" [Kaiyuan's Yulu community drug treatment model will be pushed throughout the country]. September 14.

Zhou, Yongming. 1999. *Anti-Drug Crusades in Twentieth-Century China: Nationalism, History, and State Building*. Lanham, MD: Rowman & Littlefield.

Zhu, Jianfeng, Tiashu Pan, Hai Yu, and Dong Dong. 2018. "Guan (Care/Control): An Ethnographic Understanding of Care for People with Severe Mental Illness from Shanghai's Urban Communities." *Culture, Medicine, and Psychiatry* 42, no. 1: 92–111.

Zigon, Jarrett. 2009. "Hope Dies Last: Two Aspects of Hope in Contemporary Moscow." *Anthropological Theory* 9, no. 3: 253–71.

———. 2011. *HIV Is God's Blessing: Rehabilitating Morality in Neoliberal Russia*. Berkeley: University of California Press.

———. 2018. *A War on People: Drug User Politics and a New Ethics of Community*. Berkeley: University of California Press.

Žižek, Slavoj. 1999. *The Ticklish Subject: The Absent Centre of Political Ontology*. New York: Verso.

Zoccatelli, Giulia. 2014. "'It Was Fun, It Was Dangerous': Heroin, Young Urbanities and Opening Reforms in China's Borderlands." *International Journal of Drug Policy* 25, no. 4: 762–68.

Zoubian Zhongguo [Discover China]. 2017. *Gejiu Cungui Wangshi* [The history of Gejiu's meter-track railway]. CCTV-4.

# INDEX

addiction: author's assumptions about, 6–8; challenging preconceptions, 7–8, 14; changing patterns of, 73, 149–50; class and social status considerations with respect to, 26–27; competing government responses to, 88–91; connections with employment and obsolescence, 14, 62; disorientation and, 16; in context of intergenerational suffering, 21–22; as historical condition, 10–12, 14–16, 66–67; as a Maoist problem of laboring, 88–89, 96–100, 170n22; medicalized views of, 21–22, 159nn18,19; pluralizing understandings of, 20; recovery from, stages of, 7; relationships as helping to overcome, 107–9, 115–24; rhetoric of in Chinese culture, 10–14, 66, 99; society as failing to allow individuals to move beyond, 110–12, 132–33, 177n22; SOEs as protecting from, 92–96; symptoms of, 44, 78; triggered by physical objects and places, 76–77
adoption, 120–24
Agar, Michael, 6
Ahmed, Sarah, 16–18
Althusser, Louis, 143, 179n33
Amway, 118–21
Anagnost, Ann, 159n16, 161n15, 166n26
Appadurai, Arjun, 84
Arendt, Hannah, 100–101, 172
"art of relationships" (*guanxixue*), 108
Austin, J. L., 113, 115, 173n13, 177n33

Ban, Wang, 131, 144, 162n22
Berlant, Lauren, 9, 159n19
"Big Brothers" (*laoda*), 41, 74, 138–39, 178n26
Bo (declares Heroin Generation will disappear), 69–74, 78–80
Bourdieu, Pierre, 21, 49, 59, 60, 63, 165n13, 166n25
Bourgois, Philippe, 21, 165, 168n15
Burroughs, William, 4–5, 7

Carr, David, 8, 70, 74, 76–77, 81–82, 167n5, 168n12, 171n14
"catching up" (*ganshang*), 15, 47, 62–63
Chen (Green Orchards idler), 87, 95–97, 100–101, 103
China-UK HIV/AIDS Prevention and Care Project, 5
Cho, Mun Young, 138, 164n6
civil society: blurring line between state and civil society in early Maoist period, 172; commitment to work, 177; "community" and 129, 139; conflicting Chinese translations of, 176; as contested symbol, 128; grassroots network and, 20, 129–32, 176n10; "ideals" against "making a living" and, 176n11; invoked by Yan Jun, 128, 144; purchasing service model and 137–38, 149; rights defense and, 20, 132–34; seen as in need of monitoring, 137–38; significance of language used to describe, 138–39; social organizations as, 149
Comaroff, John and Jean, 9, 12, 128

Founded in 1893,
UNIVERSITY OF CALIFORNIA PRESS
publishes bold, progressive books and journals
on topics in the arts, humanities, social sciences,
and natural sciences—with a focus on social
justice issues—that inspire thought and action
among readers worldwide.

The UC PRESS FOUNDATION
raises funds to uphold the press's vital role
as an independent, nonprofit publisher, and
receives philanthropic support from a wide
range of individuals and institutions—and from
committed readers like you. To learn more, visit
ucpress.edu/supportus.